UNSEPARATE

··· **Sensing Media**
Aesthetics, Philosophy,
and Cultures of Media
EDITED BY WENDY HUI KYONG CHUN
AND SHANE DENSON

UNSEPARATE

Modernism, Interdisciplinary Art, and Network Aesthetics

STEVEN HENRY MADOFF

STANFORD UNIVERSITY PRESS
Stanford, California

Stanford University Press
Stanford, California

Library of Congress Cataloging-in-Publication Data
Names: Madoff, Steven Henry, author.
Title: A sense of wholeness : modernism, interdisciplinary art, and network aesthetics / Steven Henry Madoff.
Description: Stanford, California : Stanford University Press, 2025. |
    Series: Sensing media : aesthetics, philosophy, and cultures of media |
    Includes bibliographical references and index.
Identifiers: LCCN 2025001748 (print) | LCCN 2025001749 (ebook) | ISBN
    9781503642294 (cloth) | ISBN 9781503644199 (paperback) | ISBN
    9781503644205 (ebook)
Subjects: LCSH: Modernism (Art) | Arts, Modern—Philosophy.
Classification: LCC NX456.5.M64 M33 2025 (print) | LCC NX456.5.M64
    (ebook) | DDC 709.04—dc23/eng/20250305
LC record available at https://lccn.loc.gov/2025001748
LC ebook record available at https://lccn.loc.gov/2025001749

Cover design: Bob Aufuldish, Aufuldish & Warinner
Cover art: Alfredo Jaar, GESAMTKUNSTWERK, 1988/2018, lightbox with vinyl mounted on plexiglass, 8 3/8 x 36 3/8 x 5 in.
Typeset by Newgen in 11/14 Minion Pro

The authorized representative in the EU for product safety and compliance is: Mare Nostrum Group B.V. | Mauritskade 21D | 1091 GC Amsterdam | The Netherlands | Email address: gpsr@mare-nostrum.co.uk | KVK chamber of commerce number: 96249943

CONTENTS

UNSEPARATE

One

A CABINET OF CONCEPTS/
NETWORK AESTHETICS

••• Even before artificial intelligences seeped into every seam of *now* and *here*, before their sleepless neural networks gathered endless bits of human making into patterns of sudden visibility, there were proto-networks that impelled us toward collectivity.

I was born in the last century, the century in which most of the artists inhabiting this book lived. And now, in this third decade of the twenty-first century, I would say I'm a typical digital citizen of contemporary life. There are no devices embedded in me for transmission and reception. No data tattoos. Nothing whose invisible frequencies, packets of ones and zeros, signature tags, and wireless pulses rise from my flesh and link me ineluctably to the protocols of control overlapping in unseen streams. Though these devices aren't (yet) embedded in me, they're everywhere around me, and I wear them and carry them in my pockets, whole ecologies of computation packed into small, lightweight machines, prosthetic others joined to me in intimate and seemingly limitless ways.

Velocity and mobility are the swerving figures of a loosened, eruptive spatiality that passes through bodies, populations, and economies toward their profound rearrangement. No surface is im-permeable to these algorithms and protocols, to computationalism and programmability—intelligences augmenting and accelerating, collecting me into the vast web, as I collect them into my virtually tentacular body. This crossing of boundaries, these flows and grids, these burst-modes of notation, significance, and chance, this overlap and blur that produce contests of legitimation and new meanings are my subject in a highly particular way.

As European modernism unfolded in the nineteenth century, it presented new practices of assemblage that led to our own times and foreshadowed our technologies—dreams of interconnectivity spoken and materialized, conjoining artistic disciplines from the visual arts to poetry, music, theater, film, architecture, and dance that link in concatenated wholes and informed and were informed by ways of thinking about the self and the self with other selves. Captured by the term *interdisciplinary art*—a species of making that still has had only limited philosophical speculation and little attention to its political roots and facets—this reading of European modernism offers an alternative to the conventional understanding of this art as a representation of an alienated world in pieces. As Albert Gelpi has written, "The critical discussion of Modernism has concentrated on the shattering of formal conventions as an expression of the disintegration of traditional values."[1]

So much has been written about fragmentation as a consistent trope and structural paradigm for European modernist production that it would be impossible to rehearse this history in full, though I'll discuss many aspects of it in these pages. A brief outline of this standard reading portrays this art's tendency toward splintered composition, inwardness, reduction, opposition to the status quo, and despair brought on by the industrial, war-riven, and private shocks of the contemporary landscape.

In the midst of the modernist period, T. S. Eliot writes in *The Waste Land*, "These fragments I have shored against my ruins," while his friend and compatriot, Ezra Pound, lamented after decades of writing one of the other great monuments of modernist poetry, his endlessly allusive *Cantos*, "I cannot make it cohere."[2] Gertrude Stein spoke of the First World War as a Cubist composition of violence that was without center,[3] just as the Futurist Umberto Boccioni described his paintings in terms of "dislocation and dismemberment."[4] Meanwhile, the composers Igor Stravinsky, Arnold Schoenberg, and George Antheil, each in their own way, announced new compositional methods and effects whose revisions of harmonic traditions refracted a previously unheard dissonance, mirroring a world uprooted and brutally revised. Antheil's *Ballet Mécanique* (1925) went so far as to incorporate noisemaking machines that he built for the work—rattlingly loud, percussive, and wailing. He described the work as "Like machines. All efficiency. No LOVE. Written without sympathy. Written cold as an army operates."[5]

The clanging bells and sirens in Antheil's score sound shattering and thrilling to this day, and the work shares in sensibility an embodiment of machinic rapture, as well as rupture, that modernist artists as various as Vladimir Tatlin, Natalia Goncharova, Francis Picabia, Fernand Leger, Hannah Hoch, Raoul Hausmann, Carlo Carrá, and Boccioni, among many others, depicted as an encapsulation, an inward turn that was a critique of past methods, subjects, and means of art-making in formalist terms, while simultaneously marking an estranged sense of self in the world, whether ironic or earnest, and often both in the same disorienting breath.

The fascination and terror that machines offered as muse to the European modernists were a hallmark of their ethos, a song sung by the Futurists in such anthemic pronouncements as F. T. Marinetti's oft-quoted words from the 1909 *Futurist Manifesto*—"a roaring motor car, which seems to run on machine-gun fire, is more beautiful than the *Victory of Samothrace*"[6]—and was still reverberating a quarter of a century later when the great modernist architect Le Corbusier declared in his 1923 treatise *Towards a New Architecture*, "A house is a machine for living in."[7] That sense of efficiency embodied in integrated modularity, in a machine's dynamic, capable, incisive, and coordinated actions among its well-oiled parts also inferred another hallmark of the modernist esprit: a heightened consciousness of its own means.

This schematic sense of artworks built like machines from parts spoke to the exultation, as well as to the cool anonymity and alienation, of industrial production, and it encompassed an internalized scrutiny, an interrogation of how to make and how to be. If war and its technologies advanced the efficiency of contemporary machines and brought both celebration and despair, from an artistic perspective they also pointed to the notion of autonomy in creative techniques and practices, artistic productions so alienated from ordinary life that their invented expressions were isolating in their willful obscurity, throwing specialized languages of one kind or another in the face of the everyday, true to themselves alone. Whatever the artistic form, it was, in a larger sense, a fragment broken off from what was considered normal and normative, with all the contested ramifications of ethical deviation and artistic integrity attached.

This is a standard formalist reading of European modernism—what, years later, the American art critic Clement Greenberg sought to champion as the great signature of modernism by focusing on the act of making as if it were drawn centripetally and almost exclusively from analytical material introspection with a rigor that approached the discipline, specialization, and autonomy of scientific method. He wrote that the "essence of Modernism lies, as I see it, in the use of the characteristic methods of a discipline to criticize the discipline itself—not in order to subvert it, but to entrench it more firmly in its area of competence."[8]

That rendering of modernism still finds notice to this day, presenting a reflexive art dedicated to the isolation of its elements in keeping with its violently industrialized, fragmentary world. So, a leading recent art-history textbook remarks: "The modernist aesthetic of autonomy thus constituted the social and subjective sphere from within which an opposition against the totality of interested activities and instrumentalized forms of experience could be articulated in artistic acts of open negation and refusal."[9]

Beneath the surfaces of chaos, European modernism's psychological affects and introspective structures are seen as windows on essence. Influenced by and in response to the fractured world, the modernists also broke everything down, concentrating on each element's internal properties—another form of splintering that, by no coincidence, replicates the effects of the new technologies around them, even if to buffer, control, resist, and negate what they've wrought. Just as Pound bemoaned his inability to make his work cohere, within these acts of fragmentary disconsolateness and protest, there is the sense in this art

of an aesthetic event whose techniques and technologies yield both turbulence and pathways out of wreckage toward refinement. So, Nicholas
Bourriaud writes in his brief book *The Randicant*, "Indexed to progress
and abundance, modernism is thus structured around the image of a
derrick planted in the depths of the individual and society, a violent
explosion of the visible."[10]

Of course, it can be said that what was being refined in the world
were the means to improve efficiencies of violence as well as the means
to temper it, including new ways to represent it. Yet what I want to argue
is that this overarching image of a shattering art for a shattered world
offers, if not a misreading, only one part of the story; that over approximately the last 175 years, there has been a counter-tendency: artists
whose conceptual precepts and practical methods intend what Jacques
Rancière calls in a different context the "power of the unseparate"—an
art not of fragmentation, but one in pursuit of wholeness.[11]

What interests me is to look again at icons of the standard European
modernist canon and propose that their art engaged strategies of the
interdisciplinary toward what can be called, in a contemporary, if
anachronistic, term, structurally *networked* works—works whose internal connectivity of heterogeneous elements toward an operative unity
point in various ways to the future of artistic thinking, production, and
technological societies today. And so I begin with Richard Wagner's
proclamations of the "total work of art," the *Gesamtkunstwerk,* at the
time of revolution in Germany in 1849. Wagner's way is followed by
thinking about Paul Cézanne in relation to Marcel Duchamp, specifically how they understood their bodies and works as organs of artistic
unification, as proto-networks. This leads me to another physical and
spatial idea of the unseparate, again in a time of war—Hugo Ball and
the brief moment of Cabaret Voltaire in Zurich 1916 that presages Dada.
I turn then to Walter Gropius's founding of the Bauhaus almost at the
same moment as the cabaret, focusing on his pedagogy of artistic-
industrial production that proposes another form of totalist thinking.

Each of them offers what can be described as an expression of
network aesthetics—a mapping of complex, interconnected systems
and the patterns that emerge from them that are understood as processes and methods for the representation of the world, systems of

representation that are immersive, variable, refractive, fluidly adjusting, contingent, and always determined by linkage, not fragmentation, among their parts.

In proposing that we look again at these familiar figures who have traditionally represented European modernism, but now through the lens of network aesthetics, I mean to point as well to the ways in which their formations of artistic systems are precedents for contemporary interdisciplinary art—paintings, sculptures, drawings, objects, videos, texts, performances, photographs, soundworks, digital media, and communal participatory events conjoined in various arrangements—which we know most readily in the forms of installation art and performance art. I hope to make clear how these earlier practices make way for what we take for granted so easily today without understanding where and when these kinds of contemporary works come from: works of assembly and collectivity whose numerous artistic disciplines are brought together as interconnected wholes and that can be said to count objects and temporalities toward the experience of interdependence, of a collective connectivity between components toward dynamics of unity.

If not the modernist narrative of fragmentation, then, with its familiar particularities of sociological and psychological duress, this counternarrative of the not-fragmentary offers a prehistory of our contemporary networked way of understanding and representing the world and, in looking back at these historical works as early drafts of network thinking, asks by what mechanisms, through what motifs, and at what cost did their artistic practices embody an ethical sociality, an ethical life embodied in artistic attempts toward visions of unity? Or did they?

I ask this, all the more conscious of the fact that these classic modernist figures, so often written about, had immense influence at the same time that they're precisely linked to the white European patriarchal model of power of which they were a part—despite their sometimes renegade status—and that is understood today in all of its oppressive violence as a negative triumphalism of brutal means. As we'll see, the urge toward wholeness, with its underlying and sometimes explicit question of being together, can veer as well toward oppressive totalism as it does toward a vitalizing commensurateness. Yet it's precisely because these figures remain so prominent in the study of European modernism that I've concentrated on them in order to challenge the canon in this specific way.

At least in retrospect, the pathos of their work lies in the implicit instability within their various aesthetic projects of unification. So, to write about their attempts to bring heterogeneous elements together in unifying forms is to speak of a very different kind of relationship to otherness than the crucial attention to gender and racial difference that in recent years is addressed in feminist and queer archaeologies of modernism, in transnational art histories, and in postcolonial and Indigenous studies. In a way, my purview lies alongside these, looking at early modernist systems of assemblage by extension as metaphors and models for the relation of self with others, and how these shift over time, underscoring the flux in the very notion of time that scientific and technological advancements pressed on these historical figures.

The structure itself of my narrative intends to reflect this. The organization of this book, with its leaps from Wagner to Cézanne and Duchamp, then back to Dada and forward to the Bauhaus, as well as the interchapter meditations on the presentness of the senses, echo the text's themes and consideration of time's fluidity in those quaking shifts that touched these artists and transformed their thinking and making. While the book invites a consecutive reading of chapters, as one interdisciplinary formation is shown in connection and contrast with the last and the next, each chapter is also a study in itself, and some readers may simply prefer to read about their artist of preference. This touches again on temporality, on the linearity of time and then of anachronism, as at least three temporal directions are implied here. First is time's arrow, the chronological trajectory of the 1850s through to the 1930s, and the ways sociopolitical and technological transformations appear to march along a straight line. Second, the sense of the individuation of each interdisciplinary practice under review within its own time, not necessarily as an instance of diachronism, of "development," but as an aesthetic formation that may be produced in time and yet, as a *type* of interdisciplinary production, nonetheless has close relations to works of the same kind made at other moments in time and therefore, in this sense, steps out of time. And so, as a third temporal direction, I come again to anachronism, re-viewing these artists and their works from the other end of time's telescope.

This sense of reversed temporality is concisely expressed by Hal Foster, who writes: "For even as the avant-garde recedes into the past, it also returns from the future, repositioned by innovative art in the present."[12] Looking back at these specimens of European modernism from the contemporary perspective of network thinking is a way, as I've noted, to give an account of the present as well as seeing the past; to offer a contemporary technological model as a means to understand how these historical co-relational structures undergird so much installation and performance art today, just as contemporary practices and technologies help us to understand what came before—all the more so as computation and specifically artificial intelligence and biotechnics contribute to forms of networked world-building in cultural production.[13]

This book focuses, nonetheless, on these specific historical accounts as exemplary, not on contemporary works in their wake or even other early artistic practices. Were this a far longer study, so many stylistic movements and artists on the path to network aesthetics could be turned in this analytical light. To name just some of these, from Futurism and its Synthetic Theatre to Fluxus and Happenings, from the visionary theater works of Robert Wilson to contemporary artistic productions as far flung as those of Joan Jonas, Pepón Osorio, Ann Hamilton, Thomas Hirschhorn, Rirkrit Tiravanija, Renée Green, Shilpa Gupta, Ryan Trecartin, Hito Steyerl, Theaster Gates, ruangrupa, Nora Chipaumire, Sarah Sze, Anne Imhof, Allora & Calzadilla, Abigail DeVille, Tiona Nekkia McClodden . . . and the list could easily go on, growing exponentially.[14]

Many concepts touch on this compulsion and longing for expressions of connection and unification—Hegel's problematic but significant notion of "Spirit" as a definition of collectivity; Wagner's Gesamtkunstwerk, so foundationally crucial; Wassily Kandinsky's "monumental" work of art and "inner necessity"; Gilles Deleuze and Félix Guattari's "Body without Organs"; Ilya Kabakov's "total installation" (in obeisance to Wagner); Manuel DeLanda's description of "emergent wholes" and "meshworks" (in obeisance to Deleuze); Nicolas Bourriaud's "randicant universe"; scientific theories of convergence and autopoiesis; Bruno Latour's thinking about actor-network theory; and various renderings of network theory by Benjamin H. Bratton, Alexander Galloway and Eugene Thacker, and Kai Eriksson, among many others.

As historical background, Juliet Koss's *Modernism After Wagner* is a decisive work of scholarship, illuminating the historical origins of the Gesamtkunstwerk as Wagner envisioned it and the ways in which his polemics and practice play out through the 1930s, particularly in German artistic and architectural production. Relevant, too, as background is Jeffrey Saletnik's *Josef Albers, Late Modernism, and Pedagogic Form*, offering a historical review of education in Wilhelmine Germany, useful for an understanding not only of Albers's training and teaching but also in relation to Bauhaus pedagogy more generally. Implicit within this frame are notions of sociality, and so it has been vital to read Judith Butler's *Giving an Account of Oneself* and *Notes Toward a Performative Theory of Assembly*, Donna Haraway's *Staying with the Trouble: Making Kin in the Chthulucene*, and Leela Gandhi's *Affective Communities: Anticolonial Thought, Fin-de-Siècle Radicalism, and the Politics of Friendship*, all resonating in various ways with societal and technological network formations.

In fact, a literature that analyzes cultural instances of network thinking is growing rapidly, with such works as David Joselit's *After Art*; Anna Munster's *An Aesthesia of Networks: Conjunctive Experience in Art and Technology*; Caroline Levine's *Forms: Whole, Rhythm, Hierarchy, Network*; Kris Cohen's *Never Alone, Except for Now: Art, Networks, Populations*, with his key thinking about group forms; and Fred Moten's *The Universal Machine*. All of these works and others join Patrick Jagoda's *Network Aesthetics* in reckoning with contemporary practices across visual art, fiction, video games, TV, new media, and social media in relation to the internet, big data, artificial intelligence, and other expressions of planetary computation. Yuk Hui, in his thinking about what he calls "cosmotechnics," juxtaposing the Western philosophical tradition and Eastern philosophical thought, in works such as *The Question Concerning Technology in China, Recursivity and Contingency*, and *Art and Cosmotechnics*, further complexifies artistic forms of systematization and assemblage toward schemes of totalism. In the

breadth of these inquiries into wholeness and networks—utopian, dys-
topian, fictive, and real—the terms applied by these authors map an
intricacy of related thinking, an expanding theoretical and critical universe of its own.

There is one further mode of interpretation, alongside my art-
historical and theoretical chapters, intended as a phenomenological
exercise, and which I've already noted in passing in its temporal condition
of presentness. As this spatial art of interdisciplinary assemblage in its
various strategies and expressions over time actively seeks to engage,
even disturb, the sensory as well as the intellectual, I've interspersed
among the chapters my reflections on six bodily senses. After all,
they're the corporeal apparatuses toward assembly in the experiential
field in which makers conceive their works and viewers perceive them.
My own sense of the senses is the most phenomenally immediate, the
most intimate I can know, and so, this other vocality in response to the
analytical call of the text is offered as a different entry into this thinking
about the production and reception of the interdisciplinary, about the
sensory omphalos of assembly per se, how it lives in the body.

Of course, these artists of the European modernist project remain
the central subject. Each interdisciplinary practitioner's work under-
goes its process of tumult that reflects, codifies, distorts, destabilizes,
and recodifies a world-picture. This is the unspooling and respooling
of meaning in their art as sites of becoming and as historical events,
as infections within social bodies. (The art of the interdisciplinary is
a metaphorical form of virology.) These practices toward wholeness
have found different hosts—music, architecture, cabaret, social events
with intensified quotients of chance interaction, enterprises seen ho-
listically. As dynamic sites, they always prefer couplings, intersections,
multiple points of exchange, multiple means of production, of poly-
expressiveness. Comprised of assembled elements that act as agents
engaged in intercommunication, viewers included, the works can be
called multi-agent systems. What are the operative behaviors of these
pieces and wholes as communicative collaborators and rogues? Under
what circumstances did artists come to the notion of the insufficiency
of a single discipline? What pressed on them, made them desire the
supplement, the aggregate in place of the single? And how did these

interdisciplinary productions change with geography, with politics in particular times and over time, and with different technologies?

I began by speaking of contemporary technologies of communication (systems streaming from my pockets, my wrist) because I see in their local and global effects the paradigm of network aesthetics as a framework for understanding interdisciplinary art in its various totalizing ambitions.[15] Media theory, from the work of Marshall McLuhan in the 1960s through to more recent thinkers, such as McKenzie Wark and Lev Manovich, have given us ways to consider how effluences of media are harvested and manipulated to influence societies, from film and television to computational machines and platforms. In some instances, media theory considers how different kinds of media not only shape but are also shaped by historical, economic, social, and cultural contexts. Within the broader frame of media theory, network aesthetics, as a specific development, zeroes in on the ways that interconnection as described by network analysis and expressions is a means to articulate how the activity of nodes, links, and data flows provide a schema for analyzing and interpreting creative practices. In my case, the task is to articulate how such connective flows dance in step with interdisciplinary assemblage and how they offer technical and philosophical tools toward thinking about the kinds of artistic interconnections that are structurally embodied as networks and breed them, pointing from art to world.

Jagoda states that "scientists, politicians, journalists, poets, and artists have increasingly framed the world in terms of the interconnection of people and nations, objects and economies, transportation hubs and computers. Networks, across these contexts, have become ubiquitous as both literal infrastructures and figurative tropes."[16] Meanwhile, Pamela Lee, in her book *Forgetting the Art World*, remarks that "the language of networks is critical to our present-day understanding of globalization."[17] She cites Lawrence Alloway's prescient essay from 1972, "Network: The Art World Described as a System," which draws on contemporary sociology, communication theories, and informatics to limn a concept of the art world as a closed system. In fact, Alloway's use of technological organization as a descriptor for art and its markets wasn't unprecedented. Precisely four years earlier, in the September 1968 issue of *Artforum*, where Alloway also published his essay, the artist and art historian Jack Burnham brought out a piece titled "Systems Esthetics," discussing systems analysis in relation to site-specific art and Minimalist art.

In 1990, Roy Ascott's essay "Is There Love in the Telematic Embrace?" moved still closer to the role of technological networks in art production, using such terms as "telematic art," "telematic culture," and "the Gesamtdatenwerk" to draw us forward toward the logics of networks in our contemporary digital era, and doing so with the historical precedent of Duchamp's *Large Glass*, which he characterized as a work of "telematic networking."[18]

Of course, technology has changed, as has the art world. But whether we're talking about simpler closed systems or the porous, expansive nature of newer mass-distribution platforms, I would argue, to return to Lee's writing, that globalization isn't simply made more vivid or explicable through the language of networks as metaphor. Instead, I would say that globalization is a *symptom* of network thinking—the thinking of totalities and totalization, and its ruthlessly efficient economic and social execution. That thinking, as I'll explicate in this book, has a longer genealogy, a modernist history that precedes and in many ways prepares for the linkage of networks with both beneficial modes of sociality and the punishing extractivist practices of neoliberal policies that still accelerate today.

To come to terms with "network" as a historical concept that undergirds our time and to delve into its ontological and phenomenological bases is to reflect on the rise of interdisciplinary practice as both speculum and speculation, reflecting on the politics of specific moments in modernist production as an impulse toward collectivity among societies of objects and their viewers that extend to notions of society itself, and particularly to notions about society and systems of control. This reading of what "network" means, invoking ideas ranging from Deleuze and Guattari's rhizomes and spastic bodies to propositions about thingness made by more contemporary philosophers, is crucial to how we can use network aesthetics to reevaluate these all-too-familiar modernist artists and thinkers in their own moment, and how their influence has seeped into our contemporary world in which each of us can be blasted out into the networked world, pored over, exaggerated, and dissected at the same moment that we are no more than anonymous data points for harvest.

Kris Cohen, for example, argues that it's inimical to neoliberal globalization that "individuality (overtly) and populations (behind the scenes) are privileged relational forms" and speaks of people as "hyperindividualized entrepreneurs," a phrase that resonates with the way nodes within networks and objects within interdisciplinary works accommodate collectivity and diversity.[19] These contemporary aspects of totalizing mechanisms and behaviors, I would say, are remarkably anticipated by the attempts toward totalization in the works of the early European modernists that point in both enriching and potentially devastating ways to the distributive models affecting individuals and populations that Cohen describes. In all of this, there's a deeper itch, a deeper human anxiety about and need for systems of unification.

In a wider purview, the use of interdisciplinarity in the hard sciences, social sciences, and humanities has its own history, its own literature and disputes. Back to the inaugural lecture at the University of Jena in 1789, Friedrich Schiller pitted *Bildung* against *Ausbildung*, the concept of the student to be forged in the fire of full exposure to the range of human knowledge versus the intensity of a focused flame that burns a narrow path toward specialization. Modern universities have incorporated both tracks, while the rewards for scholars to combine disciplines in their work have grown immensely. That the *Oxford Handbook of Interdisciplinarity* holds nearly six hundred pages and offers thirty-seven essays on interdisciplinary knowledge production in an exhaustive breadth of subjects only confirms how pervasive within academia interdisciplinarity has become.[20]

If writers who think about interdisciplinarity in general speak of "boundary work," of "the composite set of claims, activities, and institutional structures that define and protect knowledge practices"—if only to deepen and combine them—then interdisciplinary artists are boundary workers par excellence, by turns honoring, dilating, upsetting, and reorganizing bound fields of knowledge.[21] To think of the interdisciplinary artwork's constituent parts is to think of objects that are directionally transverse, whose tense is the conditional, whose grammatical form is the interrogative, whose method of building is assemblage, whose carriage is a platform, whose group order is that of the swarm and stigmergy, and whose activation is always local. And while I've emphasized the philosophical and material aspects of the historical works I present, they sometimes show a hyperintensity that evicts us from the empirical, pressing us toward the mystical or camp.

Various fields specific to art inquiry touch on the expansiveness implicit in the unbounding of discrete disciplines and identify forms of interconnection, as we see in writings about installation art, site-specific works, and performance art. I think, for example, of Rosalind Krauss's pathbreaking 1979 essay "Sculpture in the Expanded Field," in which she diagrammatically relates sculpture, architecture, and landscape, indicating a shift from art objects in their individuated forms to a coherence of relations among multiple kinds of structures and spatial experiences, a dilation grounded quite literally in site specificity and whose breadth of intersections support systems-based reorientation. Miwon Kwon's 2002 study *One Place After Another: Site-Specific Art and Locational Identity*, extends Krauss's thinking, further interrogating the concept of "site" while delving into the interaction between site-specific production and community.[22]

At the same time that Kwon publishes her book, Nicolas Bourriaud's *Relational Aesthetics* appears, describing a kind of art focused entirely on interactions among its viewers as a participatory community that co-produces the content of the work,[23] while three years later Claire Bishop (who will come to contest Bourriaud's ideas) brings out her seminal survey *Installation Art: A Critical History*, which presents the expansiveness of installation works and its relation to community. She invokes the viewer as a participant entering the works physically, at once an active agent in and with the work and a subject in turn shaped by the structure of the work. That seems in keeping with my notion of the historical and philosophical origin stories I narrate, and yet a key difference that underlines my approach appears on the very last page of her book, where she writes: "It is possible to say that installation art's insistence on the viewer's experience aims to thrust into question our sense of stability in and mastery over the world, and to reveal the 'true' nature of our subjectivity as fragmented and decentered."[24]

Yet network aesthetics as it applies here argues that decentering isn't necessarily an endpoint. Our subjectivity, our "I" as both a receiver and agent, as both an author and viewer, can also negotiate and renovate meaning structures, including those of artworks that represent the world at different moments of disequilibrium. Our behavior as subjective beings, as I hope to show in my historical accounts and the philosophical and social concepts that pertain to them, don't continually or exclusively succumb to decentering and fragmentation but instead have shown that the impulse is just as present to attend to the possibilities of anchoring linkages and the prospects of systemic wholeness.

Still, Bishop's quotation marks around the word "true" offer a little hint, a narrowing spotlight that produces an illuminating shadow with it. And it's useful here to note another viewpoint on the nature of installations, which redounds to what interdisciplinary works as networks encompass, with their vectored nodes and links. Boris Groys, in his brief 2009 essay "Politics of Installation," makes the claim that the truth shining from an installation isn't relational in a sense of democratic community at all. No, there is only one truth, one subjectivity that illuminates the space of an installation, and that's the artist's, whose "sovereign, authoritarian control" holds dominion over the community of visitors entering the work. "Here the artist acts as legislator, as a sovereign of the installation space—even, and maybe especially so, if the law given by the artist to a community of visitors is a democratic one." In doing so, in fact, the attending community "leaves the public territory of democratic legitimacy."[25]

Yet it's contradictory that the viewer, in Groys's understanding, apparently doesn't change the installation by entering it and cognizing it uniquely, altering its meaning on a local level, while in the very same text he writes that "anything included in such a space becomes a part of the artwork simply because it is placed inside this space." That would suggest the possibility of a viral intervention in the work by the viewer, a reciprocity between the work and those who enter it. In my own consideration of network aesthetics, all parts of an interdisciplinary work are nodal and interoperable, including the viewer, whose own agency or sovereignty engages the installation and acts on it. As we'll see in the foundational case of Wagner, as well as in the complicated, dire case of

Hugo Ball, what the interdisciplinary work from its start in European modernism offers is never uniform. The registers of subjectivity, control, and truth in these works have different trajectories and, by extension, present ways in which individuals, communities, and networked relations take shape.

This brings another important text to mind about installation art's relational structures and meaning-making, implicitly present in interdisciplinary works and network aesthetics, and with ramifications for society in general. The book is Juliane Rebentisch's *Aesthetics of Installation Art*. She develops a taxonomy of installation formats, filtered through linguistic analysis, the phenomenology of Martin Heidegger, and a central understanding indebted to Theodor Adorno's notion of reconciliation—a word that instantly evokes the way that objects within an interdisciplinary work are assembled to coexist productively.

Rebentisch quotes an analysis of Adorno that speaks to another view of subjectivity, truth, and control, with its human toll and prospects. For Adorno, the goal of art to offer reconciliation seems to present an aporia. Art, he claims, is always an Other, "the negation of an unreconciled reality." And still more so, he claims: "Art can thus be true in the sense of being faithful to reality to the extent that it shows reality as unreconciled, antagonistic, divided against itself. But it can only do this by showing reality in the light of reconciliation, i.e. by the non-violent aesthetic synthesis of disparate elements that produces the semblance of reconciliation."[26]

Adorno calls this knot in art's representation of the world an "antinomial structure" that lies at the heart of artistic production. In this way, it can be said that he makes a case for the unitary as a horizon line implicit in interdisciplinary practices, with its internal tensions, its constellations, its attempts to reconcile its parts. "Installation," in this light, is a term I'll often use to describe the convergence of things in various historical works, whose combinatory effects charge their complex internal relations with haptic and semantic purpose. In the co-determination of meaning with viewer-agents, as I'll come to denote viewers of interdisciplinary works, a kaleidoscopic mingling of knowledge formations takes place, which is transformational to the work in its reception as well as to its viewers. In effect, ontologically and epistemologically, the interdisciplinary work's society of objects can be said to have a being-state and a knowledge-state, individually and collectively—a matter of presence, autonomous life, and life with others.

. . .

But let me step back for a moment. As the genesis of interdisciplinary artistic production is my subject, it's important to clarify some still more basic terms, beginning with the word "discipline" itself. A standard definition of "discipline" is training by instruction with the goal of proficiency in a particular body of knowledge or making. In my context, an interdisciplinary work is the coming together of individual art objects made in different artistic disciplines, and so a shorthand that emphasizes this is to simply call each artwork within the whole a "discipline-object." Every discipline-object is both an epistemological thing, a container or dwelling of knowledge, and an embodiment of the actions of a maker who is, in this construction, the disciple. (Whether a thing has its own agency is another matter, and one of speculative interest to be taken up later.)

"Discipline" derives from "disciple," whose prefix, the Latin *dis-*, means apart or asunder, though it is also aligned with *dvis*, meaning twice, duo, and therefore by extension, coupling. These two heads are joined to the single body *-ciple*, drawn from the verb *capere*: to take hold of, to grasp. And so, the disciple grasps what he has taken apart in order to couple it, to make meaning and add to a body of knowledge. Discipline-objects, as I'll call them, are products of the disciple, who makes meaning through training and then makes that training visible through the specific materials, techniques, and construction of a discipline—whether drawing, painting, photography, sculpture, musical composition, etc. *Inter*disciplinary is the bridge, the coupling of couplings, the link between proficiencies and subsequently the creation of discipline-objects that initially begin in breaking down the making of an individual artwork into processes and parts, constructing it, and then joining these discrete discipline-objects in a network of relations among them: the interdisciplinary artwork.

In writing this, it's clear that a still finer distinction needs to be made in this terminology: the difference between "discipline" and "medium," though it will take a moment to get there. In the historical works I'll present as nascent forms of interdisciplinary artistic practice, the characteristic composition of each discipline-object is necessarily present as a physical thing. The specific elements that bring the work into being and visibility, such as its materials and the techniques deployed to marshal these materials, are the basis of the object's presence, although it isn't necessarily the case that they be considered solely in terms of the inwardly focused self-sufficiency that Clement Greenberg associated with modernism or, for my own purposes, that they be considered finally as entirely autonomous things. The point of my argument, again, is just the opposite: to bring to the fore the proposition that in these historical interdisciplinary works, and the installation art in its wake, these discrete discipline-objects are animated by relationships of connection.

Krauss famously announced the end of what she referred to as the medium-specific character of individual arts in her 1992 lectures and subsequent book, *"A Voyage on the North Sea": Art in the Age of the Post-Medium Condition*. The way that I've already defined "discipline" encompasses how Krauss speaks of "method" or, I might say, rhymes with it. She provides a trenchant and compressed description of how the notion of medium-specificity emerges in the history and theory of modernist art in what she calls its "recursive structure"—the constitutive elements, say, of a painting that "produce the rules that generate the structure [of the work] itself."[27] Her history moves forward into later historical precedents in the twentieth century of the fate of medium-specificity. She points, for example, to the conceptual thinking of the artist Joseph Kosuth, who pronounces that the logical conclusion of the kind of essentialism promulgated by Greenberg inevitably leads to generality. That's to say, an artwork's essence becomes so reduced in Greenberg's notion of modernism's entrenchment in its own competence that art ultimately becomes simply generic, it empties out all its particularities in reducing it to its most fundamental material being—a painting, for example, becomes just paint on a support, etc. Or so Kosuth claims, in Krauss's telling. This is the path to the devaluation of medium-specificity and the opening, at the very least, to the erosion of mediums as significant in themselves. In primarily focusing on the installation art of the Belgian conceptualist Marcel Broodthaers, Krauss proposes, in any case, that what she sees in and through his work is that the specificity of mediums lose their hard boundaries, and through conceptual frameworks and the increasing fluidity of mediums, a post-medium, postmodern art asserts itself.

There is far more nuance to Krauss's argument, but here I'll say that her ideas concerning medium-specificity and its erosion are obviously of great significance in thinking about the ways in which what she refers to as "medium" and what I specify as "discipline" play so centrally not only in late twentieth-century installation art but also in the modernist interdisciplinary precedents that were foundational for it. And so, to come back for a moment to a distinction between "medium" and "discipline," for my purposes "medium" denotes the material means within a discipline, underlining the concerted interrogation of means in the act of making and the physicality that was indeed a part of the modernist project. In the same breath, "discipline" is the container or platform for the medium, so that, for example, watercolor, charcoal, or bronze are the materials used with specific techniques within the broader disciplines of painting, drawing, and sculpture. It's apparent, in rehearsing this history of early European modernist art, that these artists never demoted materials or techniques in any final way—not even in the case of Duchamp, despite all the remarkable turns along the path of his work. As we'll see, regarding the music in Wagner's music-dramas, the language and sounds of Hugo Ball's poems, and every millimeter of marks in Cézanne's paintings, those works as discipline-objects were deeply and intensely worked on precisely in their specificity, while the teaching principles that Gropius formulated for the Bauhaus were specifically focused on materials and techniques.

This specificity within each discipline-object is crucial to the dynamics of those objects together. The reciprocity between discipline-objects in the history of European modernism and its interdisciplinary impulse adds genealogical layers and resonates differently, yet I hope usefully, with what Krauss has written so persuasively. To those ends, the physicality of the discipline-object in its thingness is considered below and then expanded on in its own chapter in my narrative. In a way, what I quoted above from Groys's argument underlines just how crucial medium and discipline are, as they're the tools of the artist as legislator—or, perhaps, dictator—and I'll soon enough quote the artist Ilya Kabakov, who elaborates on the artist's willful control of every aspect of an installation. In many ways, this was already characteristic of the early European modernists, whose works bring into relief the potency of interdisciplinary constellations of discipline-objects as conveyances for sensations and meanings accrued through networked relations among their specific material qualities, in concert with other dynamics, such that we can speak of "medium" and "discipline" as nodal elements with their own internal protocols that are activated in turn through the protocols of the networked whole of the work.

In this light, Joselit notes that art objects, rather than spoken of as the product of reified mediums, should be thought of as "format," which he defines in terms of "nodal connections and differential fields" and which "channel an unpredictable array of ephemeral currents and charges."[28] Through the optics of network aesthetics, "medium," "discipline," and "format" are constituents of this interdisciplinary conveyance of sensation and meaning, a platform that links internal properties to external ones in permeable relations that are often contingent and unpredictable—the immutability of laws and rules questioned, longed for, enforced, or denied. I've already linked the words "format" and "platform" in passing, and they both serve to identify these kinds of creations as containers and conveyances conceived, even if intuitively, as differential fields in which heterogeneous elements come to life. They are, to use a computational phrase, difference engines.

Yet it's important to go one further step in defining these terms, differentiating "interdisciplinary" from nomenclature that has entered critical writing and is often used interchangeably to describe this kind of art. Intermedia art, multimedia art, and mixed-media art have at various times been used as synonyms for interdisciplinary art. Krauss does this herself, and we find instances of this as far back as the 1960s, to the writings, for example, of the early media theorist Dick Higgins.[29] But "multidisciplinary" is the term most commonly used without any seeming sense of difference from "interdisciplinary," and so a clarification is important. For my purposes, in the case of the visual arts, "multidisciplinary" signifies that an artist produces works in a variety of mediums and disciplines, but they remain individual works. So, let's say, an artist does a suite of drawings, a moving-image work, and a series of sculptural objects for an exhibition. They aren't meant to be interconnected, or perhaps only thematically.

In contrast, interdisciplinary art strategically joins together various artistic disciplines as communicative agents within a *single* work. This is the case in the historical works I address. To make one further distinction, interdisciplinary works as I define them in relation to the historical examples in this book are distinct from the common contemporary practice identified as "transdisciplinary"—works that aren't primarily centered on the essential medium- and discipline-based properties of their individual parts and their integration into something singularly unified but seek to create entirely new frameworks through the expansion of the apparatus into fields of knowledge and practice other than artistic ones such as economics, fields of scientific inquiry, ethnography, etc. Transdisciplinary works may organize themselves as single entities or may, again, simply be related as works within a common theme displayed alongside one another.

Still, in thinking about the term "interdisciplinary," it has to be said that there's nothing in the term itself that indicates the *degree* of integration of parts within the whole, which is so central to the notions of networks and network aesthetics that I'm proposing in re-reading European modernism. This isn't to deny the material, processual, and procedural introspection that Krauss calls the recursive structure crucial to modernism, which remains an interiorized conception of discrete parts, of constitutive elements. Certainly, to begin thinking about the linking of discipline-objects is to begin with an understanding of them as precisely that, as individual things.

Heidegger considers a thing as a gathering of qualities, just as Hegel before him wrote about essence and form: "Precisely because the form is as necessary to the essence as the essence to itself, absolute reality must not be conceived of and expressed as essence alone, i.e. as immediate substance, or as pure self-intuition of the Divine, but as form also, and with the entire wealth of the developed form. Only then is it grasped and expressed as really actual."[30]

In turn, Heidegger conjectures how essence and form present what he calls the "thinghood" of a thing. He writes: "The thing as such is the thing which has many properties. The thinghood of the thing is that whatness of the particular this, the universal. This universal (thinghood) includes the following essential moments: the 'also' of many properties and the one of the unity of the independent object, which we now call thing."[31]

These ideas of essence and form, of a thing's properties as they inform network aesthetics and the networked relation of discipline-objects, are the way each object, each thing radiates in each viewer's perception, its apparatus seeming to unfold its points of energy in space. The discipline-object as a thing incites my recognition that it is not myself. It's a separate entity, even if, through my cognition, it enters my sense of being in the world. And from this condition of relation, I come to its existential emergence in my experiential field. This is to say that the actions of artists and viewers, in constructing and contemplating the work, inaugurate the event of its being, its emergence into sensation and meaning as we look at it, listen to it if it can be listened to, smell it, touch it, perhaps even taste it, or imagine its surface against our hands—the senses engaged through the artist's physical and intellectual means.

Still, as I say, the work as a thing is not me, its otherness exists alongside me, presenting an edge, a possibility of sociality, query, provocation, and negotiation. So, Moten writes: "How might another understanding of the thing, an understanding of the thing from the position of the thing, of the radically other, a position heretofore conceived as beyond thinking's frontier, serve to rehabilitate—which is to say, to bridge—separation and the touch in all of their interinanimate necessity?"[32]

The thing in its thingness as both bodily and social constructs presents itself to me. It inserts itself into my story. Its gathering of qualities addresses itself to me just as I address myself to this thing and to the assembly of things. Each and all together bridge matter and thought, a narrative of sensory, social, and political meanings in my personal narrative of self. In this act of self-consciousness, discipline-objects form a multiplicity. They amplify what the artist intends as their directed being, and their potential meaningfulness seems to move toward me.

In actuality, I move toward and around them. The path I enter among the work's parts compels me to sense the physical size of individual discipline-objects and as an interdisciplinary whole. I cognize this materiality. I know from the vocabulary of sensory memory the weight of things, their feel, smoothness, roundness, what density is, what cool and heat are, the manual use of things, and so on.

In the contemplation of this collection of things toward a narrative of myself and myself in relation to the world of others, this reciprocity, this bridge, is a vector line of energy that lives within what Deleuze and Guattari call "a plane of consistency" that envisions an expansive gridded structure whose multiplicities continually redefine themselves through their connections.[33] Each thing within the matrix of the interdisciplinary work has its properties, its essence and form, its medium-specificity, its technical apparatus within its disciplinary being. These are at the base of the interaction—all the histories of each kind of discipline-object, its way of announcing its individual being and mutable presence as a node, a data point, a semiotic projector in interaction with the other objects constellated in its proximity. As I experience the work, whether I'm still or moving, I, too, am part of the plane of consistency, entered onto the platform, and each thing, though separate from me, seems to run toward me, through me, and away from me.

This ground of connective relations projects an interface from its surface, rich with physical information and representational presence. As Benjamin H. Bratton writes in his book on planetary-scale computation, *The Stack: On Software and Sovereignty*, for a thing "to be known, it must be locatable as a discrete entity among all other things."[34] He speaks of this as "addressable flows." And while one thing may be intricately or grossly different from another in kind and quality, nonetheless, all things linked in a network share what he calls "an ambient field of systematic intercommunication and assembly"—an apt description of interdisciplinary artworks. Just so, an artist attempts to give each discipline-object singly and in concert with others an address, a locatability, where meaning and feeling can be found. The artist puts in place the rules of governance that give the work its particular logic of being, while simultaneously presenting to viewers an apparatus for the actuation of their own agency, their own subjectivities altering their perceptions of the work, and so, again, they can be described as viewer-agents.

We can call the relation of discipline-objects within the work "hard" relations, embedded as they are in the materiality of each object, while the subjectivities of viewer-agents as potentially dissensual actants, like Lucretian clinamen raining down, introduce into the work's dynamics a "soft" relation that affords its porousness, its elasticity. This is characteristic of network aesthetics and, in its internal and centrifugal mobility, points to the sense of movement and change intrinsic to interdisciplinary assemblages and their reception. The velocity of each viewer-agent's thinking immersed in the work can be said to crack the empirical shell of its discipline-objects. This cognition shimmies the co-relation of objects between their materiality and interfacial surfaces, their outward presence toward the viewer precisely for cognition. Each discipline-object is loosened from its shell of wood, paint, film, time-based narrative, sociality, whatever its container, and transforms its substance into meaning, unstable and individual as that meaning may be for each viewer-agent in turn. It is a matter of moments, the tiniest leap from the flesh.

The artist, the constellation of discipline-objects, and viewer-agents constitute a triangulation of power relations in which contingent intensities of difference and pressure, of varying expectations, backgrounds, (un)freedoms, and behaviors intersect, transact, and continually adjust their interoperability along the work's plane of consistency. This fluid schema presents an emergent becoming, an algorithmic condition of networked relations among things in the particular sense that Luciana Parisi states as fundamentally open to indeterminacy and contingency.[35] The word "algorithm" itself is based on accident—a corrupted transliteration of al-Khwarizmi, Arabic for "native of Khwarazm," the surname of the great mathematician who brought what became known as algebra to the West—and has come to signify a computational sequence of instructions broken down into parts toward the solving of a problem.

The artist imagines and attempts to work through the algorithmic sequence of discipline-objects laid out within its network—a solving of the problem of the work as every artwork is a form of problem-solving. The artist imagines and attempts to establish the protocols of the work, both internal and in active relation among the interdisciplinary work's parts; what he, she, or they intend to signify; and how these significances are meant to be received. "In the broadest sense," Alexander Galloway and Eugene Thacker write, "protocol is a technology that regulates flow, directs netspace, codes relationships, and connects life-forms."[36]

This braiding of nodal and network protocols activates the individual rules and group rules for discipline-objects in a flow of woven communication; production and interpretation modulate the making and perception of the work. The emulsification of discipline-objects in the process of the viewer's cognition of the whole is always in motion, and so it can be said that the algorithmic and protocological structure of the work tests my self-consciousness, the narrative of myself with others emanating from the work, which is always a lure, a spider's web, a paradoxical locatability of semiotically shifting things, and therefore a negotiation, a microcosm of the world's scale within a logic of multiplicities and the enunciation of assembly.

Naturally, as the chapters to come will bear out, artists bring varying intentions with regard to wholeness in the assemblages they construct. In his remarkable series of lectures, "On the 'Total' Installation," Ilya Kabakov, speaking of his Constructivst forebears, states: "The coordination of forms, their simplicity, the nakedness of the 'device,' all function with iron necessity in a total installation that 'works' well."[37] His fifteen lectures are a veritable how-to for the creation of an installation, saying explicitly at the end of the first lecture that his total installation is nothing more or less than a new Gesamtkunstwerk. He details everything from ideal space dimensions, sound level, colors, lighting, materials, even that the installation can change with the movement of the viewer. And "well," of course, means well for the artist as legislator, as sovereign; well for the producer whose decisions about the characteristics of each discipline-object and its relation to other objects spatially and temporally mean that they strictly follow the protocols that define their closed system—the network as a walled garden in which viewer-agents are frictionless observers, not essentially considered in the regulated character of the work. This type of installation is based on a notion of central command in which all components of the work encode an idealized union in which there is no impurity of the signal, although specters of ideological danger loom whenever schemes of purity arise.

That is one kind of strategy within the triangulation of power that I've proposed is always at play in the interdisiciplinary work. And while the case of Wagner, for example, leans into centralized control, as we'll see, the constructed space of the interdisciplinary work in its orientation toward distributed forms of wholeness is also prevalent—what has been called "node-to-node relations with no backbone or center."[38] Hugo Ball at the Cabaret Voltaire was one such interdisciplinary strategist. And so, let me return for a moment to the subject of formatting and platform to speak more fully about the intentional network structure of these works, with Bratton elaborating on what I've said about governance and communication, about the interdependencies and motions of transaction that the interdisciplinary work presents.

> A platform's systems are composed of interfaces, protocols, visualizable data, and strategic renderings of a geography, time, landscapes, and object fields. [. . .] Even as the majority of information they mediate may be machine-to-machine communication (as, for example, today's Internet), the specific evolution of any one platform, in the ecological niche between the human and the inhuman, depends on how it frames the world for those who use it. It draws some things in and draws other things out, but foremost a platform is a drawing and framing machine.[39]

Bratton's vision for his "Stack" draws relevance from Michel Foucault's notion of the *dispositif*, or apparatus, in its crucial aspect as a vast structure of connections among different levers of knowledge and power. "What I'm trying to single out with this term," Foucault explains, "is, first and foremost, a thoroughly heterogeneous set consisting of discourses, institutions, architectural forms, regulatory decisions, laws, administrative measures, scientific statements, philosophical, moral, and philanthropic propositions [. . .]. The apparatus itself is the network that can be established between these elements."[40]

In relation to interdisciplinary artworks and network aesthetics, the inverse of this is also the case: the network is the apparatus that draws energetic links between elements of subjective expression and administrative power. Discipline-objects and their interactions are a *dispositif* for communicative means of address, a matrix in which artistic flights of imagination create a ludic communality bound by fluid codes of operation. They generate a sense of shared being, a framing of the world within the work and the world that the work frames. The artist may intend to control as much as possible as a walled garden or may be more open to contingencies. Discipline-objects may be revised, changed, or replaced. The interface of the work may be altered in the arrangement of objects coterminous with the pressures and influences bending their reception by viewer-agents. The organization may share something with Kant's notion that "every science is a system in its own right [. . .] a separate and independent building. We must treat it as a self-subsisting whole, and not as a wing or section of another building—although we may subsequently make a passage to and fro from one part to another."[41]

Yet a building is presumably stable, a fixed structure, while the interdisciplinary work, whatever the artist's intentions, has all of that sense of vivid complexity Bratton delineates and has a more vital organicity. Each discipline-object can be thought of as an organ within a body. Just as the whole of the work, in the Deleuzian sense of fluidity, acts as a "Body without Organs," its shifting formations inflected by the mercury-like nature of viewers' projected subjectivities—all to be thought of as chemical combustions of combined properties, an architecture of aleatory possibility in reaction to an artist's initial instruction set.

Pierre Bourdieu describes this effect in *The Field of Cultural Production*: "The auto-constitution of a system of works united by a set of significant relationships is accomplished in and through the association of contingency and meaning which is unceasingly made, unmade and remade."[42] And Bratton notes that "platforms centralize and decentralize at once, drawing many actors into a common infrastructure. They distribute some forms of autonomy to the edges of its networks while also standardizing conditions of communications between them."[43] Deleuze is more poetic, but underlines the relativism and viral relationships among the component parts of assemblages when he writes:

> What is an assemblage? It is a multiplicity which is made up of heterogeneous terms and which establishes liaisons, relations between them, across ages, sexes and reigns—different natures. Thus, the assemblage's only unity is that of a co-functioning: it

is a symbiosis, a "sympathy." It is never filiations which are important, but alliances, alloys; these are not successions, lines of descent, but contagions, epidemics, the wind.[44]

Once the platform and its operating assemblage are activated and brought into the public sphere, the interdisciplinary work instantly initiates what the sociologist Geoffrey Bowker has referred to as a "legitimacy exchange." For Bowker, the term represents the crucial interaction among scientists and mathematicians who lent each other languages and logics that gave credence to new modalities and the birth of the interdisciplinary field of cybernetics, as the cultural historian and communication scholar Fred Turner points out. He notes: "As Bowker suggests, cybernetics facilitated not only the interlinking of research, development, and production activities, but also the development of new interpersonal and interinstitutional networks and, with them, the exchange and generation of a networked form of power."[45] Manuel DeLanda has similarly spoken of "legitimizing narratives" that code authority structures. These are the rules, rituals, regulations, standard procedures, histories, traditions, and narratives of social institutions and practices that operate within rational-legal forms—or, counter to them, are "overcoded," as DeLanda calls it, when a new social code superimposes itself and dominates.[46]

If the interdisciplinary artwork's discipline-objects are containers of administrative traditions, regulations, and procedures, the legitimacy they draw from one another is dependent on the degree to which their organicity is fully labile and effective from within and without. The activities of the interdisciplinary assemblage as a drawing and framing machine comprised of nonhuman and human elements indicate a process of coding and overcoding that produces a virus of sympathies and irritations, its components coupling, decoupling, and recoupling their phenomenological effects and semantic meanings, shifting through each viewer-agent's cognition to form different unities.

The process of the work unfolds in time as well as space. The way, for example, a painting's physicality (its material gestures, the light on its impastoed surface, the density of its marks, its palette, even the passage over time of its smell) stands against the temporality of a video or a work online; all of them pictures, yet different modalities of picturing, different tempos, different material resistances and limits, different tasks involved, a different duration inhabiting the eyes. Sound, too, is an active durational component—music, recorded sounds, live aural events—integral as well to so many of the historical works surveyed here, from Wagner's music-dramas to the Cabaret Voltaire, the sounds and music Duchamp envisions to accompany his works, and Bauhaus theater.

A body standing and moving between discipline-objects in an interdisciplinary installation senses these phenomenological activators: the apparatus of sight gauging depth, volume, color, light, motion; hearing that senses nearness and distance; different forms of harmony, dissonance, composed time signatures, randomness; and spatial sensitivities impregnated with time. The sensory operations of the assemblage constitute its being-state that I noted earlier, the protocols of the work activating them. These activations enliven the agency of viewers, whose entry into the work as mobile nodes performs another linkage within it, the knowledge-state of meaning production, of interpretation, that overcodes the assemblage. Viewer-agents process the specific transmissions of information relayed between nodes, instantiating their legitimizing narratives. They cognize the parts and the whole asynchronously, instantly, and in incremental flashbacks of sense accumulation—an irregular, chunked temporality of meaning formation. For viewer- agents, each discipline-object within the work and the work as a whole present a form and a spatial and temporal process, a motion of expression in a convivial or troubling order of call and response, an exchange of values continually enacting a form of social swarming that presses and alters the boundaries of the work in the volutions of shifting influencers. "How a set of simple, local actions," Galloway and Thacker say, "culminates in complex, collective organization, problem solving, and task fulfillment."[47]

Objects within the work have different energies of attraction, like actors of different magnetisms—what the sociologist Clay Shirky calls "power law distribution," noting: "In systems where many people are free to choose between many options, a small subset of the whole will get a disproportionate amount of traffic (or attention, or income), even if no members of the system actively work toward such an outcome."⁴⁸ Power law distribution adds still more complexity to the roiling interior of the network, indicating that there is never a single topology that describes the interdisciplinary work but, to use Bratton's term, a continuous "geo-graphic" inscription; meanings inscribed within the situated arrangement of things develop through the interactions of object with object, node with node.

The artist establishes the physicality of the work for this geo-graphic arena, the agora of meaning-making in which calibrated protocols seek to legislate interactions, while viewer-agents in their continuous intersections with discipline-objects hack the network, erupt its syntax, distend its framing of parts as confirmation of the interdisciplinary work's intricate multivocality, its pluriverse of sovereignties. As Galloway and Thacker note, "Thus any type of protocological control exists not because the network is smooth and continuous but precisely because the network contains within it antagonistic clusterings, divergent subtopologies, rogue nodes. [. . .] The problem of 'control' in networks is always doubled by two perspectives: one from within the network and one from without the network."⁴⁹

The interdisciplinary artwork operates in the same register as a platform in which the protocols of artistic production allow contingency into the nodal interactions, including those of each viewer-agent, each rogue node, whose entrance and passage through the work creates unforeseen transitory ripples of generative meaning. As Jagoda states, "network aesthetics emphasize not merely that everything is connected but that people and things connect, intersect, disconnect, become, atrophy, transform, or emerge over time."⁵⁰ The role of contingency that impinges on artistic protocological control—that's to say, dynamizes it—is a feature of network aesthetics in which generative meaning is created from the persistence of noise, of double signals, triple signals, layers of data and interpretation folding over, intertwining, delaying, and intervening with one another.

Each interaction of viewer-agents within the framing machine of the work is a hermeneutic event of its own small magnitude that opens the swarming society of discipline-objects, ineluctably revising the interfacial effects of the work, presenting a new geo-graphic encounter, a newly catalyzed sociality. There is never one edge between discipline-objects but the layering, superimposition, and radiation of their links, generating manifold meanings from their materiality and the immaterial traces of other things, other events and times that stream through them. In this regard, Latour's thinking is useful. He anatomizes interactions as they occur in society, which stand as true for viewer-agents' interactions in the society of discipline-objects inhabiting an assemblage.

Latour speaks of what he calls the "not isotopic" character of an interaction, meaning that every social transaction is influenced by other transactions that occurred in other places. This aligns with the "synchronic," that tracing of overlapping moments across a temporal spectrum so that, in offering a reverie of a teacher's presence in the classroom near the office where Latour is writing, he muses:

> The desk might be made of a tree seeded in the 1950s that was felled two years ago; the cloth of the teacher's dress was woven five years ago, while the firing neurons in her head might be a millisecond old and the area of the brain devoted to speech has been around for a good hundred thousand years. . . . Time is always folded.

To these features he adds the synoptic, the heterogeneous, and his own description of power law distribution. Their chorus should already seem familiar from my thinking about the interdisciplinary work, with its multivocal distributions and unities, its causal chain of human and nonhuman agents, and what Latour refers to as the "not isobaric," meaning the relative intensity of presences that interact and shift a balance of power. "In most situations," he argues, "actions will already be interfered with by heterogeneous entities that don't have the same local presence, don't come from the same time, are not visible at once, and don't press upon them with the same weight."[51]

Every interdisciplinary work's internal dynamics are a rheostat, each with its external influences inflecting the interior conditions of the system and its path of diffusion. As Anna Munster notes, "The human, for instance, is not an object 'in' the environment; rather, human-environment is a coupling that, already a network/relation, generates a network/relationality of interactions."[52] The viewer, as a rogue node within the work, introduces a shift in the collection and organization of knowledge that always revises what the work is, how it can be read, as each viewer brings to these discipline-objects and their assembly a different knowing and different pressures, external and internal, that impact the measure of the whole. In sum, the interdisciplinary work seen through network aesthetics is a spongy reactor, spatially and temporally vulnerable, at once projecting its properties and acting as a reflector of viewers who are always present and remote, parasitic and generative, always agents of contingency.

In this reciprocity of meaning production, discipline-objects are, of course, put in place to influence and affect, to transfer meaning, and so the total operation of the work, of the platform in its true interoperability, means that the viewer-agent is controlled in turn. Bratton writes about what he calls "platform sovereignty," which he notes (with his appetite for idiosyncratic capitalization) is "derived from the *Interfacial* line, surface and partition, and how its designation influences how it will *Address* its *Users* and how they *Address* the platform and one another through it."[53] Sovereignty, in its fusion of aesthetic and political aspects, is especially germane to the geo-graphic impulse of Hugo Ball at and after the Cabaret Voltaire. But in the general case of network aesthetics, the idea of platform sovereignty and its interfacial relations propose, in the fluid exchange of discipline-objects and viewer-agents, something spectral in which each component and the properties within it seem to leak.

In the discourse of the body and technoculture, this leakage is a form of resistance and liberation, what Legacy Russell describes as a glitch that refuses, that unwinds and rewinds the protocols of societal threads of gender code in the name of greater agency.[54] Her glitch feminism speaks of the body as componential, relating its agency in relation to computational machines. There's something essentially modernist in this, and it's a useful metaphor for the interdisciplinary work as well. For the work's discipline-objects constitute a body of bodies whose protocols are as determined by contingency, by the dynamics of external forces, as they are by internal codes, often incorporating forms of interference, latency, noise, and hiccups in form as a means toward a critical aesthetics of liberatory resistance and revision. Discipline-objects exist as solids, as locatable addresses and identities, yet they simultaneously deliquesce, penetrated by the will of the glitch, by rheostatic influences, as Latour's anatomy of interactions also proposes.

If the protocols of the network are administrative and the artist is the administrator, then the viewer-agent as a subjective force, as the glitch in the system, de-bureaucratizes the whole of the work. From above, the scene of the interdisciplinary work is seismic and erotic—models of undulation, explosion, and reformulation driven by the impulsive might of internal pressures and external forces acting on one another. It can be said that both artist and viewer-agent have their own limited repertoires. The protocols of the works they produce and receive are always already to a degree portable, carried from one work to the next. Yet political ideologies and political forces of coercion, scientific and technological theories, historical references, social influences, and memes, along with personal histories and events, are like mist around a light or an infection, movers of molecules that affect a work's discipline-objects and the whole.

A mise en abîme appears in this perpetual tumult of vying productions of meaning. Why is this viewer-agent here if not as an intrinsic component of the work to make self-consciousness apparent? Within the sitedness of the work is its visibility, its legibility not only as a framing machine but also implicitly as a reciprocity machine, which is what its legitimizing narrative, internally and externally, entails. The mechanisms of data exchange among the interdisciplinary work's society of chattering objects, their protocols, their elements of interaction and viral incursions are fueled by the energetic economy of self-consciousness, of each viewer-agent's conflicting and complex ideas about inside and outside, of which the phenomenological reading of the self by Maurice Merleau-Ponty is a profoundly eloquent example. So he writes about perception:

> Taken exactly as I see it, it is a moment of my individual history, and since sensation is a reconstitution, it presupposes in me sediments left behind by some previous constitution, so that I am, as a sentient subject, a repository stocked with natural powers at

which I am the first to be filled with wonder. I am not, therefore, in Hegel's phrase, "a hole in being," but a hollow, a fold, which has been made and which can be unmade.[55]

Latour radicalizes Merleau-Ponty's intricate conceptions of human sentience when he proposes that "individuality, subjectivity, person-hood, and interiority" are entirely permeable, arguing that "nothing is inside which has not come from the outside."

> But what about me, the ego? Am I not in the depth of my heart, in the circumvolutions of my brain, in the inner sanctum of my soul, in the vivacity of my spirit, an "individual"? Of course I am, but only as long as I have been individualized, spiritualized, interiorized. It is true that the circulation of these "subjectifiers" is often more difficult to track. But if you search for them, you will find them all over the place: floods, rains, swarms of what could be called psycho-morphs because they literally lend you the shape of the psyche.[56]

Both notions of the composition of self-consciousness stand in relation to Hegel, arguing, struggling, rejecting but never freed from the long shadow of inherent antagonisms and suspensions in Hegel's thinking—the "compositional struggle," as Fredric Jameson calls it[57]—that permeates his writing about self and other, about the individual, the collective, unity, and totality that bear so directly on the jurisdictional arena of the interdisciplinary work and of network aesthetics.

Hegel writes in *The Phenomenology of Spirit* that no self-consciousness, no "being-for-self," is finally fulfilled without the recognition of another, "when each is for the other what the other is for it." What he defines is the being of the social, of the power relations and responsibilities of beings-for-self—what's called the "for-us"—as a worldly expression of a collective that he speaks of as "Spirit." Spirit isn't used by Hegel as we use it, to describe the ethereal. He calls Spirit the "actuality" of ethical substance and states that it is "the unmoved, solid ground and starting-point for the action of all." This is the "purpose and goal" he demands of every self-consciousness, and in this we find the relentless-ness of his mind to forge unity in his systems. About essence, he writes that it is the "sublatedness of all differences." Things must be given up, handed over, in order to be subsumed by the satisfaction of totality. He writes, "Spirit is the ethical life of a nation in so far as it is the immediate truth—the individual that is a world." The collective subsumes the individual, and the danger of this "substantial unity," as Hegel calls it in *Outlines of the Philosophy of Right*, is that it offers a teleology in which the might of political authority "has supreme right against the individual, whose supreme duty is to be a member of the state."[58] So Michael Hart and Antonio Negri remark that "Hegel revealed what was implicit from the beginning of the counterrevolutionary development: that the liberation of modern humanity could only be a function of its domination, that the immanent goal of the multitude is transformed into the necessary and transcendent power of the state."[59]

With Hegel's words, the agon of inside and outside arrives at a terminus, a pulverization, a ladder of doctrinal prohibitions, which are nothing less than the rigid triumph of protocol over contingency and chance—an arrow pointed at histories of brutal oppressions of all kinds to follow. Frantz Fanon, for example, argued that Hegel's "being for other" is essentially a colonialist privilege in which "ontological resistance" is always unattainable for oppressed Black societies.[60] As I will use it, "for-us" is a term indicating an ethical impulse of positive value in co-relations, but this is not to ignore that who the other is has been bracketed by power, constraint, and violence. The triangulation I've drawn between Merleau-Ponty, Latour, and Hegel is meant to serve as an index of theorized social relations that reside within the self and between the self and other selves, positively and negatively charged, that operate variously in the European modernist examples laid out in the chapters ahead.

To think of the self and others is, to a degree, metaphorical as an illustration of the ways in which discipline-objects under the governance of the artist form haptic and semantic relationships, whether harmoniously or not, whether dominated by a single component, more evenly distributed, or simply without complete connection among its parts. So, Bratton contends, "an interface that may be open for one User at one moment may be closed to another."[61] Yet to extrapolate from the cognitive-behavioral operation of the viewer-agent as one force of

contingency suggests the larger complexities at work of chance and ramification (from the Latin verbs "to fall away" and "to branch out"), so
that the broader ground, the platform for the interdisciplinary artwork,
is the baize on which the billiard balls of war, technology, and social
change collide, compelling both artists and viewers, with and beyond
their innate experiential predilections, to do and think reactively.

Such is the case in Wagner's music-dramas, the aftermath of Cabaret
Voltaire, and Gropius's Bauhaus in Dessau, drawn as they were to the
seductions of totality in different forms. Others were enthralled by
the shine of the most mercury-like pools of shape-shifting identities
in which all elements of their works swam—the lesson that Cézanne
taught to Duchamp and Duchamp to everyone afterward. In this way,
the interdisciplinary work as a Gesamtkunstwerk, as a totalizing work
of art, reproduces its historical society, just as Latour remarks, "Society
is not the whole 'in which' everything is embedded, but what travels
'through' everything, calibrating connections and offering every entity
it reaches some possibility of commensurability"—even if commensurability, as an operative aspect of the network of the work, is never fully
accomplished or is the zenith of the artist's intention.[62]

This is all to say that network aesthetics, as a way of understanding the European modernist works assessed here and their relevance
to future works, describes a system of systems, a framing that is always
refractive, a microcosm of the flux of the world. Bratton is useful
again when he remarks that one "jurisdictional vision" may touch
any given set of interactions, but "multiple or incongruous strategies"
from without—what he calls "state, nonstate, transstate, superstate, or
substate actors"—impact the sovereignty of any claim to totality.[63] The
matrix of measurements of the relations within the society of the interdisciplinary work and of societies themselves is, one can say, a matter
of models to scale.

In this refractive condition, there is no terminus in the sense of a
teleology of the self, only the littoral actions of behaviors, jurisdictional
orders, individual subjectivities, and the group assembly of intersubjectivities that are briefly joined, exercise their eddying judgments, plebi-
scites of nodal conjunctions, and then wash back into the ocean of the
human and nonhuman mass, dispersed. When Bourriaud speaks with

a predictive flourish in the last pages of *The Randicant* about a twenty-first-century art and culture that "will give rise to a new common intelligibility,"[64] he is gesturing toward a communalist inflection that had already emerged in these modernist interdisciplinary proto-networks as salutary gestures, yet that were most often unstable and had to contend as well with what political tyrannies (which rhetorically advertised themselves as communal fealty) imposed.

Now we look through the lens of an era of accelerated developments in artificial intelligence, when the very notion of one thing connected to another is recalibrated by the most pressing sense of immensely efficient platforms for concatenation and infection. Wholeness refracted in these ways is predicated on an irony of contagion and the viral—the virality of autonomous, nonhuman agents in power relations with humans that magnify hybrid entities and operations in asymmetrical dynamics that will continue to shift what wholeness means in micro and macro registers of sociality.

It is all the more poignant to review those artistic enterprises that took as their imaginary the constructs of unity, though they may have been far from consistent in the ways their creations align unity with benevolence. Whether toward a self-affirming or self-sublating impulse of totalism, the Gesamtkunstwerk, cabaret, *poème simultan*, painting as nature, body as machine, readymade, and *Einheitskunstwerk*—reconsidered in these pages not only through the optics of network aesthetics but also as the foundations for it—rose from the specters of fragmentation, seeking the splendor of coherence, the power of the unseparate, settling, dissolving, and leaving their traces in the silt of generations, pointing toward now.

The Senses

SEE

• • • The dark. I remember Dante's first lines in *The Inferno*: lost in the dark woods. Or at the end of the journey, when he climbs up and stares at the stars falling through time on the figure of Love. But to be without sight or to stand in the low light's half-glimmer isn't Love or the embodiment of Grace. It's the loss of the body, body leaking into air. First the eye is an apparatus for surviving prey, weather, the riddled landscape with its fissures, its obscurities. The passage from unknowable to known, the stepped grammar of recognition carried by photons to cognition, to understanding, to action. . . . Sight stands at the entryway of this causality, where being makes itself known in the ground of our blood and tissue and the tiny fierce engine of continuance. I'm used to sight. I'm the *why* that mates my eyes to my I-ness. But not my eyes alone. I share the field of communion in a consensus on colors or that the small drops of glint running down the window like a snail's slick will come to be called "rain" or that the particular thickness I sense through my eyes is a thing then shaped in my mouth as the word *leather*, *cuir*, *Leder*, with its wrinkles and seams like the dead trace of the animal it was. Seeing is survival's language, the breath of my eyes.

I start with sight as the generality of my being, the sense from which the encyclopedic taxonomies emerge. I count the lamps in a room, trees in the humped blue air, all those things around me (their materialities, structures, transparencies and weights, their patterns), which are first not metaphors, not science, not abstractions, not indexical signs. I begin with the dark because I imagine my eyes first being closed as the absence of a primal location of the self in space. I'm leaking into the air without the boundary of skin, though I know I have skin and boundary. My eyes are closed, as the beginning of the world is closed until it's opened by what is inferred and assumed but not said—that *sight* is the beginning and that the Logos, the Word, is enunciation of what is *seen*. I write with the instrument of seeing. I speak words as we've long imagined sight as the progenitor embodied in the figure of Adam who first saw and then named and is himself the figuration of light made flesh, made Word. Light fills his mouth and projects concretions, formed sounds, a mirroring language, an organ of codes deriving shapes in the air, formed whispers, exhalations of meaning.

We say, *You see? Do you see what I mean?* In the dark, I'm not sure of meaning because my I unlearns its shapes, and when my eyelids lift as the light comes, the first *yes* of being re-forms, strikes the time of being and place, the visible *qua* of every thing in its thingness that comes after as the enumerated, the catalogued furnishings of the world, the winding chain of knowledges spooled first from the eye's primacy, inward into memory, outward as the lapidary art of interpretation. But what I want, here, isn't the more-than-sight, woven and weight, but light in its firstness.

I had gone far into the dark. It doesn't matter why or what it was. Each of us has this in our lives. Many times. My eyes had fallen shut to firstness, to the locus of what arrives in the empirical from the authorless state of *is*. To lose this is Dante's wolf, the dissolution of the Word, of knowing, epistemological zero, (Bataille's spit). The ambition of every artwork is always in some way to reconstruct firstness, to intimate the birth of knowing, the being of personhood, the constructs of the social again and again. Out of nothing, something. It says to us: Each time you enter, *see*.

Two

ABSOLUTE INTEGRATION AND
TERMINAL UNITY/WAGNER'S WAY

• • • Totality is a lure, a danger, a promise. We look across the landscape of the divisible in time and in the being of parts. Every fragment is a call to a *once*, of what is remembered or imagined of a prior wholeness, the lost health of the body or polity. The native land of the self inevitably seeks unity as an act of recuperation, and so it was in 1849, as Richard Wagner sat in exile in Zurich. The historical record has long noted his complicity in Germany's failed revolution that played out before his eyes in Dresden that year. The dream was to end absolute monarchy, joining the country's thirty-nine independent states into a democratic union under constitutional monarchy, and Wagner, in typical revisionary mode to improve his fortunes, later emended his recollections to suggest his political zeal was only youthful folly. He wrote: "In my own country I had, without quite realizing it, come to be considered a criminal owing to the peculiar connection between my disgust at the public attitude towards art and the general political disturbances."[1]

Yet 1848 and into the spring of 1849 were filled with plans for insurrection, mass demonstrations, and violent skirmishes in Germany (as throughout Europe), and planning sessions took place in Wagner's own home, in the company of the anarchist Mikhail Bakunin and his confederates. The composer gives public form to his radicalization in the speech he offered on June 14, 1848, to the local *Vaterlandsverein*, in which he combines swollen metaphors of fatherland, soil and labor, and the *Volk* with the equally swollen abstraction of "the idea [*Begriff*] of Prussiandom," which must, like faulty munitions, be detonated—an ambition in keeping with Nicolas Bourriaud's image of the derrick that symbolizes the wrecking will of modernist aesthetics.[2]

Wagner speaks of a "great war of liberation" and imagines emancipated citizens "exchanging the products of their activities to mutually enrich and benefit each other"—so telling for his future art and its legacy in interdisciplinary production. The language of campaigning for radical unity enters Wagner's theorization of a renovated artistic practice in thrall to collectivity, a politicization embedded in art by profound, if delusively imagined, structural means. "When art held her peace, the wisdom of the State and philosophy began. Now that both the statesman and philosopher have breathed their last, let the artist's voice be heard again."[3]

Four days into the revolt, on May 7, 1849, the opera house where Wagner was the resident conductor was set aflame; an event of symbolic note in his private rebellion-to-come against the conventions of musical form. With the uprising resolutely demolished by Kaiser Wilhelm IV the day after the destruction of the opera house, Wagner deserted Dresden under the threat of arrest. Others were less lucky than the composer. Bakunin and many of his political associates were imprisoned or scattered. Over the next three weeks, he fled through Chemnitz, Weimar, Magdala, Jena, from there through Bavaria, and settled finally in Zurich.[4] For the next twelve years Wagner stayed, the recent champion of the demise of despotic monarchism enjoying the sinecure of customary noble patronage—self-contradiction intrinsic to Wagner's complexity. In that first year of exile, he wrote the long essay "Art and Revolution," and then, with a title bearing homage to Ludwig Feuerbach's philosophical work *Principles of the Philosophy of the Future*, he composed the ur-text of artistic interdisciplinarity, "The Art-Work of the Future."

Wagner spoke of his abiding devotion in later years to Schopenhauer's philosophy, but Feuerbach was his early philosophical enthusiasm. So, Friederich Nietzsche, who once admired Wagner and then turned against him, states: "Let us remember how enthusiastically Wagner at one time walked in the footsteps of the philosopher Feuerbach. Feuerbach's words 'healthy sensuality' struck Wagner in the thirties and forties very much as they struck many other Germans—they called themselves the young Germans—that is to say, as words of salvation."[5] Fresh from the rhetoric of revolution, Wagner couldn't be more blunt in his deployment of a socially inflected lexicon to determine the future course for art and society.

> I was forced to recognize that it is not the individual, but only the *community* that can bring artistic deeds to actual accomplishment, past any doubts of the senses. The recognition of this fact, if hope is not to be entirely abandoned, means to raise the standard of revolt against the whole condition of our present art and life.[6]

He goes on to argue that all art must be seen as a "factor in the life of the State" and to embrace it finally as a "social product."[7] His social and aesthetic omphalos is ancient Greece, his dream of unity knit from Athenian tragedy's strands of choral song, dance, and narrative that together, in Wagner's words, "brought forth the highest conceivable form of art—the DRAMA."[8] The fall from this unity, made manifest in art, is the collapse of the Grecian state. "As the spirit of community split itself along a thousand lines of egoistic cleavage, so was the great united work of tragedy disintegrated into its individual factors."[9] That fragmentation is a mirror of Wagner's ruined hopes for Germany, as he wrote from exile. Yet there is more to the simple equivalence of state and artifice as a fragmented *demos*. An implicit sense of the pure and impure struggle there; Wagner ties this ethics to the formation of forms, whether political or aesthetic, and entwined as they are.

Now his language becomes more interesting. "The Grecian tragedy denoted the culminating point of the Grecian spirit; but ours is the efflorescence of corruption, of a hollow, soulless and unnatural condition of human affairs and human relations."[10] What lies beneath this bloom of corruption is something corporeal, sulkily sexual, something about the unclean body, unclean makers, unclean relations. The unnatural. Wagner sees the art of his times as a corruption in the body, a transrevolutionary condition to be attended to. Failed political union is replaced by a programmatic insurrection through artistic vision that performs a purification of commingled bodies. The body of the artist, of the citizen, of the state are cleansed and conjoined in a Grecian retrotopia made wholly German in this new operation of unity. Wagner calls this "the genuine Drama; that one, indivisible, supreme creation of the mind of man."[11]

He means, of course, his own mind that now fixes on a precise inversion of what he said earlier in the same essay. It isn't that art is merely a social fact poured from the crucible of revolution, art that begins and ends in community and universal commensurability. Instead, this teleological *volk*-ness, this collective destiny, is a product of art itself. "Art and its institutions, whose desired organization could here be only briefly touched on, would thus become the herald and the standard of all future communal institutions," Wagner writes. "The spirit that urges a body of artists to the attainment of its own true goal, would be found again in every other social union which set before itself a definite and honorable aim."[12] That is: *I am the embodiment of the artist-body and the social-body.* The revolutionary future is built from a union of parts, as Wagner had plotted in Dresden, a union now fused in the notion of artistic disciplines both as armaments for a new kind of unifying insurrection and as organs of radically embodied change.

And so, "The Art-Work of the Future" is, in the most fundamental and also the most evocative ways, a call to arms in militant and erotic rhetoric, an essay fixed on copulation. A copula is a bridge—a comma is a copula that ties together a community of phrases. Buried in our genetic code is that need to make these joints that communities are made from, a communion of individuals, of individuated parts, so that we avoid the *horror vacui* of existential voids and social chaos. In Wagner's text, we read the proclamation of the political rendering of the copula through art. He calls it the Gesamtkunstwerk: the total work of art.

Still, the production he envisions and produces isn't total. Totality would be that from which nothing can be excluded, an object in which all other objects are present. And then, what about networks themselves, as the Wagnerian Gesamtkunstwerk is a proto-network of connected disciplinary components, of musical motifs that attempt to tie stories, gestures, and images into one continuous tonic flow under the final protocol of the drama? The total network is the simultaneous coexistence of multiplicities of infinitely connected nodes of communication in which all protocols are algorithmically different and yet interlingually unified. This network would need to be defined as a platform of interconnectivity among things, a ceaseless nodal production, and the interconnectivity of all things would define the network as one with a supra-protocol that allowed the infinite legibility of this infinitude of nodes one to another. The network of networks would be, to borrow a phrase from Quentin Meillassoux, an "unencompassable pluralization"—simultaneously limitless and absolute, and all simultaneity paradoxically timeless.[13]

In this light, Hegel speaks in his *Logic* of "the identity of identity and non-identity," which he says "could be regarded as the first, purest, that is, most abstract, definition of the absolute."[14] There is a moment in which, he says (and Marx said after him in his *Grundrisse*), an *Umschlag* occurs: an inversion in which the contradiction between identity and non-identity is negated, suspended, transformed into its opposite and a new form transpires, not less contradictory but self-encompassing.[15] The power relations within this ultimate network allow unceasing asymmetries, contingencies, and regulations within irregulations and their inverse. The infinite network swallowing the idealized Hegelian *Umschlag* is always an event unfolding and refolding itself, always a process of accommodation to the heterogeneous elements within, outside and inside seamless with one another, the endless accommodation to the otherness of nodal others.

This is what Meillassoux remarks on when he speaks of Hegel's notion of the absoluteness of a supreme entity that "remains in itself even as it passes into its other." It "absorbs both difference and becoming into its superior identity" and "harbors the superior form of eternity because it is at once temporal and atemporal, processual and immutable."[16] Of course, the prospect of ruin also hovers when the theological and political combine and claim superiority. In its continual autopoiesis, the supreme network encompasses and displays its generative and ceaseless state of becoming, while also offering the peril of its oppressive omega. We can read all of this into Wagner's Gesamtkunstwerk, with its stain of Hegelian absolutism, just as Meillassoux's mentor, Alain Badiou, states that Wagner "is the Hegel of art in the sense that he brought to an end, through his systematic failure, the project of high art as a project apposite to the absoluteness of its subject matter"—an "aestheticization of totality."[17] With far less sympathy, Nietzsche called Wagner "the heir of Hegel. . . . Music as 'Idea.'"[18]

It can be said, at least, that the proposition of Wagner's total work of art isn't so much a realizable totalization as a conceptual problem to be worked out through specific artistic maneuvers within a smaller circumference, though more loftily told. What Wagner described was a work that brought together a handful of disciplines that comprised his new form of "DRAMA": music and voice, which he called "tone," along with poetry and dance. If painting, sculpture, and architecture are considered secondary integrative elements of the Gesamtkunstwerk, as "The Art-Work of the Future" notes almost dismissively, his essay leaves strewn across the imagination the possibility not so much of the impossible object of a total creative expression, but of the larger extent to which the network aggregation of disciplines and discipline-objects advances the unifying inflection of interdisciplinary practices.

If Wagner's work could never reach the idealization of what might be seen as an unencompassable pluralization, what he proclaims in his call for the deployment of artistic disciplines united in their phenomenological and cognitive impact on an audience is, as I've said, a proto-network, a language of linkages meant as an answer to the failure of the 1849 revolution; a language that willfully conjoins the copulas of politics and artistic disciplines as a seduction of heterogeneous bodies to render an ecstatic commensurateness.

Wagner's notion of the Gesamtkunstwerk, in fact, predates him. Juliet Koss, in her remarkable work of scholarship, *Modernism After Wagner*, cites the term's first appearance in a text from 1827 by the Berlin philosopher Karl Friedrich Eusebius Trahndorff, who writes:

> The four arts, the art of wordsound [*Wortklang*], music, facial expression [*Mimik*], and the art of dance, contain within themselves the potential to join together into one presentation. But this potential is founded on a striving that pervades the entire

artistic sphere; a striving toward a total work of art [*zu einem Gesamt-Kunstwerke*] on the part of all the arts.[19]

The Germanic root of the idea comes still earlier, in an 1803 lecture by Friedrich Wilhelm Joseph Schelling.

> The most perfect combination of all the arts, the unification of poetry and music through song, of poetry and painting through dance, itself brought once again to synthesis, is a theatrical manifestation in its most complete composition, equivalent to the drama of antiquity, of which has remained for us only a caricature, opera, which could be developed into a higher and more noble style from the side of poetry as well as from that of the other competing arts, to lead us back to the mode of production of ancient drama, linked with music and song.[20]

Yet in Wagner's revolutionary-period writings at mid-century, this clarity of interdisciplinary artistic production becomes a confusion of metaphors that encompass sexuality, gender, politics, and art that is still curious to read today. They describe a spectacularized, patronizing sexualization of artistic forms that spreads analogically in his argument from politics. Wagner is continually talking about manliness, manhood, the "real man"—a term he uses near the start of "The Art-Work of the Future." He already wrote in the opening pages of "Art and Revolution": "To hold this art-work up to life itself as the prophetic mirror of its future appeared to me as a most weighty contribution toward damming the flood of revolution within the channel of the peacefully flowing stream of manhood."[21] Art is strangely cast as an opposition between something apart from flesh, an "artificial product," and yet a thing understood as an appetite of the untainted male body. It isn't an "arbitrary issue, but an inbred craving of the natural, genuine, and uncorrupted man."[22]

His argument means to shore up the stature of his artwork-to-be, yet the framing of art as a bodily embrace is difficult when Wagner himself has spent so much time arguing for the combination of artistic forms as a contrivance, a willed machine. How does he square the difference? By the twisted merger or sheer elision that the artwork is a body in need of being purified that is equivalent to the human body as a natural machine of coordinated parts. And still more so, in the dominance of the male body as art-body, he sees this vitality as a means to establish wholeness through the authority of the masculine body, an authoritarian body equaling an authoritarian wholeness that determines society itself. This layering of bodies, art, and social institutions has to be imposed on the weakness of the individual against the strength in union of the many. And this translates still more particularly as a gendered hierarchy: the weak, by the imprimatur of nature, are always the lesser female, awaiting the domination of the manly hand that sanctifies.

A scene in the first act of Wagner's *Lohengrin*, completed in 1847 and first performed in Weimar the year after his escape to Zurich, captures this arrangement by seduction as a contractual form. Lohengrin binds his promise of marriage to Elsa with the demand, "Never ask me, / or trouble yourself with wondering, / where I traveled from, / what my name is or my origin," and she answers in the perfect obedience of the subaltern to his request, "Never, sir, will this question come from me."[23] So it is in art as in nature for Wagner, as the authoritarian body may take individual (male) form, which in its will to communal wholeness can only imagine and seek it through autocratic tyranny. In "The Art-Work of the Future," dance, tone, and poetry are the lesser bodies that he calls "the primeval sister arts," each clinging to the other, seeking unity in body and spirit.[24]

Beneath the legalistic gaze on what is claimed to be feminine frailty and is structurally and erotically servile to the male organizing principle of totality, it remains salaciously Wagnerian to imagine these sisters, no, to *propose* them as craving each other literally as objects for copulation, bridges from limb to limb. They're absorbed by one another with a hint that nature has a taste for the involutions of what is implied to be homoerotic sin, the ingestion of one another that, by logical inversion, is ultimately in the name of the communal, of the Gesamtkunstwerk, of the *Volk*. "She reaches out her hand to her neighboring art in unrestrained acknowledgment of love," Wagner intones, and continues:

The very grasping of this hand lifts her above the barrier; her full embrace, her full absorption in her sister. [. . .] And when every barrier has thus fallen, then are there no more *arts* and no more boundaries, but only *Art*, the universal, undivided.[25]

Wagner's "sisters," codependent, entangled, finding satisfaction first in each other (certainly an interesting form of Bowker's "legitimacy exchange"), are of prime interest in the lineage of interdisciplinarity and network aesthetics. But their subsequent arrangement—penetrated and subsumed, free only through transformation in Wagner's idealized absolute of muscular Germanic music-drama, dominant over the soft bellies of French and Italian opera, which he deemed trivial and trivially sensual in turn—eschews any real reciprocity and remains a simple and defective hierarchy: male on top. Female absorption, in the specific case of music, as he proposes in his 1852 essay "Opera and Drama," opens itself to the male in the most explicit way: "The necessary bestowal, the seed that can only in the most ardent transports of love condense itself from his noblest forces—this procreative seed is the poetic aim, which brings to the glorious loving woman, Music, the stuff for bearing."[26]

The shudder of climax, driven by priapic authority, is fused with society, in fact with the "life of the future" that now, by means of the biological contortion of his rhetoric, takes this art-work of the future "up into its womb."[27] As it is in the Gesamtkunstwerk, constitutive fusion is fundamental to all that nature and society can hold in its becoming toward a new order of being. This contortion of the biological reaches its apex in Wagner's last completed musical work, *Parsifal*, in 1882. The protagonist's body, envisioned as a chalice, incorporates gendered opposites into the single hybrid form of his hero/heroine: the icy figure of Parsifal himself/herself as the total body of the future; a superior being whose theo-erotic ascendancy vanquishes the impurity of difference through biological revision, destroying and absorbing it simultaneously, while summarizing the more general coercive buckling of otherness entrenched in Wagner's art.

Nietzsche, with his usual hyperbolic intensity, wrote that *Parsifal* was "a work of rancour, of revenge, of the most secret concoction of poisons with which to make an end of the first conditions of life, *it is a bad work*. The preaching of chastity remains an incitement to unnaturalness: I despise anybody who does not regard 'Parsifal' as an outrage upon morality."[28] Yet in essence, he was chastising Wagner for the very opposite of chastity, whose offense of ethical promiscuity is literally embodied in a perversion of bodily convention that redounds to the music itself in Wagner's will to impose its false wholeness. The composer, in Nietzsche's stridency, is *against* nature, a corruptor of nature through this perversion performed in the making of artifice. Each art form is forced to contort itself so that its ultimate condition for health is submission. For Nietzsche, the joining of artistic disciplines, like the joining of bodies, is at once demanded, salacious, and denies individual dignity.

The figure of Parsifal, as the apotheosis of engineered completeness, would seem to signal an ultimate twisting of virility, of authorial force, that speaks to Wagner's overarching ambitions. So, Matthew Wilson Smith remarks: "It is an androgyny that can only occur under the sign of the gentile male: Woman must die in order to be raised up and preserved as a symbolic discourse between men, just as the Jew must die in order to be raised up and preserved as a symbolic discourse between Christians. Wagner's final Gesamtkunstwerk creates totality through the translation of excluded others into acceptably symbolic form."[29] Here again is the mystification of myth, legend, and spiritual longing retold as foretelling, with the music-drama as bellwether, as itself the chalice of totalism.

Yet long before Parsifal's arid embodiment of the totalized self, Wagner's great monument to totality remains *The Ring of the Nibelung*— *The Rhinegold* (1854), *The Valkyrie* (1856), *Siegfried* (1871), and *Twilight of the Gods* (1874)—his bulwark against a political as well as ontological sense of belatedness and incompletion. In the *Ring's* four linked works, sixteen hours of musical innovation and repetition unfold a narrative told in a series of nomadic, minatory quests that swoon before an arching anxiety over structural continuity and a nascent meritocratic capitalism awash in connivance, selfless love, and greed among gods and men. The story of a gold ring whose owner will bear ultimate dominion never portrays power as a supra-protocol in a universal scheme of commensurateness. Instead, the bearer of the ring wields the absolute sovereignty of authoritarian right and obedience, already familiar in Wagner territory as a masculine verticality of force.

As the vast machinery of the *Ring* winds down, the telos of its plot, telegraphed in the words "Twilight of the Gods," would seem to be the exhaustion of supernatural administration and the final revenge on 1849 with the rise of democratic agency. Yet the terminal conflagration of the gods never resolves humankind as ultimately less in thrall to the same urges: to make continuity over discontinuity a political ethos of domination; to ensure wholeness through the repression of anything unlike the mass; to simply shift power from an exclusive group, the gods, to the larger patriarchal group of a hierarchical, power-driven, materialistic human society that enacts its will to sameness.

The implicit critique of capitalism, torn between resistance, capitulation, and complicity, points simultaneously to Wagner's self-contradictions of political consciousness and personal interests. After all, he's at work in the times of Marx and Engels, of whom he was fully aware through his revolutionary meetings with Bakunin. In "Art and Revolution," he writes: "What has aggrieved the painter, when he must immortalize the repugnant visage of a millionaire? What the musician, when he must compose his music for the banquet table? And what the poet, when he must write romances for the lending library? What then has been the sting of suffering to each? That he must squander his creative powers for gain, and make his art a handicraft!"[30] Yet his history of sinecures and swindling direct us to other sentiments, and the culminating immolation of Siegfried and Brünnhilde only underlines the hierarchical, recursive nature of the Wagnerian Gesamtkunstwerk's closed system. His monumental work, stretching across a continent of all-too-human impulses, never fully convinces, in the end, that it is any different from its beginning in the nature of power and the ring, such that capitalism reads backward as nascent within the materialist greed of the gods, and not of them alone.

The appetites for flesh, money, and ethereal ascent conflate in Wagner's desire for willed uniformity and his fascination with bodily hybridity, a hybridity by force, confused yet ceremonial and ritualized, Olympian in its striving for totality as a Grail-like Prussiandom detonated and remade in his own contradictory image as the imperious progenitor, lord, and *man* of the people. The body in all its forms (assembled as a codependency of parts that commingle sexual identity, artistic practices, and political institutionalization spread over vast topologies of time and space) is schematized as a nodal arrangement under the authoritarian protocol of the music-drama—if a proto-network, not finally a distributed one; instead a closed network, an absolute code, a theater event entirely scripted for its components and its captured users under Wagner's central command. (Soon enough we'll see the way Kandinsky critiques Wagner's sheer exteriorization of the disciplines and how that critique in turn influences Hugo Ball at the moment of the Cabaret Voltaire.)

Yet to more fully understand this trajectory toward suppressed individuation in the name of a politicized aesthetics of unity, first we need to reverse it. We need to systematically undo its copulation of parts and think of its engulfed sister disciplines not just from the viewpoint of networked nodes but still more elementally. If interdisciplinary works can be thought of as micro-totalities, then each discipline-object as a thing with properties internal to the production of its being is always turned outward toward its reception—a thing whose inner being is cognized through the viewer-agent's hermeneutic act that overwrites its essence with subjective determinism, constructing different gestalts, different forms of wholeness. The behavior of these elements must take into account the relationship between their internal properties and what lives outside of them.

Bruno Latour's argument for the permeability of the ego has already been invoked, claiming as he does that "nothing is inside which has not come from the outside" and that the world around the self swarms with "subjectifiers" that shape the I we each become.[31] This echoes Hegelian self-consciousness, which I've already spoken of, captured in his phrase "when each is for the other what the other is for it." That self-consciousness as a dynamic, reciprocal, codependent, and potentially destructive interactivity—evident in Hegel's *Phenomenology of Spirit,* in which master and slave, lord and bondsman, are bound by the tortuous gravity of their power relations—is what Slavoj Žižek usefully calls in Hegel the "antagonism between *ground* and *condition*, between the inner essence ('true nature') of a thing and the external circumstances which render possible the realization of this essence."[32]

The always proximate and intimate danger of authoritarian force implicit in Hegel's notion of self-consciousness is also implicit in Wagner's assertion, his overcoding of the sister arts that forces relations on them without true equivalence. And yet, despite his intentions, placing his audience in the dark, immobile in their seats, the viewers of Wagner's *Ring* cycle inevitably find in each art form and in all of them together their own perceptions and judgments that just as likely bend against the artist's will in one way or another. The formational power of external subjectivities, the action of rogue nodes, as I've called them, who enter a work and shift its meanings, derails Wagner's programmatic intentions to some degree, and, in a more general way, is a subject that rises again and again among philosophers, considering the ambience of the self in the world with others.

So, Edmund Husserl argues: "We do not experience the object and beside it the intentional experience directed upon it, [. . .] only one thing is present, the intentional experience."[33] Merleau-Ponty asserts: "The very experience of transcendent things is possible only provided that their project is borne [. . .] within myself."[34] And Jean-Paul Sartre remarks at the beginning of *Being and Nothingness* that "the phenomenal being [. . .] is nothing but the well-connected series of its manifestations."[35] Each notion is a different turn of the outside-in, the proposal that the thing in itself may be an indwelling of being, alive in its internal aspects of thingness, but whatever its internal life may be, its availability to me, its surface of inscription, is the projection of my subjective cognition and of the many subjective consciousnesses that cognize it—the many I's that are themselves whorls of subjectifiers in the continual play of presence. Žižek's description of ground and condition underscores this: the final quiddity of each discipline-object and the assemblage's combined effects are dependent on their interactions, which occur with every individual gaze, every ipseity, every filter of signal and noise that viewers bring with them and through which aesthetic meanings are drawn.

Here, too, Wagner wants to go two ways at once. He speaks of the democratic ethos, with his vaguely lubricious sisters delving into each other's bodies and somehow, on the other side of the spectacularization of the arts, are taken up into the womb of the people. This delirium of body metaphors is fundamentally a scheme in which the nodal communication of parts is supposedly toward equivalence and communality, while it's actually held within a vestigial hierarchy of weak and strong. What that creates in practice is an experiential friction among his disciplines, of node against node, so that they never entirely coalesce and instead highlight, once again, the internal contradiction of Wagner's way as a formal antagonism, despite his rhetoric, his innovations, and the sheer breadth of his artistic efforts.

The weak connection of his proto-network among linked discipline-objects finds a particular starting point in Wagner's theorization of the Gesamtkunstwerk. What we see in his music-dramas as a constant note of reference to this structural model is a certain kind of nomadism, a wandering of his characters across time and landscapes such that all relations become distended, with a coincident musical equivalence in what he calls "endless melody": an unceasing flow of harmonic suspension and narrative strands that Wagner likens to a sense of perpetual imminence hovering.

Let me reiterate briefly what I've stated about things in their inwardness and the outward effects on them, now seen specifically in the case of Wagner's music-dramas, of disciplinary components joined on the stage and made manifest in the actions of characters singing, gesturing, and situated in massive stage sets, with the music as an equal protagonist in the dramas as they play out over hours and, in fact, days, in the instance of the *Ring*. When we look at the interdisciplinary work as a combinatorial formation that establishes a kind of network, we can say that its discipline-objects each stand as a thing with internal properties that resides in its specific material and historical characteristics that make it the object that it is. Each has its own temporality in three senses: first, simply, the time of its making; second, the duration implicit in our experience of it; and third, the aesthetic time of the object that we call "period style." Within each object of expression there also resides the potentiality of the Hegelian notion of the "for-us," that intention and trajectory of outward reception, individual and communal, in its temporal aspect: the possibility that the work is taken up in another time, the time of posterity, and this, too, reaches back as it reaches forward, transforming the object in another time, an *afterness* latent in the artwork that brings it into co-relation with another audience, another for-us, even an endless chain of plural temporalities in which the interdisciplinary work in its ticking assembly presents itself for further interpretations and reimaginings, both current and anachronistic—just as this reading of European modernism does and future readers will do.

In the equality between this essential object character and an external reflection, what's offered, then, is another time and other thing: the simultaneous *something-else*—another object character superimposed and entwined, a hybridity of inward and outward; what can be called, in keeping with Wagner's own metaphors and the fate of Parsifal, an invaginated supplement. This object as a dual event of internal properties and external reception is the temporality of the interdisciplinary network that establishes its catalytic ability to circulate difference. The interdisciplinary work is always a difference engine, as I've previously noted, an engine of essence and affect, of disciplinary noumena and disciplinary facticity, whose nodal interactions include the viewer-agents whose interpretations continually revise what is there, hacking the system.

For sensitive viewers, what lies underneath the discipline-object's palpability is something possibly flickering. This is the object's and the assemblage's ontological immanence—the *live-ness* within, unseen, without which its coming forth as a visible thing wouldn't enter into the process of its eventuation. This vitalism is an emanation in which the object would seem to have its own life, as much as any animal presence does. How did this live-ness and the contested possibility of its internal necessity come about? Those speculations, crucial in the history of philosophy, aren't my central subject here. But at least it's appropriate to say that we can conceive of the relationship, again, of internal qualities and outward projection as a layering. Here Žižek is helpful once more when he notes in Hegel's thinking that "the inner potential of the self-development of an object and the pressure exerted on it by an external force are *strictly correlative*."[36] Merleau-Ponty gets at this in another way, positing that the surface of the visible is "doubled up over its whole extension with an invisible reserve,"[37] which suggests that what appears to us and has meaning for us is layered over what is internal to it in its thingness.

Meaning, of course, is what makes the visibility of things cohere—what makes a network a network, with its constant interactions. Each significance within the interdisciplinary work's network can be understood as an event that is a subaltern of time, time planned and the contingencies that alter its temporal plan. The very idea of the Gesamtkunstwerk and its precedent for the imagination of interdisciplinary art and network aesthetics is the volatile, uneven, promiscuous, continuous, and prodigal production of significances that change over time in the course of reception. All possible relations of significance between discipline-objects and viewer-agents are potential because it isn't possible that there is only non-significance if all such objects are coded by protocols of making, history, and reception—that's to say, communication protocols, protocols to facilitate reception. Each discipline-object has meanings applied to it by artists and viewers alike, as we are all in our human nature signifying beings.

If this is so, then it's also so that discipline-objects are always potentially significant to viewer-agents and, therefore, that all discipline-objects within their particular networks as makers and reflectors of meaning hold an infinite combination of significations that unfold at relative temporal rates, based on the contingency of its variant viewers. The network, then, can be understood as a platform of meaning-contingent distribution, as contingency is a motor of variation, and here contingency is the producer of variations in the narrative of any object, any work, and so of any aggregation of works that we call interdisciplinary. Within the network of the interdisciplinary work and the contingency of meanings applied to its discipline-objects and to the work as a whole, meaning isn't based on its premise of stability but on the multiplicity of its revisions.

An archaeology of the Wagnerian notion of relations among disciplines toward a unity of meaning for the *Volk* reveals the way meaning is produced in light of these notions of ground and condition, inside and outside, the internal thing and its outward projections, the in-itself and the for-us. If every discipline is pure at its core but must melt into the others, as Wagner proposed for the "sister arts" in "The Art-Work of the Future," that act of melting/melding is to make another surface for what lies within, this inner reserve. The membranes of these copulated disciplines are, as I've already noted, the surfaces of inscription for the producers of meanings: first the artist and then our rogue nodes, our viewer-agents whose vectors of force impose on the work's manufacture the living spokenness of things felt and thought about in the cognitive production that becomes the work's received and interpreted meanings, an articulation impregnating matter.

This is what the network theorist Kai Eriksson, in his thinking about the ontology of networks, calls the "actualization of multiplicities."[38] To experience interdisciplinary works is always in this way to participate in and witness acts of becoming. The interdisciplinary work presents a temporal dance of beings together in which contingency is the mode of its musicality, and the questions and satisfactions of resolution, of a finished object in total, are at once solid and liquid. This clinamen of meaning-making is an implicit agreement between motion and the production of significances that flow asynchronously and together in time.

In the *Ring*, as Badiou remarks, Wagner's characters seem congenitally incapable of staying still. They're nomads, as I've said, perpetual wanderers. To think of them as interconnected nodes, they're always in a double-state of struggle against the eddies of contingencies built into the plot, though the plot itself has nothing contingent about it. It's fixed—the bound inscriptions as issued from Wagner's pen. His Wotan and Alberich, his Siegfried, his Brünnhilde and Günther roam in a closed network whose protocols are intended to be unyielding. They're a mirror not only of the formal challenge of Wagner's Gesamtkunstwerk to marshal all of his artistic disciplines into unity within a rigid hierarchy of exhaustive sonic continuity but as an incubator of political modes of organization, as Badiou describes:

> The question of the relationship between the local and the global, between continuity and discontinuity, or of the nature of transitions, is a major question in every branch of philosophy and specifically (I'll just mention this in passing) in politics. If, in effect, discontinuity is no longer expressed politically in the traditional figure of revolution, how then *is* it expressed? Should we conclude that there is no longer any discontinuity whatsoever (an idea that is ultimately analogous to the idea of the end of history)? Or should we instead think that the discontinuity

is concealed behind the overwhelming appearance of continuity? The latter question is in my view a typically Wagnerian one. Indeed, Wagner has generally been interpreted as someone who submerged discontinuity in continuity [. . .], whereas I think that Wagner displaced discontinuity in such a profound manner that it came to act as a new figure of undecidability between narrative drama and music, and that in so doing he invented a new model of the relationship between continuity and discontinuity.[39]

But isn't it so that Wagner's goal, his overcoding of individual disciplines and the audience's reception of them as a whole, was precisely to mitigate undecidability? It's true that inimical to undecidability is a sense of suspension, of time in limbo, which is so much the feeling in the twilight zone of the *Ring*. Yet it is decidedly not of a piece with Wagner's proclamations for unity: to make an art, as he put it, that is "universal, undivided." Or, as he announces in "Opera and Drama," the goal is always for the "unitarian," which hardly seems undecided at all. (Decisionism will play a central role in Carl Schmitt's proposals for authoritarianism, as we'll see in relation to the interdisciplinary enthusiasms of Hugo Ball.) In fact, Wagner speaks in "Opera and Drama" about "continuity in presence" as a quality that could be construed as mystical or psychological[40] but could just as well be ascribed to the political will that makes its impression in the name of coerced reception that's protocologically defined as the rule of order.

What remains at odds is the structural paradox intrinsic to Wagner's artistic willfulness. His methods are absolute, relentless, and his characters are pressed forward in the old forms of the saga and quest-journey, with their archaic gestures and ancient contracts, impelled across the fields of their eventual undoing. Decidedness is all. Yet the sheer length of the *Ring*, the weight of its physical and rhetorical machinery, and the breadth of its nomadic circuits invite a sense of endless deferral that rides its endless harmony. The trajectories of his characters seem to advance, stutter, repeat, and rotate, minutely adjusted, in ways that spell a future for Samuel Beckett (the Comedian of the Impasse, in Hugh Kenner's phrase) and the latency of data packets along the routinized paths of networks.

Yet Badiou's attention to the structural question of discontinuities in flows of continuity is crucial, as this is the historical, political, and aesthetic knot of these Wagnerian packets in their labors of love and greed. Wagner's is a world quaking under the hand of a politically longed-for synchronicity in which a hard sovereignty correlates "unitarian," "universal," and "undivided" with Hegel's "supreme right against the individual, whose supreme duty is to be a member of the state." This is precisely a matter of a forced administrative continuity. Wagner's fervency for that nascent form of central command over his interdisciplinary nodes seeks to produce his own artifice of supreme right that is, as I've already quoted, "the herald and standard of all future communal institutions."

Like the sister arts, all are to be absorbed into the composer's artist-body as public-body. Wagner is the network himself, it could be said, the apparatus of a great tide and immersion, a washing clean as a precondition for the future. And so, he offers another precedent in this way, as the programmatic agenda of the Wagnerian music-drama corresponds to what would later be called *Gebrauchsmusik*, utility music, music specifically assigned a political identity in Germany as a representation of collective will.[41] The concept is indebted in part to Heidegger's notion of "equipment," as opposed to the autonomy of things, and Wagner's work is just such equipment, just such a *dispositif*, wielded for its collective use. Yet the apparatus of Wagner's system to accomplish absoluteness, of discontinuity in some failed or new relationship to continuity, even in its attempts at aesthetic and political utility toward the highest ends of the highest art, proved, so Badiou contends, that such reparative utility could not succeed. "One can observe in Wagner a relationship that instrumentalizes the state of dereliction to which music bears witness precisely in order to stage a forgiveness or salvation that is actually impossible."[42]

The *Ring* as the signifier of this unreachable summit of salvation is embodied in its own structural struggle between mobility and weight. Its instrumentalization is always meant to be in service to ascension, to lift up and mobilize German-ness. But its formal means produce an ultimate *immobilization*, bilaterally suppressing the autonomous identity of disciplines and peoples under Wagner's idealized totalization of spectacle. This *Gebrauchswerk* is lit up with moments of beauty and invention. We sit in the theater's darkened place of reception, the orchestra's music welling up from its pit as an invisible force (an innovation from the music hall in Riga that Wagner brings to Bayreuth), and we receive what Friedrich Kittler calls the music-drama's three "data fields" of the verbal, the sonic, and the visual. As Kittler says, "The text is fed into the throat of a singer, the output of this throat is fed into an amplifier named orchestra, the output of this orchestra is fed into a light show, and the whole thing, finally, is fed into the nervous system of the audience."[43]

Wagner spoke of the orchestra pit as "the technical hearth of the music," and when we think of a hearth, we think of a center for gathering, the gathering at home, the site of reception of a family that shares an unspoken bond, unspoken because it is always already present, shown in the genetic mirror of one with others in the biological sympathy of code-bonded selves.[44] Around this place of combinatorial selfhood where similarity warms itself, repetition flourishes as sameness, as commonality. What Wagner promulgates is the braiding of data fields fed into the audience to produce this warmth of sameness. "The spectator transplants himself upon the stage," Wagner suggests, "by means of all his visual and aural faculties; while the performer becomes an artist only by complete absorption into the public"—which, as I've said, is really for one and all absorption into Wagner himself.[45]

The viewer and the artist are imagined by the composer as consorts of reciprocity and mutual conviction—the viewer as citizen, fellow traveler, and adjutant to Wagner's implicitly political savoir faire. The medium and the message—set to seduce and overwhelm the audience in this cave of enchantments—are dedicated to amplification as it coincides with its opposite, diminishment, and the claim that all parts, every discipline-object in its individuality, are in debt to the collective. Nature itself is failed by separate expressions that aren't compelled into unity.

So Wagner writes: "But the individual man, in full possession of the health of his body, heart, and mind, can experience no higher need than that which is common to all his kind; for, to be a true need, it can only be such as he can satisfy in community alone." The "separate arts," he continues, are "indefinite, obscure, unfree," which is to say their freedom is only gained inversely by a submissive devotion that allows them to be overcoded, making them "universally intelligible."[46] Benjamin Bratton makes a telling remark apposite to this, writing: "The logic of absolute communication for which any haecceity must appear to a common, commanding network platform is a utopian gathering of all into one (the first hint of totality and totalitarianism blurring)."[47]

Any haecceity, any thing in the particularity of its internal properties, is meant to be overcome by Wagner's compulsion to drive difference beneath the overarching interface of universal intelligibility, the über-platform of his Gesamtkunstwerk, which is what its tilt toward domination portends. Whether in terms of artistic disciplines or individual subjects of the state, heterogeneity and otherness are vulnerable to characterizations of disturbance and insufficiency—forms of unintelligible noise, dropouts in the data stream. To clarify his rhetoric of communal allegiance, amplification and monumentality are the maximal means of the Wagnerian *Gebrauchsmusik* by which he can reconfigure singular identity as ideological uniformity among the *Volk*, as if in compensatory triumph over the past.

Nietzsche was the first to speak to Wagner's bottomless antipathy toward the single thing and his ultimate failure to overcome it. He calls Wagner an "old magician," a "clever rattlesnake." The first thing Wagner's art does, Nietzsche claims, is to thrust a magnifying glass into our hands so that "we no longer trust our eyes—Everything grows bigger, *even Wagner grows bigger.*"[48] Amplitude and amplification produce the obligatory scale of his rhetoric to compel.

> As a matter of fact, his whole life long, he did nothing but repeat one proposition: that his music did not mean music alone! But something more! Something immeasurably more! ... "*Not music alone*"—no musician would speak in this way. I repeat, Wagner could not create things as a whole; he had no choice, he was obliged to create things in bits, with "motifs," attitudes, formulae, duplications, and hundreds of repetitions, he remained a rhetorician in music,—and this is why he was at bottom *forced* to press

"this means" into the foreground. "Music can never be anything else than a means": this was his theory, but above all it was the only *practice* that lay open to him.[49]

So it is that, along with the compulsory force of endless melody, Wagner deploys another binding instrument to persuade his audience: the leitmotif. It distracts our attention, it hypnotizes by accumulation, by the sheer mound of recognizable musical phrases like the longest pop song in the world with its "hooks" that drum themselves into our heads—a formal practice of subjugation. The leitmotif is a lever that pries and inclines all the elements of the music-drama to slide into seeming contiguity, unceasing copulation, so that what is discontinuous can be buried beneath the total. I've already spoken about what Galloway and Thacker call the "antagonistic clusterings [and] divergent subtopologies" contained within networks.[50] Those fluid arrangements of nodes and links operate within a logic of multiplicity that is always *toward*, always enacting becoming and deploying protocols that support heterogeneity among connections. What we see in Wagner, to the contrary, and what's so fascinating about Wagner is the nascent state of antagonism that seeks to enforce vertical hegemony in the face of his idealistic claims for the Gesamtkunstwerk's democratic ethos. For Nietzsche, and for Theodor Adorno after him, what Wagner offered instead was an ethical nightmare unfolding into terror.

On this razor's edge lies precisely the question of individual sovereignty and a subservient populace, of a Hegelian self-consciousness that streams with grim inevitability toward destinies of authoritarianism and the ashes of Auschwitz. For Adorno, Wagner is the cautionary specter in perpetual orbit, a lodestar of Germany's inexorable ethical destruction—or so he expressed in *In Search of Wagner* (1952), where he calls the composer "the diligent lackey of imperialism and late-bourgeois terrorism."[51] Fourteen years later, toward the end of *Negative Dialectics* (1966), he writes with regard to Hegel that "the unity of world history which animates the philosopher to trace it as the path of the world spirit is the unity of terror rolling over mankind." Then suddenly, in the same paragraph, without having mentioned Wagner previously in more than 300 pages, he claims that the *Ring* "is more Hegelian than would ever have occurred to Wagner."[52] On the horizon of Wagner's totalist aesthetic is the catastrophe of individuality buried under a musical mountain of authoritarian universality, or undifferentiation.

Nietzsche, of course, would disagree with any underestimation of the link between Hegel and Wagner, but Adorno's structural troubles with the author of the *Ring* echo Nietzsche's argument to a considerable degree. Adorno reiterates the criticism that Wagner deals in "bits" when he writes that "the intermittent gesture becomes the fundamental principle of composition," and further that the "tendency of Wagner's compositional technique as well as that of his texts is to dissolve everything definite and specific into an undifferentiated mass. [. . .] Wagner's hostility to standard form ends in absurdity, in the nameless, the unspecific and the abstract."[53]

Still, there's a small but signal leap from Nietzsche's complaint to Adorno's. If Nietzsche rails that Wagner couldn't make the work cohere organically but only by the sheer force of elongated aggregation, for Adorno this diminishment assumes a specific terror in the phrase "the undifferentiated mass": the terror of the dissolution of racial identity. The correlative of condition and ground, of the essence of individual beings and a monolithic One that consumes the sanctity of the self, of the *Umschlag* in which the individual's unique otherness becomes through oppression a specimen rather than an individual and is subsumed by the total collective under statist control, this imposition is the end of discontinuity as the haven of difference and is a purely political solution—what Badiou calls an "ideological operation"—materialized in the work of art.

It isn't simply the German-ness of the (self-)mythologizing Wagner that Adorno, like Nietzsche, holds to the flames. It's the specificity of German-ness after the Holocaust that casts for Adorno a rearward pall on the ideological suppression of difference that instrumentalizes the music in a way that leads to the terrorist destruction of otherness per se. The key terms are identity and non-identity (though with a very different meaning than in Hegel) or, in parallel, unification and disunification. This transformation is mirrored in Wagner's own writing, since what's later seen as a will to destroy the integrity of the separate, and in this sense, of self-sufficient properties, is seen in Wagner as a process of enthused communalism. Sympathy and self-estrangement are instead the words that describe the Wagnerian aspiration. As Koss notes, quoting Wagner,

> fellow-feeling and fellow-creating friends [*mitfühlenden und mitschöpferischen Freunde*]" would help create the total work of art of the future. [. . .] For Wagner, as for later theorists, the experience was inherently linked to that of self-estrangement, a hybrid emotion that he likened to "a thorough stepping out of oneself into unconditional sympathy [*Mitgefühl*] with the joy of the beloved."[54]

Wagner's craven desire is for audiences to become one with him and support him, to be absorbed into him, as I've said—"those who, out of their general sympathy for him, can also comprehend his position and, by sharing in his striving . . .," as Koss quotes him in the same passage. What Wagner says in relation to art is only what he said in his 1848 speech to the *Vaterlandsverein*, already quoted, that revolutionary liberation must bring "vigorous" human beings who "combine in well-ordered unions, exchanging the products of their activities to mutually enrich and benefit each other."[55]

That particularly German vigor and striving, that collaborative distribution of value captured in the words "exchanging the products of their activities" (*im Austausch ihrer Thätigkeit*) is chiseled in the most obdurate stone of Adorno's judgment. For him there is no recuperation of the self in unification, and he joins collaboration and well-ordered unions in *Negative Dialectics* in the brutal aphorism, "Genocide is the absolute integration."[56] The only recourse is non-unification and non-identicality or, in Adorno's more radical term, non-identity. Non-identity is the suspension of the authoritarian identification of the other: an ethical act that accepts the other rather than exterminating it.

As a concept of survival, non-identity aligns itself, both ethically and biologically, with Adorno's use of disunification, again from *Negative Dialectics*, in the most obvious sense that the rounding up of each person whose self may be individual but whose racial identity is seen in terms of a terminal unity. So, Adorno comes to the nightmare determination of "absolute integration," which is understood in opposition to the Wagnerian platform of the Gesamtkunstwerk. The struggle *against* identity, as Badiou notes in Adorno's philosophy, is about the thing against itself, the thing that is always in relation to its own destruction, a form that must refute the will to form, as the historical trauma of resolution that's the burden of Adorno's consciousness is intrinsic to the inherent evil of humankind, the mournful resolution of the Shoah. Adorno famously said there could be no poetry after Auschwitz but later recanted this in a statement still more extreme:

> It may have been wrong to say that after Auschwitz you could no longer write poems. But it is not wrong to raise the less cultural question whether after Auschwitz you can go on living—especially whether one who escaped by accident, one who by rights should have been killed, may go on living.[57]

The dismal hyperbole of this thinking is essentially deployed in his war with Hegel, who is the subject of Adorno's continual battle over the autonomy of individuals in relation to the state. He condemns Hegel's judgment that "for us, the individualities disappear and are noteworthy only as those who realize the will of the popular spirit," and a section of *Negative Dialectics* is entitled "Hegel Siding with the Universal."[58] Adorno's linking of fascism with resolution and absolute integration with death exemplify his counter-stance of what he calls "waiting in vain," a temporality antithetical to conclusiveness that brings us back to Wagner's intentions for the Gesamtkunstwerk, seen through the philosopher's eyes as aesthetically, politically, and racially ruinous. (Entirely consistent with Adorno's attraction to a notion of waiting in vain is his defense of Samuel Beckett's theater, saying of the play *Endgame* that it was emblematic of the culture built after Auschwitz.)[59]

In Adorno's view, the *Ring* is fundamentally a badly written manual presented as allegory for the totalization of the German spirit and what it will lead to. For Wagner, the *Ring*'s heroic structure is the embodiment of its heroic sentiments. Its primary action is to raise up and repair the weakness of individualism, to supplement the insufficiency of isolated disciplines and deeds with a unitary purpose at once ecstatic and wise. Its temporality is meant to bring the resolution of human triumph over former ways. Its mechanisms, through Wagner's invention and argument, close up all lack and disillusion, all disobedience to greater principle in the example of the gods' endless mendacities.

Yet, as it is night to day between them, mendacity is the very word used by Adorno to describe Wagner's art. Adorno's *bona fides* as a musicologist allowed him to roam over the technical history of musical composition and wield his knowledge as a cudgel to revoke the powers ascribed to leitmotif and endless melody, referring to four-part harmonics, polyphonics, chromaticism, and "the lack of melodic articulation of the interval E natural—F#," etc.[60] Yet at the base of his pyrotechnical disquisitions is the almost querulous refrain that the great oceanic wash of this music beating on the shore of his stranded patience—the will of Wagner to implicate the audience in the dissolution of difference through the sheer ego-sublime of his outward-turning power—is a mendacious illusion of totality.

Consider these two statements by Adorno. Again, first from *Negative Dialectics*, second from *In Search of Wagner*. The first I've referred to already in passing, writing about the loss of individuality: "That in the concentration camps it was no longer an individual who died, but a specimen—this is a fact bound to affect the dying of those who escaped the administrative measure." And here, in his assessment of Wagner, is a drastic and similar notion of administration, bound up in totalizing music.

> The very seamlessness of the form of the music drama, the Wagnerian "style" itself, is what is at fault. Music no longer possesses its decisive power: its ability to transcend imprisonment, in the context of an action. This is why it is reduced to overwhelming the listener with a passion and excitement that does not even pause for breath. The aesthetics of duplication is a substitute for protest, a mere amplification of subjective expression that is nullified by its very vehemence. But the individual arts whose rules are violated by the Wagnerian magic take their revenge by mocking the union and emphasizing their differences, which the work failed to fructify.[61]

The individual arts and, by extrapolation, individuals themselves appear in Adorno's argument as unwilling to be ruled by the administration of a totalist imposition on others, in which the intention is to disavow any existential autonomy and, beneath this, any ontological one. This isn't the political light of democratic ethos in a condition of collective determination but an incipient darkness. The alleged falsity of the Wagnerian method of imposing unity, of overwhelming us with a fundamentally uneasy sensorial imbrication of stimuli, is assailed over and over by Adorno. He often employs the metaphor of inebriation, proposing that the compounding of disciplines by force is Wagner's means to trick the audience into an intoxicated, ascendant experience of a new universality from which they will awake with a hangover of historical proportions.

Reading *Negative Dialectics* after Adorno's earlier excoriation of Wagner, this illusory wholeness in the music-drama is exposed as a seduction that makes way for national acquiescence and the Jewish march to the camps. The subjugation of the separate in whatever form must be identified and pilloried. So, Adorno writes in *In Search of Wagner* that "the radical process of integration, which assiduously draws attention to itself, is already no more than a cover for the underlying fragmentation." Wagner's recourse to "small-scale models" strung together "provides a substitute for true development." "The whole no longer achieves unity, because its expressive elements are made to harmonize with each other according to a pre-arranged design." Wagner's will to bring aesthetic totality into being bears witness to his "defiant unconcern about the absence of the social conditions necessary for its survival."[62] But of course we know what those conditions would come to be. Every critique by Adorno is a belated retort to the violent wages of resolution so that they might not be repeated.

The profoundly difficult relationship between interdisciplinary practice, communal politics, freedom, and absolute authority finds a typically exultant expression in Wagner's late essay "What is German," written in 1878, nearly thirty years after "The Art-Work of the Future." The essay is a celebration of the flows of energy and influence that overtake the rest of the world and presume an almost ecclesiastical dominance of the Other in codependent terms of cultural and national sovereignty. He writes:

> When Goethe's "Götz" appeared, its joyous cry went up: "That's German!" And, beholding his likeness, the German also knew to show himself, to show the world, what Shakespeare is, whom his own people did not understand. These deeds the German spirit brought forth of itself, from its innermost longing to grow conscious of itself. And this consciousness told it [. . .] that the beautiful and noble did not come into the world for the sake of profit, no, not for the sake even of fame and recognition. And everything done in the sense of this teaching is "Deutsch"; and therefore is the German great; and only what is done in that sense can lead Germany to greatness.[63]

Elsewhere, Wagner would only seem to call for something opposite—inclusiveness and tolerance—when he remarks on the German's accommodation of Slavs in the cosmopolitan character of Bayreuth, where he would ultimately build his groundbreaking theater of 1875 to house the annual performance of the *Ring*. "Here first were Slavs transformed into Germans, without a sacrifice of idiosyncrasy, and amicably shared the fortunes of a common country," he writes. "Good witness to the German spirit's qualities!"[64] Yet it's clear that what he thought of the Slavs is symptomatic, reflected equally in his approach to the individual disciplines within the music-drama: submission is required, whatever his semblance of respect for individual identity may claim. As Matthew Wilson Smith remarks on this passage: "Wagner held Bayreuth to be the mirror and microcosm of Germany at its most essential and a crucible in which the non-Germanic would be Germanized."[65]

The Wagnerian centrifuge attempts to emulsify difference result in a shimmering slick of essentially unrealized unity, precipitating the reality Adorno wrote about with such mournful grimness and the quality of resentment he inherited from Nietzsche in disassembling the dissemblances of the Wagner machine. The mendacious prospects advertised for the Gesamtkunstwerk invoke a black magic whose sleight of hand is not sleight enough, leaving the immobile viewer in the spectatorship of stuttering connections awkwardly revealed, seams showing, in a delirium of time slowed by schemes, conquests, and musical structures dependent on redundant coding.

Yet what Badiou says, in a statement concerning the Wagnerian enterprise, initiates for me a turn in thinking about Wagner and the interdisciplinary on the road to network aesthetics. He sees the mirror-opposite of Adorno, particularly on the matter of the significance of resolution in Wagner's work. Approximately halfway through his *Five Lessons on Wagner*, Badiou states five rules for greatness as he sees them exemplified in Wagner, and the fifth is the most striking, as it encompasses a critique of Adorno's trouble concerning resolution, while capturing an essential aspect of what happens within a network. He writes: "The last rule has to do with the notion of transformation without any finality as the principle of development, in the sense that the giving of a form to the development can be found in the resources of the transformation."[66]

In other words, he's offering the counter-supposition to Adorno (and Nietzsche): What if resolution *isn't* Wagner's aim? To the notion of the total work, the absolute contrivance, the colossus of hegemony, Badiou introduces a small but significant puncture, an aperture. About absolute contrivance we could say that it is, of course, an impossibility, as I've already argued: no total but a supra-total constructed by a supra-entity fulfills such terms in their logical extension. Absolute contrivance proposes that by force the other becomes the same as the not-other. And in essence this is Adorno's accusation of Wagner's will to overcome difference by fiat, the Germanizing of the non-German, the "concealment of the process of poetic production for the sake of its aim, that is to say, its rationale."[67] For Adorno, neither the Gesamtkunstwerk nor the Final Solution of the Holocaust come to an ultimacy of resolution—and so he writes of survivor's guilt.

What is Wagner's failure, then? That the synthesis of his ur-interdisciplinary practice is not a totality of continuously linked interfaces but is no more than an immense kludge that never makes its assemblage frictionless enough? So, Adorno writes: "The eternity of Wagnerian music, like that of the poem of the *Ring*, is one which proclaims that nothing has happened; it is a state of immutability that refutes all history by confronting it with the silence of nature."[68] But if, as Adorno protests, the *Ring*'s end is no different than its beginning, that it falls short of definitive resolution, that each of its moments simply aggregates without conclusion, hasn't Wagner's actual Gesamtkunstwerk in the particularity of its failings satisfied Adorno's existential requirement of the persistence of difference, no matter the composer's intention? And isn't Wagner's constant loop of elements and glacial, minute recodings without finality, then, not the opposite of Adorno's critique but akin to his notion of disunification that spoils authoritarian hegemony? Is Badiou's radical claim for a Wagner who is after totality but not finality— a Wagner who so redistributed discontinuity within continuity that "it came to act as a new figure of undecidability"—a cousin (though less extreme) of Meillassoux's notion of "unencompassable pluralization"? That is, having combined but *not unified* the disciplines in so vast and complex an enterprise, the work finally enacts a form of aesthetic metastasis instead of synthesis. And though this isn't triumph, nor does it excuse Wagner's hypocrisies belying despotic will, there is the work itself, standing outside the artist's dream and intention, the thing as it is in the close analysis of its operations.

To think of this in terms of the future of interdisciplinary art and network aesthetics isn't a matter of Badiou being right and Adorno otherwise. It's a question concerning the ways in which heterogeneous elements exist within a system toward the act of interoperative communication, of systemic legibility, of legitimacy exchange, of likeness and difference coexisting, of the layered coexistence of material and formal properties and their outward effusions of feeling, idea, rhetoric, ideology, whim, wisdom, and apparatus for change. What Badiou offers is the provocation that difference and sameness, counter to what previous arguments in this regard assume, aren't end terms.

I would only emend his prescription to say that Wagner's efforts are not so much a case of undecidability or, as I said before, just of decision. No, what Wagner proffers with continual iteration and recoding is *re*-decidability, which is of a piece with the ultimate instantiation of his work's redundancies, repetitions, and final lack of finality. So, in "Art and Revolution" Wagner claims that the "DRAMA" is the dominant form above all other disciplines, including music. Eight years later, in his essay "On Franz Liszt's Symphonic Poems," he re-decides: "Music can never, and in no possible alliance, cease to be the highest, the redeeming art."[69]

We could say that the instability of the protocols of Wagner's system, or rather its continuously asymmetrical relations, is concentric with the iterative and reiterative nature of his work—for what are endless melody and the leitmotif if not forms of ceaselessness, of suspension and emplacement in continuous oscillation? If, in holding Wagner's slipperiness against him, his work is deemed a failure, then it is also failure as possibility, as the potentiality of the condition of "flows, movements, alliances, and detachments," of entities in the throes of communicative adjustment and mutation.[70] The jurisdictional field of the work can never be adjudicated strongly enough; it's always slipping away from the rule of law because of that disjunction between a suggested horizontality and its unrealized distribution of true equality. Exactly because of the untamed obstinacy of the heterogeneous rising beneath the attempt to accomplish monolithic totalization, the community of discipline-objects in Wagner's works takes on the network character of what the sociologist Darin Barney calls "thin relationships," which are always on the point of being revoked within a society based on voluntary, common interests—revocable because they react to the protocols of control, renegotiating their identities, adjusting their interoperability.[71]

The Wagnerian project recast along these lines returns us to the sense of itinerancy of the figures wandering through the *Ring*. They are like Wagner's unruly disciplines: unsettled, their unities transient, never truly joined, a world of bits stuttering across their evental field. It's the thinness of these relations, the upheaval of parts erupting along the sonorous surface, that presents an ontological feature that will resonate in the interdisciplinary works to come and is fundamental to networks and network aesthetics: the continual unfolding of becoming. Wagner points to this himself, when he writes in "Opera and Drama":

> In his farthest strayings, the Absolute Musician fell into the error of copying plastic art, and giving the Finished in place of the Becoming. The drama alone is the artwork that so addresses itself in space and time to our eye and ear that we take an active share

in its becoming, and therefore can grasp the *Become* as a necessity, as a thing which our feelings clearly understand.[72]

This *Become* is always on the cusp of finding another form that spreads (just as Deleuze and Guattari will write more than a century later that "becoming is a rhizome"), though he interpreted it as the congenital weakness of the sister disciplines.[73] In turn, this meant for him that identity was never finally resolved, despite his efforts, and the fluidity of becoming is both the ontological and formal status of Wagner's re-decidable art, with its logic of multiplicities, its ramification, circularity, transformation without finality, its inability to attain the organic unity for which Adorno took him to task so furiously.

In place of that Nietzschean/Adornoesque mirror of punitive correlation between statement and object, theory and practice, is another form of organic organization that sheds a more usefully nuanced light on Wagner's actualization of the Gesamtkunstwerk, which we find described at the very start of Hegel's *Phenomenology of Spirit*—where Wagner likely found it, too. A well-known anecdote about Wagner has him laughing in dismay at Hegel's book, but historians surmise that he got at least as far as the first pages of the preface. There the philosopher develops a metaphor that is key to the dialectic and to an understanding of organic transformation, as unlike forms enact the becoming of a wedded whole.

> The bud disappears in the bursting-forth of the blossom, and one might say that the former is refuted by the latter; similarly, when the fruit appears, the blossom is shown up in its turn as a false manifestation of the plant, and the fruit now emerges as the truth of it instead. These forms are not just distinguished from one another, they also supplant one another as mutually incompatible. Yet at the same time their fluid nature makes them moments of an organic unity in which they not only do not conflict, but in which each is as necessary as the other; and this mutual necessity alone constitutes the life of the whole.[74]

Hegel's perception of unification imagines transformation in which micro-totalities are processual, simultaneously changed from within and without in mutual relation and reconstitution, an ongoingness of becoming—and one, interestingly, that includes a sense of falseness perceived and then revised. In the context of the theorization of networks, we find a logic of the processual transformation of nodal objects such that there are always codes that describe these objects and their operations, but also codes that are self-healing for the system, that present interoperable flexibility in reciprocity, a state of "vicarious causation," in Graham Harman's phrase, transforming without finality, continually redrawing the state of play. To learn from Wagner as a progenitor of interdisciplinary practice and to schematize his proto-network is to see the way his longed-for totalization becomes the internally refutational, re-decidable, non-totalizing total, just as a network "opens up a possibility for a non-totalizing frame that still functions as a whole."[75]

The conditions of predetermined and contingent development, of constriction, tumult, latency, redirection, and transformation—all are fundamental to interdisciplinary works as networks, Wagner's and those to follow, hacking absolute totality. After Auschwitz, we can say to Adorno that the idea of a network aesthetics in Wagner finally opposes the totalitarian logic that extinguishes poetry, offering an open syntactical scheme of protocols, nodes, and linkages in recombinant copulations—which is simply to say that the network-as-model ultimately retorts the trauma of identity as a suffering sameness. In network aesthetics, the itinerancy of nodes, of discipline-objects as they enter and leave their networks, and as they are visited and continually transformed by the contingency of viewer-agents as rogue nodes, isn't a waiting in vain but a readiness to interoperate that offers a wholeness *with* difference. Identity and non-identity are coexistent and serve the network in varying operations of interdependency, different vectors, and an ethical imperative whose openness promulgates transformation without finality.

This, we could say, is what Wagner's works fail toward. He is, in this particular sense, an accidental inventor, an inventor so given to the monumental gamble of his task that in his ultimate inability to satisfy completed-ness as such under the stubborn reign of the heterogeneous, his error implicitly proffers that opening for future artworks that are inclusive of otherness. With Wagner—who so instinctively senses the seductive power and danger in Hegelian self-consciousness but can't resolve the one for the other—we have just begun. We are on the road to a fuller, entirely more pliable technical interdisciplinarity, one whose boundaries aren't nearly so priapic, nor so vertically imposed.

The fleshliness of his disciplinary imaginary, with its absorptions, its leaning sisters, its politically inflected audience as *Volk* taken up into the womb, advertises, however egomaniacal and inadvertent in its contradictions, the concupiscence of an urge toward a seamlessness with the world, melding the somatic and the social, inside and outside. So Merleau-Ponty, in his own thinking, remarks: "The presence of the world is precisely the presence of its flesh to my flesh."[76] After Wagner, through Wagner, because of Wagner, alongside Wagner, and despite Wagner, soon enough the body of the artist and the body of the interdisciplinary artwork will become still more blurred, still more open and joined, blossom and fruit.

The Senses

HEAR

• • • The blurs—shapes, sounds, sound of my mouth crying out. Eyes not clear yet, and hearing nods toward the immaterial. First, the physical waves of sound, the ear is meat, the timbre of things in the canal, an internal stem of flesh, an involution, but when the head turns to hear, listening is a shapeliness of air. Sound enters me unfelt like touch. At first an innocence, the first brief entry of a sound, a *pre*, before cognition, the entry of the world were we able to listen that way. Or a heaviness of my head under water, bursting up into air, into the brightness of the known, of sounds with faceted markers of signifying sense along their ribboned surface resolving into structures and limits, into semantic modules, into laws. The spool in my head over all my time could be unwound if only memory were strong enough. You would have to be Nabokov, who seems to have remembered everything. And so the title for his book closest to him begins with a word denoting sound. *Speak, Memory.*

Adorno says in his treatise on Wagner that hearing is the lazy sense, passive, unlike the eye that seeks, hunting. It's true, the ear doesn't blink. It's not a net but a basket filled interminably. We try to block it with plastic, with noise cancelling, to put off the inevitable surf of *more*. Like Didi and Gogo, our ears are the waiting servants of horizonless time. All the properties by which we learn to distinguish sound from noise—language, melody, the growling threat of animal or gun—all are invisible engines of my body transformed, lifted in status, reduced, sounds turning us into what? True, among us are those without it, never given or taken away. Lack adds a compensatory intensity, which means sounds become cognitive energy, not physics alone, and open wider elsewhere: tongue, nostril, epidermis, pupil.

Hearing is the adding machine, apparatus of accumulation, and how many of us are we, when sound, transcribed on this ribbon, writes its temporal script, starting, ending? With the sound of my mouth, sucking, or a bee suddenly at my ear? With the voice of my lover? With musics, each different, penetrating not through ears alone, but through stomach, groin, my legs shaking. And I am different selves. Voice of the schoolteacher, the boss, reasoned syllables unfolding in semantic units of control, voices turning, each I a self bored or fearing or filled with promise. To hear is the chorus of the socius, knotting sonar affiliations, the what of what it is to be among others. But *this* thing, *this* self, the braided and unbraided sounds of thisness, quiddity, haecceity. A loop of thrumming, falling, loud again. Those harmonies, those discords marking our sonar accord of likenesses shared or a turning away—the call of *this is me*, of *will not be*, of *yes*, constellated or alone.

So it is that hearing in its hearing marks boundaries, makes them. As always, I'm the center, noise rushing inward, my own noises oozing, barked, murmured, enunciated to offer rim and tender core, margin and center, a roundness of lines of intensity, growing in density until skin indicates the demand or hazard, goosebumps and hairs rising, sheath of alarm: *Stop!* Is it first the seen, then the heard, or reversed, or smell, or touch as the cry and soothing of proximity? Impossible to say, or the chorus of all-at-once, orchestral machine, mammal. But how remarkable, how much a statement beyond just creatureliness—climbed that ladder from bare need to ornament, barbaric yawp to language and music. A jewel from the heap. As if all the world's orphan noises found their home in the cognized imagination of the self. Though noise, too, is an ocean of particulars we turn at times to purpose. I will fold them into shapes. I will speak them, sing them. I will make instruments to make other instruments so that I can play them, hear them. *Poor Beethoven*, I think. And yet he amplified.

Three

PAUL/MARCEL

Two Bodies

1.

But let me begin with two bodies. Two at least. Bodies inscribed in practices both proto-interdisciplinary and proto-networking. Bodies embodying the instability of identity, spatial orientation, and time. So: a touching moment in a letter Rainer Maria Rilke writes to his wife from Paris. The date is October 19, 1907. Nearly a year to the day has passed since Paul Cézanne died. "I'm sure you remember [. . .] in *The Notebooks of Malte Laurids Brigge*," Rilke writes to Clara, "the place that deals with Baudelaire and his poem: 'Carrion.' I was thinking that without this poem, the whole trend toward plainspoken fact which we now seem to recognize in Cézanne could not have started; first it had to be there in all its inexorability. First, artistic perception had to overcome itself to the point of realizing that even something horrible, something that seems no more than disgusting, *is*, and shares the truth of being with everything else that exists."[1]

Baudelaire's poem rhymes the rotting corpse of an animal covered with maggots found bursting in the sun with a meditation on love and the fate of every person, no matter their beauty, no matter our devotion. "Do you remember the thing we saw, my love, / That beautiful, soft summer morning, / The stinking carcass at the turn in the path, / On a bed of stones."[2] What Rilke sees in this equivalence is a leveling, the apprehension of an old propriety and of venerable hierarchies broken down. Baudelaire gives permission, in a sense, to Cézanne and to other artists after him to move without hindrance across "everything else that exists," which is to find in things a recalibration of connections, a revised connectivity and distribution of significances now flowing over the opened plane of potentiality. Rilke's radical "*is*" foreshadows the fundamental idea of networks as events of connectivity in which meaning and interpretation are dynamic, revocable, contingent, and conditional, determined by protocols whose codes are given to continual revision. Perhaps this characterization does not change a conventional interpretation of the poem in its fundamental anthropomorphic sentimentalization of nature. And yet the incipient revision of epistemic borders between things in their thingness and affect ripples the surface of connectivity per se, pointing toward what "network" will come to mean and be.

Baudelaire's poetry was valued deeply by Cézanne. But the painter's understanding of the equivalence of things begins in a more direct indebtedness to the Impressionists and to his mentor and friend, Camille Pissarro. Equivalence in Cézanne's case isn't about disgust—just the opposite, it's about the pleasure of the eye, the eye and mind caught up in a particular relationship to time. That relationship is captured in the word "spontaneity," a break in time, a dis-homogeneity with the past, the spontaneity of the hand recording the movements of light and shadow. We take spontaneity for granted. We have mobile devices whose speeds are the consequence of this very need to steal the eloquent fluidity of time and contain it in various ways: cameras with blindingly fast shutters, video cameras, digital voice recorders, mobile phones with all of these combined. For the Impressionists, the visual revelation of spontaneity was new.

But an asterisk needs to be placed next to "spontaneity": *. Whim, impulse, the presumption of freedom from determinism must be questioned. Consider, for example, Slavoj Žižek's observation concerning Hegel, and Kant before him, touching on the true character of what we deem an unbridled sense of being. "According to German Idealism," Žižek writes, "when we act 'spontaneously' in the everyday meaning of the word, we are not free from but prisoners of our immediate nature, determined by the causal link which chains us to the external world."[3] Our impulses, he continues, are always an interchange between our sensations determining our actions and a consciousness of this determination, such that we're always responsible for what seem to be unfettered reactions, which are always already a choice bound to the limits of the self, just as they scrape across the experiences of others in all the relations in which obligation finds us.

Impressionism seen through this lens took on a triple task. First, the burden to undo previous painting's sense of deliberateness and stillness, while beneath the surface of this "free" hand that rendered the quickness of the light were two other weights: the phenomenological weight of being bound by the chains of animal response and, at the same time, the ponderousness of bourgeois life as critiqued in *plein air* painting that represented an ambivalence toward material delight, a contestation in the throes of industrial capitalist change.[4] In this implicit sense of conflict and loss was an aching precession, the rearward trail of nostalgia for the health of nature confronted by the trajectory of the machinic, the non-organic, of an ultimate externality with which the self and nature could no longer seem to form an abiding circuit.

It's a well-rehearsed chapter in the history of European modernism that Cézanne struggled heroically to find those sensations that were truest to his experience of nature and that bound him to it. In a letter to his old friend, the novelist Émile Zola, dated October 19, 1866, he writes: "You know, any picture done indoors, in the studio, never equals things done outdoors. In pictures of outdoor scenes, the contrast of figures to scenery is astonishing, and the landscape is magnificent. I see superb things and I must resolve to paint only out of doors."[5] There are indoor eyes and outdoor eyes. From this moment forward in Cézanne's work, a rupture opens in the history of art-making that will not close again. Or rather ruptures: in the stillness of representation; in the surface of continuous time and the advent of multiplicity; of the body that becomes more than one, its organs mysteriously transmuting, riven by heightened, ramified sensations. What Cézanne offers is a phenomenology of the *open*. Pissarro summarizes this suppleness, this jumping momentariness in Cézanne's art, in a letter from November 21, 1895. He writes simply: "Sensation is there!"[6]

Pissarro means that sensation is snared in the representation—though, of course, sensation must first be in the body and projected from it. We can say most fundamentally that art addresses the body's organic attraction to the worldness of the world as a generator of physicalities embodied in artifice in order to create resemblance, recognition, and recollection. They form our sense of placefulness. (If the teleology of disruption and discontinuity so crucial to modernism argues against this placefulness, it always presupposes it.) The physicality of this presence is the home of sensation, as the body is its living sign of reception. Around this reception, the conventions of enclosure have come to stand. Each organ has its boundaries of tissue by which it preserves itself. Each person has his, her, or their borders of physical feeling: pain feelings and pleasure feelings, with subsets of hot, cold, wet, dry, intoxicated, sexually heightened and released. Each group has its borders of fellow-feeling, hostility, incursion, lawfulness, and the unlawful. Each society has its borders of civitas. Sensations and borders are intrinsic to one another. The representation of sensations, which is how we come to the subject in the work of Cézanne, is a questioning of this relationship of sensation and the conventions by which the borders around physical objects and feelings are represented and redefined in order to recollect them or imagine their recollection or note their disruption.

So, to return to spontaneity*, now with its asterisk and its conflicted relationship in Cézanne's art. On the one hand, as art historian Joseph Masheck notes, Pissarro's influence on Cézanne to catch the swiftness of light is obviously there in the work. But as Masheck says, "Even *en plein air*, C spent much time making scrupulous adjustments to a particular painting; so that as regards its 'rate' of construction, its real-time execution, such a work might not be considered spontaneous at all. [. . .] He releases himself from any obligation of impressionist spontaneity in the interest of formal contrivance."[7] Cézanne's contrivance, his reading of spontaneity as an unending labor toward a very different offering of what Rilke called "truth" (and one that shares a likeness with Žižek's description of spontaneous acts), tests the painter's body and presses it toward de-articulation and re-formation—and leads to the production of another modernist body equally given to diffusion, displacement, and corporal ventriloquism: Marcel Duchamp.

But let me return for a moment to Rilke's radical "*is*," the little blind in which an existential assumption sits waiting, an assumption about being—specifically that a common essence flows through being, this "*is*" that "shares the truth of being with everything else that exists." The problem of truth here will hold momentarily in order to pay close attention to "everything else," to the interrelations of elements as a complicity of common matter. Louis Althusser gets at this in a different but useful way in relation to the fundamental question of "*is*," of essence and structure, with his proposition of "expressive causality" that speaks to the "effectivity of a structure on its elements."[8]

Althusser came to his concept in the context of reading Marx's *Capital* on the way to a revisionist philosophical understanding of Marxist production and political economy, yet the idea of expressive causality and its relation to what he called "overdetermination"—by which he proposed that historical events and social phenomena are shaped by multiplicitous interactions of political, ideological, and cultural factors that bear down on one another and therefore overdetermine each individual element—offers another way of articulating the dynamic relations of inner necessity and outward projection, of the processual and eruptive network dynamics of co-related things in dense connections effecting and altering both part and whole.

Expressive causality stands in relation to Rilke's *is*, and for that matter with respect to Hegel's bud, blossom, and fruit, as it gives us a sense of the profound reciprocity between ideas concerning the becoming of things, of both structures shaping what is internal to them and the internal, roiling nature of inner necessities that in their collisions and adjustments give outward form to their expression. Perhaps both exist together, a conjugation of emergence made visible in Cézanne's works as platforms whose material structures and ideational expressions offer, in the most literal sense of "sensational," a causal visuality, a proposing of nature as an intrinsic structure that becomes the structure of painting; a construction of painted things as an embodiment of nature that takes on a material correspondence among its parts of visualized essence, intending to perform a kind of ontological mimesis.

This fluidity of natural and human expression is so hard won in Cézanne that the causal expressivity intensely, even achingly, packed into his images implies an impassioned sense of responsibility of thing-to-thing, an ethics. In this there's an informal resemblance to what I've previously noted as central to network aesthetics, what Benjamin Bratton calls "addressable flows" between objects in networks that accumulate and allow the complexity of data to build exponentially.[9] Precisely this interpenetrability of flows, this openness and equivalence suggesting a vast plasticity, evokes that sense of conjugation, of thing in relation to thing reaching up from essence into structure and down again. In thinking about Cézanne, as he struggled to get beyond the outward look of Impressionism's spontaneity that seemed to him insufficient to get to the unseen and tumultuous presence of *is*, what was this essence he imagined at the core of Being?

Here is his *Still Life with a Ginger Jar and Eggplants* (1893–94). The lines around its objects are heavy, boundaried—how they mark a lemon's place, for example, on this densely patterned blue tablecloth, so folded, as if terrain. The rendering engages the lemon's being as a thing unto itself, a representation of a thing physically real now brought into contact with another represented thing in its evocation of thingness—a roiling pattern, in the same passage of our glance, that's both "cloth" and a visualization of abstractness. The contrasting presence of phenomenon and idea, far from whim, far from stealing the quickness of light and atmosphere, is a contrivance that argues for the deliberated representation of the potency of the visible in relation to a non-retinal, noumenal immanence.

Roger Fry, the influential art critic who wrote at the end of the nineteenth century and into the twentieth and who coined the term Post-Impressionism, went too far when he spoke about Cézanne's profound ability to see matter with a distanced eye, writing of his "complete detachment from any of the meanings and implications of appearances."[10] No, it's Cézanne's detachment that *allows* him to understand the implications of appearances and, in the spirit of expressive causality, hint at the structuring of phenomena. Nonetheless, Fry senses an eruption in appearances, and here the stability of essence suggested by Rilke begins to trouble, as if it were an unperturbed flow along a flat plane of connectivity now coming undone. That roiling tablecloth is the effect of Cézanne's insight into what lies underneath, inside, and around him, around us. It is an interior confluent with its exterior, a living inconsistency breaking up the homogeneity of a totalizing force. Every object in the picture is precarious, at once drawn into a network of connectedness and seeming to float peculiarly in isolation. Each thing would seem to have its own life, and the network of *Still Life with a Ginger Jar and Eggplants* distributes this agency among its parts so that its wholeness as an image doesn't depend on the consistent behavior of its components, its nodes, but on their differences, their contrariness, brought into correspondence as mutually addressable flows. They refuse a system of closure while nonetheless abiding together, organized in their precariousness on the lip of control.

Cézanne has his own protocols of control to follow, his own tensions among the painting's network of parts in their jittering flows of energy.[11] One such control is time—time is an essence that expresses itself in the phenomena of the objects we see in the painting. A temporal wind blows through, an unsettling. This lemon's outline is, of course, a delineator of space, yet it lives as well in a symbolic order. It tells us that what a line is isn't only a line; it's a sheath, if porous. This darkened outline is an index of time that burdens and relieves the artist's imagination. It signifies the organic object held still in a moment between ripening and rotting, and it is juxtaposed with this blue cloth that is both inert and yet tumultuously folded, as if it, too, is caught in a moment of mysterious transformation. (Meanwhile, the tablecloth is oddly fructive, holding a deep contiguity with what rests on it: in its folds is the strange tracing of a ghostly or incipient new vessel emerging, echoing the vases and bottle in the picture.) The lemon is a sign of time's continuum, time flowing forward and back between new and ripe and rotting fruit, in which the internal and unseen palpable material of the lemon, its pulp and juice, the *thingness* of its matter and being, are the fuel of time's engine.

The tablecloth's elaborate folds suggest this specter of continuous discontinuity. The image, of course, is fixed in place, even heavy, and yet it's alive with the volatility of its structure and its effects, a doubled impression of stasis and flow. Time is folded in on itself, a perturbation, an inconsistency that adds to the growing sense of the pervasive turbulence of thingness in the picture. Time seems to distribute its agency to each thing, some flattening out before the eye, some fully volumetric, some appearing solid, while surface incidents suggest erosion and ethereality here and there. The Rilkean "*is*" becomes a plane of tension, disruption, correspondence, and autonomy in the painting. And it isn't the objects alone that bring this tumult of mobility into sight but the spaces around them. That sense of repeated and discrete spatial isolation of fruits and eggplants, vessels, tabletop, and textiles is created by the outlines around them that circulate across the image's structure to create its connective and undulating pulsation.

Between material bodies and the deep, shallow, weighty, and ghostly spaces depicted, this rippling mobility brings into relief not only the activation of an expressive causality but an aspect of Cézanne's picture-as-network that speaks to its phenomenological projection and its diaristic commentary on the aggregations and dissolutions in time and over time of living and life. "Multiplicities are not defined by the elements involved but rather by the interstice, the space in between the elements, which simultaneously both connects and separates these elements; it is what links them and separates them, incessantly forging and dissolving the relations between them," as Kai Eriksson writes about networks.[12]

A question, then, of essence emerges: "Inside" these things that populate Cézanne's still life, is there another level of what might be called a value of energy, a *quale* that is the essence whose effects are the elements we see, fistules of material expressiveness bursting up from the surface of Being and that, most urgently, call Cézanne to Being? And so, what do we make of the painting's richness of palpable things and the equally apparent presentation of things shifting, dematerializing before our eyes? What is the state of essence to be inferred? Not an evenness of all that exists, but a being-state clumped, broken up, and uneven. Time itself would seem in Cézanne's picture neither a clear flowing forward or a suspension, but, as I've noted, a bidirectional motion, perhaps recursive, or simply, in the bucking character of the painting, various rhythms, various temporalities that are all simultaneously at play. This optical sensation of no one state of Being emergent from the image inevitably raises this question in turn: Is it possible to get at the painting's *"truth"* of matter since what Cézanne offers is an excitement of instability? In order to get to the essence of essence in the picture, maybe it's best to imagine an infinite regression of what lies beneath every level of facticity, since fact and truth were so crucial in the ardor of the painter's labors. And so, what swims before our eyes is precisely an *imprecision* of material fact and time, of essence in a state of continually tremulous formation and re-formation, an instability of sensation, and the canvas as an object of animistic passion, sensitive in its quaking evanescence, unsure, backward and forward in time, always on the road to . . .

These possibilities are the *against* in Cézanne's picture, the going-two-ways, the implicit chaos and equally nascent meshwork of overlap: a still life that isn't still; a painting lush with the flesh of time that also imagines time folding in on itself and multiplicitous; a painting of things present and things dissolving. Look at the blue wall, wrapping strangely along the upper half of the picture, with its shadow half-dissolved, as if the wall itself were caught between states, caught in a dreaming space that loosens—a wall still aching to become.

But this impression of destabilized matter isn't merely an abstraction about time's plurality. It is a consequent of times physically captured in the numerous viewpoints from which Cézanne painted the picture and then compressed them into a single representation brimming with polarities and juxtapositions. We see a plate that holds its fruit at a floating angle in which physical law has another canon; where the lemon, which is one of seven essays on roundness in the picture, is heavy with flesh, juice, color, acid, and smell at the same time that it presents a lightness that isn't weight, a richness that isn't only the opulence and fullness of its sensual meat but is also the meat of a philosophical abstraction. Space, as I've already said, is not uniform among these objects, with a wall inexplicably warped as a backdrop, that are all arranged in a vectored array of nodal linkage, pushed and pulled to exude a noumenal suggestion of immanence.

To kneel here before the power of Cézanne's "little sensations," as he called them, is to bear witness to a believer in the continuum of essence and form who has gone in, as Heinrich von Kleist said in the context of his "Essay on the Marionette Theater," through the back door of Paradise, through knowledge to innocence or, more precisely, to a new rendering of the phenomenal, where all palpability has ascended to spirit and yet breathes fruit, breathes matter, *is* matter, is outside of time and yet within it, and will not give up the fullness of time and matter.

Cézanne's message in *Still Life with a Ginger Jar and Eggplants* concerning Being is that the internalization of Impressionist spontaneity leads to an ethics of limitation with which and against which the body recognizes its obligation and, in Cézanne's extraordinary case, seeks a way through to a second body. It is the remarkable stubbornness, melancholy, and heroism of Cézanne to work in the orbit of this visual struggle with the monsters of time and sensation, of intrinsic and apparent chaos joined to a will toward the most peculiarly imagined harmony and wholeness, that would seem to describe a network aesthetics in the making.

To say that the network per se is a causal platform on which actions of relation unfold in correlation among its parts is also to say that cause may lead to actions whose ambitions are univocal in intention, but they're won not through homogeneity but through the presence of nodes exhibiting their differences. In terms of the artwork and its maker—and this is as true for Cézanne as it is for the work of installation artists more than a century later—the input of phenomena as cause leads to the expressive causality that influences what happens among the work's parts. Fistules, I called them, to evoke clumps of energy restlessly in play with one another. This wholeness through difference is crucial to network aesthetics, and Cézanne's picture isn't simply a representation of nature, a record of facticity, but, as I've said, a representation of relations themselves, of interrelated multiplicities with the most profound personal encoding dredged from the painter's deep well of observation and inference in which everything is recognized as unstable and alive, including representation itself, and beyond it, essence and phenomena.

This is the heartbreaking testament of Cézanne's work. He is like Beckett's Didi and Gogo who wait for Godot, never acknowledging that Godot is the unending susurration of time's waves wearing away and building and wearing away. Cézanne is the painter of the multiplicity and unfinishedness of Being unto death. He can never resolve the disjunctions of phenomena, though he is always seeking (an impossible) consistency. His inquiry into and struggle with the matter-flow out of essence is also, in that sense of linkage and temporal asymmetry, a nascent inclination toward what will be the interdisciplinary impulse, the expression of joined multiplicities as will soon emerge in the history of other art, with Marcel Duchamp as one example and Cabaret Voltaire as another. Such are the hollows in mark-making and object-making in which multiplicity pools, tied to warring heterogeneities laid out as contestations of energy.

The Impressionists' record of sensation as presence, finding a surface of appearance approaching the skittering brilliance of light as the mind apprehends it, may have been foundational to Cézanne, but their version of spontaneity worked on him toward a different lesson for the future. Burdened by an immense sense of his own limitations, spontaneity became a recognition of impulse as agon, of the self in difficult relation to the world and to others, of things elementally in relation to other things as never simply harmonious: all things shuddering, harnessed, released, clotted, breaking open, shifting toward and away from integration, never totalized. For Cézanne, the jots and specks of the scintillated surfaces of Impressionism descend downward and inward as a flaking morphology of the self, an auto-geography whose subterranean, volcanic history is part of the mark-making of the self in the complexity of new means of emergent assemblage, a new form of object construction and distribution in picture-making.

This is no less so in his work *en plein air* than in his still lifes. If sensation was there, as Pissarro proclaimed, it was there to advance the condition of the multeity of elements whose separations are incessantly dissolved. This palpable sense of the multiple is detailed by Merleau-Ponty in his extraordinary essay "Cézanne's Doubt":

> The task before [Cézanne] was, first to forget all he had ever learned from science and, second *through* these sciences to recapture the structure of the landscape as an emerging organism. To do this, all the partial views one catches sight of must be welded together; all that the eye's versatility disperses must

be reunited; one must, as [Joachim] Gasquet put it, "join the wandering hands of nature." "A minute of the world is going by which must be painted in its full reality." His meditation would suddenly be consummated: "I have my *motif*," Cézanne would say, and he would explain that the landscape had to be centered neither too high nor too low, caught alive in a net which would let nothing escape. Then he began to paint all parts of the painting at the same time, using patches of color to surround his original sketch of the geological skeleton. The picture took on fullness and density; it grew in structure and balance; it came to maturity all at once. "The landscape thinks itself in me," he said, "and I am its consciousness."[13]

Is the landscape a multiple projection issuing from Cézanne, or is Cézanne a projection of the landscape? He answers with the phrase, "The landscape thinks itself in me." It isn't, at least for the moment, that interior and exterior are without boundaries. These agents exist alongside one another. But then the other penetrates in reply, "and I am its consciousness." Is that to say he is the expression of this essence? Perhaps. That's still unclear. In any case, the painter believes that he and the landscape reciprocate a common code. His self and the selves of nature's objects are joined in a hybrid subjectivity. Not a fragmentation, but an economy of power relations, a tension between nodes, a distribution of agency between two bodies, between many bodies. Merleau-Ponty continues:

The lived object is not rediscovered or constructed on the basis of the contributions of the senses; rather, it presents itself to us from the start as the center from which these contributions radiate. We *see* the depth, the smoothness, the hardness of the objects; Cézanne even claimed that we see their odor. If the painter is to express the world, the arrangement of his colors must carry with it this indivisible whole, or else his picture will only hint at things and will not give them the imperious unity, the presence, the unsurpassable plenitude which is for us the definition of the real. That is why each brushstroke must satisfy an infinite number of conditions. Cézanne sometimes pondered hours at a time before putting down a certain stroke, for, as [Émile] Bernard said, each stroke must "contain the air, the light, the object, the composition, the character, the outline, and the style." Expressing what *exists* is an endless task.[14]

This description, nonetheless, is what exists as exterior. It offers the act of painting, Cézanne's hand and canvas, in a finalizing process with its final surface, its formal presence. Yet Cézanne's mark-making is an instrument of porosity; it drills little holes in the phenomenal. All the objects in his gaze erupt in flows that seep among the layers of matter and beneath it, inside it. Or so he claims. This could be said to be a Hegelian self-consciousness, always dependent on the other: "only when each in its own self through its own action, and again through the action of the other, achieves this pure abstraction of being-for-self."[15] These fruits, this light and shadow, these vessels, or, in other paintings, a figure in a landscape, or the landscape itself, each thinks itself in him, has agency and cause, and Cézanne thinks himself in them—all of their times, their phenomenal skins shrinking and shifting, their outsides (where time is visible) and their insides (from which their sensual properties radiate), becoming linked and progenitive.

In reading Merleau-Ponty, it seems that each stroke, as Bernard suggested, had to embody so many aspects of the transfer from essence to artifact that there was an enormous downward pressure, a compacting of thought and feeling, into the visual. All of this is undertaken in the attempt to complete experience, though the completion was an attempt in itself to express the internal sense of upheaval there in his subjects, their energy of immanence captured in a moment of *becoming*. In looking at Cézanne's work, particularly in the later paintings from the close of the 1880s until his death in 1906, what is apparent is that sense of the raw, the ripped open, the quality of the image as something that doesn't totalize but keeps visible within the picture the motion back and forth between fragment and whole, between the painter's self and nature.

The phenomenal perpetually turned inside out, as if the picture were an oscillating I/it machine, has its complement in the visual drift of objects in the pictures themselves, which is to say their manifestation of

Cézanne's internal need. To the degree that the interdisciplinary work may be considered a network of interoperative differences interlaced, this is what we see in Cézanne's premonitory assemblages that strive toward an uneasy balance among relationships on the move, a shifting continuity in differential wholeness, as he ascribed to nature. Responding to a question from Bernard about classical artists, Cézanne answered: "They created pictures; we are attempting a piece of nature." When Bernard asked, "But aren't nature and art different?" Cézanne replied: "I want to make them the same."[16]

He means to erode the separating tissues, to weld in a single image multiple states of being, reinventing the self, dismantling the painter as a body, as a boundaried thing, and fusing it with nature, dismantling the picture and its hierarchies of planar division, too. For Cézanne to get rid of painting's single point of view and its stasis, he must dismantle the single stream of time and aggregate times in the picture (a project that shoots toward the future of cinema and, later, of installation art). This is why he must loosen the painting from the frame of the self and make instead a flesh with nature, of nature, through nature—or attempt it, imagine it, even in vain. The permeable, the seeping, the erosion of boundary, the dilating possibility/dream of the self that isn't alongside an otherness but combines with it and yet is still somehow individuated, this is a true derangement, a movement away from the orderly row or line, a little bit of madness. The demands Cézanne put on himself to dismantle convention in this exploit were intense and taxing. They were in keeping with what Quentin Meillassoux writes in an argument about necessity and contingency:

> We are no longer upholding a variant of the principle of sufficient reason, according to which there is a necessary reason why everything is the way it is rather than otherwise, but rather the absolute truth of a principle of unreason. There is no reason for anything to be or to remain the way it is; everything must, without reason, be able not to be and/or be able to be other than it is.[17]

So it was that in Cézanne's imagining, some ground between reason and unreason sought essential congress in the fluidity between landscape and self—a congress for him that had a precedent in the writings

of Gustave Flaubert. In 1874, two decades prior to Cézanne's completion of *Still Life with a Ginger Jar and Eggplants*, Flaubert published *The
Temptation of Saint Anthony*, a novel he labored over for twenty-five
years. Cézanne knew the novel well. It was a primary source for his
painting of the saint's temptation, executed in 1874–75.[18] Toward the
end of the final version of the story, Flaubert writes: "Plants are now
no longer distinguished from animals. [. . .] Insects identical with rose
petals adorn a bush. [. . .] And then plants are confused with stones.
Rocks look like brains, stalactites like breasts, veins of iron like tapes-
tries adorned with figures."[19]

These imagined associations, which resonate so much with
Meillassoux's remarks about a liberating principle of unreason, were
touched on before Flaubert and after; a condition of organic fusion that
lies on the cusp of aberration and aspiration. In Georg Büchner's 1836
novella, *Lenz*, we read: "He thought that it must be a feeling of endless
bliss to be in contact with the profound life of every form, to have a soul
for rocks, metals, water, and plants, to take into himself, as in a dream,
every element of nature, like flowers that breathe with the waxing and
waning of the moon."[20]

Nearly a century later, Roger Caillois writes in his essay "Mimicry
and Legendary Psychasthenia" about what he calls a disturbance in "relations between personality and space," citing the same Flaubert passage and commenting on it in a way that also echoes with uncanny
likeness the sentiments of Cézanne: "In thus seeing the three realms
of nature merging into each other, Anthony in his turn suffers the lure
of material space: he wants to split himself thoroughly, to be in everything, 'to penetrate each atom, to descend to the bottom of matter, to *be*
matter.'"[21] Then, seventy years after Caillois, Jacques Rancière calls up
Flaubert's novel again, noting in the rendering of Saint Anthony something that alerts us as well to Cézanne's process of what the philosopher
calls a "movement of dissociation of the body from the world of representation." He quotes another passage from the novel that ends with
the words, "inert things that seem animal, vegetative souls, statues that
dream and landscapes that think."[22]

But then such evocations of bodies fused with landscapes and in-
terspecially with other bodies resound all the way back to Ovid. In

Cézanne, perhaps channeling Flaubert at least, the struggle is to find a way to break both the body and representation, allowing an emergent reinvention of both, a new formation of becoming in those terms of Meillassoux to undo and redo in violation of natural laws, of convention. This violence and yearning, so evident in *Still Life with a Ginger Jar and Eggplants*, is what Cézanne works toward in his dream of ontological fluidity. He said to his friend from Aix-en-Provence, the French art critic Joachim Gasquet, "Personally, I'd like to lose myself in nature, grow again *with* nature, *like* nature, have the stubborn shades of the rocks, the rational obstinacy of the mountain, the fluidity of the air, and the warmth of the sun. In a green my whole brain would flow in unison with the sap rising through a tree's veins."[23] The landscape is thinking itself in him. He is modeling a network of affiliation and distribution. Yet what he desires is still something more viscous, an associative hematology, blood = sap, or rather blood + sap = the redistributed, hybrid Cézannescape.

There are the two bodies, then: Cézanne's, with his own agency, and the Cézannescape's, with its loosely described new consciousness. They call to mind Deleuze and Guattari's concept of a "Body without Organs" (BwO) that they discuss in relation to the suffering corporeal fantasies of Antonin Artaud and which they illustrate as well with a passage from William Burroughs's *Naked Lunch*: "No organ is constant as regards either function or position, . . . sex organs sprout everywhere, . . . rectums open, defecate and close, . . . the entire organism changes color and consistency in split-second adjustments."[24]

They tie this prodigiously unsettled body to concepts of schizophrenia, of "desiring-machines" whose production rises from the amorphous, opaque, primordial BwO envisioned as miraculously self-generating: "Machines attach themselves to the body without organs as so many points of disjunction, between which an entire network of new syntheses is now woven, marking the surface off with co-ordinates, like a grid."[25] Elsewhere they write that the BwO "reveals itself for what it is: connection of desires, conjunction of flows, continuum of intensities. You have constructed your own little machine, ready when needed to be plugged into other collective machines."[26] They are speaking of networks and protocols, and might as well have been describing attributes of network aesthetics, with its connection of intensities through links and nodes as bodies of difference intersecting so that new multiplicities of meaningfulness are assembled. All of this touches Cézanne's desires to cultivate his body incessantly revised.

Another painting: *The Bather* (circa 1885) in New York's Museum of Modern Art. The figure approaches a quasi-geological formation in the sharp cut of his elbows, in the way his left foot is flat against the gray rock he stands on, as if he's formed from it, emerging into the air. That gray suffuses the bather's flesh, just as the landscape on the right of the figure has a fleshlike color. And there, under the figure's chin and below his right shoulder, is that green Cézanne uses to evoke plantlike growth, though no specific bush or grass is delineated. The bather is that plant, too, and that rock. His left nipple is barely perceptible; it's hardly there; it is in process. He has already shifted into something hybrid. His right nipple is a diamond-shaped shard, as much stone as skin. Like Burroughs's imagined hyperbody, Cézanne's bather is sprouting, his flesh one thing and other things, a rendering of Flaubert's imaginings and Caillois's conjuring of minds in the snare of space, which has as much agency as its human occupants and swallows them, pulls them into a state of dematerialization and reformation, an urge to become that BwO, that nodal entity among other heterogeneous entities whose divergent sub-topologies are linked in a network, subsumed.

The Bather's meshwork of animal, rock, and flora includes the sky as well, which takes on the same narrow range of hues—a touch of that sky lies next to the green just beneath the figure's right shoulder. Paint's pure materiality takes on a highly imagistic quality, with its shimmer around the body and in the air embedded in the flatness of the brush's marks. Time, too, is woven here: time of that hand making marks across the canvas; time implicit in the age of the figure and time also implicit in the momentarily halted locomotion of the bather stopping for a moment; time of the figure melding with all around him; the geological time of rocks, and the time of sky and clouds and light and climate; cycles of change and cycles of meaning all generative and invoked by the bather standing, foot lifted, a world tilted on an axis of metamorphosis.

The flesh of Cézanne's bather is brought into equivalence with each element of the landscape, things speaking to other things. When Merleau-Ponty writes in *The Visible and the Invisible*, "every relation between me and Being, even vision, even speech, is [. . .] a carnal relation, with the flesh of the world" and "the presence of the world is precisely the presence of its flesh to my flesh," Cézanne's bather and his landscape are captured in their networked being-state.[27] This collectivity intensifies as Cézanne comes to the end of his life. Flesh, of course, is not simply a unidirectional simile, a likeness that runs from human to landscape. In the phenomenology conceptualized by Merleau-Ponty, flesh as such is that sheath of Being manifest between all entities connected through space. The fleshness of the world permeates.

So we see in such works as *Seated Man* (1905–06) and *The Gardener Vallier* (circa 1906)—the penultimate and last year of Cézanne's life, in which the Cézannescape is instantiated in the ambient continuity of interlocked flakes of matter that both scintillate and lie flat, as if a horizontal terrain, an aerial map of figure and ground, a network. Once again we see in the painter's ambition a sense of urgency and hope, sublimation and willfulness in the reorganization of dominion.

This doubled space of intimate materiality and distance as a continuum of Being was already suggested in the intervening years between *The Bather* and these late figures. For example, in his *Rocks in the Park of the Chateau Noir* (1898–1900), where the myriad little interlocking colored planes, whose near blur presents the movement of matter's mutability, unveil the desiring, convivial need of variousness itself, of the fulgency of multiple forms speaking one to another, the internal bloom of essence rising in the flesh of the world. Expressive causality is alive in the most retinal way. Cézanne replaces the use of chiaroscuro with the deployment of contrasting hues placed consecutively to create a blanket of illumination so that the semblance of unified presence emerges. "I produce my planes with the colors on my palette," Cézanne said to Gasquet, "do you follow me?"

> You have to see the planes [. . .] clearly [. . .] but fit them together, blend them. They must turn and interlock at the same time. [. . .] I sometimes imagine colors as great noumenal entities, living

ideas, beings of pure reason. With which we can commune. Nature is not at the surface; it is in depth. Colors are the expression, on this surface, of this depth. They rise up out of the earth's roots; they are its life, the life of ideas.[28]

Reason is rooted deeply in this thinking, but so again is Meillassoux's notion of unreason, the proposition that anything can *be*, even a man's body that melts into the thingness of nature that is itself conceived as an equivalent subjective agent, such that they are simultaneously sprouting, separate and joined, rhizomatic, inconsistent, nomadic, horizontalized, nodes in a network. Cézanne is always looking over his shoulder, assuming all positions of perception and sensation at once. All things are seen in this way, all as if a single skin—the various pictures of Mont Sainte-Victoire that emerge in the last years of his life akin to Vallier and the faceted surface of trees and air and rocks alive in the park at Chateau Noir. Everything is seen in the act of assembling, just as Cézanne constantly struggled to enter oblivion, in the anthropologist Marc Augé's use of the verb, to rebegin.[29] Of course, this BwO in its hyper-fecundity is an idealized extreme. "You never reach the Body without Organs," Deleuze and Guattari say, "you can't reach it, you are forever attaining it, it is a limit."[30] And so, as Merleau-Ponty notes, just a month and a day before Cézanne's death on October 22, 1906, the painter is still in turmoil, still striving at the limit to meld his art and his self with nature. On September 21, 1906, Cézanne writes in a letter to Émile Bernard:

> I was in such a state of mental agitation, in such great confusion that for a time I feared my weak reason would not survive. [. . .] Now it seems I am better and that I see more clearly the direction my studies are taking. Will I ever arrive at the goal, so intensely sought and so long pursued? I am still learning from nature, and it seems to me I am making slow progress.[31]

He could not possibly arrive there. That place is a field of imminence, throbbing beneath the Rilkean "*is*" in a state of continual potentiality and progeniture. Nonetheless, the painter gives permission in art, as Rilke understood in his own way, for the possibility of extreme equivalency. This, too, is glitch thinking, a hacking of the body's codes. The onto-phenomenological proposition of Cézanne's work to record the liquid, viscous, shape-changing condition of matter and self, pressing far beyond Impressionism's spontaneity, leads in its reasoned unreason, in its bleeding of thing into thing, in its redistribution of the flesh of the world, to the dogged revision of representation's codes and stability—codes that Marcel Duchamp will soon revise in his own way.

2.

Without the late Cézanne, there would be no Cubism as it was and no early Duchamp as he was, riffling through the styles of the vanguard artists around him; no Duchamp as a retinal artist who the later conceptual and purportedly non-retinal Duchamp would rebel against.[32] Without the late Cézanne, Cabaret Voltaire and Dada after it wouldn't have had the visual precedent and the correlative ideational model for their willed chaos, because just as there is a will toward harmony at the core of Cézanne, there is also a fear and presence of chaos embedded in the work and is not tamed.

In *Pictorial Nominalism: On Marcel Duchamp's Passage from Painting to the Readymade*, Thierry de Duve lays out a clear lineage for Duchamp from Cézanne's painting *The Card Players* (circa 1890–95). He first cites Duchamp's *The Chess Game*, painted in August 1910, that shows Duchamp's brothers, Gaston and Raymond, facing each other over a chessboard and who, as de Duve notes, "are painted in the same poses as Cézanne's famous *Card Players* . . ."

They open up an iconographic trail that is easy to follow, and that will lead, in August 1912 in Munich, to the *bachelors*, a new avatar of the ego-images of Duchamp, his imaginary identifications with the symbolic father-painter. In December 1911, the *Portrait of Chess Players* begins to multiply the portrait of the two brothers and to expand on chess players through their "mise en abyme." In May 1912, in *The King and Queen Surrounded by Swift Nudes*, the players will explicitly become chess pieces, and one of them will be feminized. Finally, in August 1912, *The Bride*

Stripped Bare by the Bachelors will rename as bachelors the now doubled paternal image inscribed on either side of the bride; they borrow their iconographic form from *The King and Queen*, and thus from *The Chess Players*, and thus from the two older brothers of *The Chess Game* in 1910.[33]

In tracing this reverse chronology that originates in Cézanne's *Card Players*, de Duve inscribes an Oedipal figure buried in Duchamp's painting; another fleshly contiguity by which

a symbolic father, Cézanne, [. . .] bars the young Marcel from access to an imaginary mother, painting, by seeming to offer him—in the pressing context of the avant-gardes of the period— no other path by which to realize himself as a painter than that of undergoing, and then assimilating, Cézanne's influence by transgressing it. [. . .] Bluntly put, kill the father (Cézanne), marry the mother (painting as it will be after Cézanne).[34]

The iconographic bloodline is evident, with de Duve's Freudian gloss, if a bit fanciful, proposing a deep-seated connection between the two artists that will play its generative role as well in the formation of interdisciplinary art. Duchamp tries out the style of a dominant master and, not being satisfied with the result, pushes toward his own expression by way of Cubism, which is itself derived from late Cézanne, and then of Futurism. But the profound communication between the two artists, in light of the Freudian reading and of Hegelian self-consciousness, is never truly killed. Instead, Cézanne's corporeal code is transformed in Duchamp's legitimizing narrative that reformulates the Cézannescape through a typical inversion.

This is what Duchamp's *The Bride Stripped Bare by Her Bachelors, Even* (1915–23) and his readymades tell us. If Cézanne's influence was already clear, both in its tension and viral consequences, Duchamp helps us to see all the more strongly the double edge of Cézanne's work— intensely visual and equally non-retinal in its seeking after essence—as an ontological undertaking of physical urgency yoked to the most unforgiving standard of conceptualization. Cézanne's desire to merge his consciousness and identity with the landscape was so radical a notion of overcoding that it proposed a remarkable revision, a new definition of the word "reify" as it applies to representation. What he attempted to make real was the abstract concept of the viscous body of the self turned inside out and dispersed, subsumed by an external reality, the picture of the self extruded and absorbed into the surround, into nature, into the landscape. This urge toward distributed horizontality, this thought of the inside made outside, of eroded boundaries, of an I and an it that meld to become another being, as the dispersal of individual subjectivity in the name of a liberated objectification . . . these are the links that tie Duchamp to Cézanne, and the connection ramifies in its animation of interdisciplinary practices to follow.

For each of them, the wish for alterity, the longing to fuse the shell of apparent identity with an alternate form, is a yearning on the fundamental level of ontological being to make altogether new peer-to-peer relationships, however alien they may first appear. This is a wandering away from the self toward an absorption in a structure of heterogeneity and linked forms. The systematic deferral of the self in its reasoned unreason loosens the membrane of law and boundary, of the skin of assignment, and offers in its place a network of edges between varied forms. We can say that the field of energy between things is precisely the field of the plenipotentiary force of unlikenesses that transforms them through new linkages. While Cézanne dreamed of a new finality for his re-formed being, for Duchamp there is instead the strategically and gnomically ambiguous character of transformation without finality that he proposes again and again in a practice that envisions the representation of the self and the representation of representation as twinned reflexive bodies.

The Bride Stripped Bare by Her Bachelors, Even, begun in 1915 and left "definitively unfinished," as Duchamp put it, in 1923, is a vertical glass construction more than nine feet tall. He painted images on the glass, drilled nine holes in it, affixed wire and dust to it, and later stabilized the work in aluminum frames to brace it after it was cracked accidentally while being moved in 1934, leaving a delicate tracery behind. The work's bipartite structure shows a "bride" above and her "suitors" below—a subject the artist had already addressed years before, as de Duve's chronology indicates. The piece is commonly known as *The*

Large Glass, and it is worth thinking about glass itself for a moment: hard to the touch, a border between sight and sight, and yet in its most transparent state a material border that borders on the immaterial. It violates the physical in another way as well, for glass as a magnifying instrument of sight moves us across space without touch, without gravity. Sight is entirely annunciatory rather than designatory: it reads an impression before it assigns any meaning, name, typology. Sight is Being in its state of being whatever *is*, and so transparency is an instrument of frictionless conjunction, a perfect medium for a readiness of alliance, a facilitation of connection.

The rectangular, bisected frame as a blunt metallic joint that sutures the two pieces of *The Large Glass* represents connectivity as an infinitely recursive circuit of skewed address: desire to connect, material connection, activity of connecting, and content that indicates an attempt and failure to connect. *Attempted* connection is projected as a network of biological, mechanical, and psychological impulses charged and discharged in an energetic cycle of disruption. The operation of expression within the work is based on antinomy, an implicit opposition of parts assembled to enact an anecdotal ambivalence, an enumeration of equalized, though contested, values. So, for example, in David Joselit's seminal analysis of *The Large Glass*, such value systems as capital and gender, as they suffuse the semiotics of imagery and reference in the work, are presented as a droll agon riddled with contradiction.[35] If we see in Cézanne a leveling of the self and nature, we see in Duchamp an antinomic trajectory between a flattened self, horizontalized and altered, and his embodiment as machine. Of course, machines are much on the minds of many artists of the period who lived through the Great War—this, again, is the origin of the trope of modernist fragmentation—and the production of *The Large Glass* is contemporaneous with the years of the war and its immediate aftermath.

Duchamp had already placed war at the center of a vision of dismemberment and mechanical assemblage in a note entitled "Eloignement" that took its place in the *Box of 1914*, in which he collected sixteen facsimiles of notes about *The Large Glass*. "Eloignement" refers to the French government's requirement for extended military service, and the note begins with the statement, "Against compulsory military service," then advances to Duchamp's facetious, bitter (though coolly futuristic) idea that mortally wounded soldiers could have their parts replaced "telephonically." This anxiety about the war and the conflation of the body's parts with mechanical apparatuses sheds a mordant light on *The Large Glass*'s mechanism of images. So do the erotic musings in another set of notes, the "Jura-Paris Road" collection that describes a 1912 road trip by car, a machine with "5 hearts," Duchamp writes— among them, those of the poet and art critic Guillaume Apollinaire, the painter Francis Picabia, his own, and Picabia's wife, Gabrielle Buffet. Hers mattered most, as Duchamp's infatuation with her went unconsummated, a connection in this eroticized quintupular machine never made.[36]

Years earlier, F. T. Marinetti proclaimed in his 1909 "Futurist Manifesto" the new ecstasy of the machine in a fusion of racing cars, men, and the lust for war. Duchamp had already absorbed Futurist art's staccato rhythms into his own hand in that same year of the trip from Jura, as *Nude Descending a Staircase, Number 2* so evidently shows.[37] It is all of the moment. Alongside the Futurist impulse implicit in Duchamp's evolving work, then, is the anti-authoritarian vehemence of Dada enterprises, as we will see, with its practitioners taking Duchamp as a peer (ambivalently on his part). It's in the air, this sense of entwined and intensified destruction and allure in syncopated motion, human and mechanical contraption combined.

And so there's something programmatically chilled yet animated, mortal, vincible yet distanced while intimately imagined in *The Large Glass*, its sleight of being twined with the transformation of self. But unlike Futurist bellicosity or the situation of Dada, it isn't as dire, even if the trauma of war still hovers in the air. Duchamp's rendering of the nude and her suitors reduced to mechanical contrivances is physical comedy, and black comedy at that: a machinic slapstick in which the bride is a motor filled with what the artist whimsically called "love gasoline" and is described in a numbered diagram for the work as *Pendu femelle*," a female version of a hanged man tricked out with a "wasp or sex cylinder." Bodily fascination is transferred from subject to object, as in Cézanne, the I becoming it. To the bride's right is the floating oblong Duchamp identifies as the Milky Way, a cosmic transfer between science and faith. The notion of the bride as a re-articulated, machinic virgin—or more to the point, Holy Virgin—is an ideational extrusion of the natural body: somehow organic yet motorized; an impure and frustrated complexity of a carnal self set to an alter-human repetition; autopoietic, contradictory, and radiant; a blunt fact and the instantiation of a supernal Logos.

Duchamp incorporates this impossible corporeality into his yearned-for and what might be called de-copulative *Pendu femelle*, this hanged female form whose hybrid mechanical/human presence entices and exhausts, is exhaustion itself, alluding to the war's technologically accelerated eradication of a prior order; the romance and devastation of machines in the service of a world sped up, ruthlessly revising itself, spilling destruction and invention, vaporizing what was. The *Pendu femelle* is trauma against itself, and in the harsh and dazzling light of an era of techno-military ruin, the recuperative imagination draws toward radical reassemblage. So, Duchamp calls the bride

> a new human being, half robot, half fourth dimensional. [. . .] Simply, I thought of the idea of a projection, of an invisible fourth dimension, something you couldn't see with your eyes. Since I found that one could make a cast shadow from a three-dimensional thing, any object whatsoever—just as the projecting of the sun on the earth makes two dimensions—I thought that, by simple intellectual analogy, the fourth dimension could project an object of three dimensions.[38]

Duchamp is speaking of an immaterial form now reasonably unreasoned in a calamitous, war-torn world that had given so much permission to the sundering of reason, a nonsense of essence casting its "shadow" as alter-thing made apparent. This tie to essence suggests the ultimacy of a salient unboundedness, an omega of transparency, just as the glass of *The Large Glass* is a canvas that (almost) can't be seen as a support for images that are. The fourth dimension, if it is unseen, is a sign of the network, of the vectored relations among objects on the glass, as Willis Domingo has noted.[39] The glass is the sheerest materiality Duchamp can manage to support his seriocomic allegory of thwarted communication among a community of dunces; a mechanical landscape of madly rigid order that ensures an antic continuum of failure. If Cézanne was riven by doubt, the loosening of the body as a way to unlock essence remained his goal. For Duchamp, essence itself is a matter of doubt, a playful intellectual speculation that figures in his sardonic calculus of an unstable world controlled by wholly questionable laws (a form of juridical expression, by the way, that will be played out entirely differently at the Cabaret Voltaire).

He makes his way toward a counter-sovereignty. He intuits that the laws of the machinic world can apply to a specific kind of machine that encompasses more than individual contraptions, and into which doubt in the form of contingency and chance can be built. He intuits network thinking, and he states this outright the year before he begins *The Large Glass* with the title he gives a painting of ramified lines and points laid down on top of a sideway rendition of an earlier work, *Young Man and Girl in Spring* (1911), joined to a schematic of *The Large Glass*. He calls the painting *Network of Stoppages* (1914). It isn't that Duchamp has worked out network theory's analyses of interactions among nodes, links, and protocols before its invention and the advent of electronic computation. No, his images remain true to the romance with machines of his day, yet linkage is also there as an operational means.

The network of his 1914 painting is a more basic use of the word: an interconnection of elements. Caroline Levine notes that "network" originates in "the language of metallurgy and textiles used in the sixteenth century to describe objects made out of fabrics or metal fibers interlaced as in a net or web."[40] This makes perfect, even amusing, sense in relation to *Network of Stoppages*, with its segmented lines that refer to the pieces of thread used in a work made the previous year, his 1913 disquisition on authoritative measurement, *3 Standard Stoppages*. Still, if Duchamp nominates the idea of a network as his operating principle in *Network of Stoppages*, he implicitly expands the character of networks (and does so with an eye toward metallurgy in the imagining of *The Large Glass*'s bride), seeking hybridity between nature and contrivance.

Deleuze and Guattari write at the start of *A Thousand Plateaus*, "Every rhizome contains lines of segmentarity according to which it is stratified, territorialized, organized, signified, attributed, etc., as well as lines of deterritorialization down which it constantly flees."[41] The rhizome is the seed of the network's structural impulse; it points to the network's joining of diverse, extensible elements and the multiple directions of its flows of energy. Yet the distinction between rhizome and network isn't a matter of the quantity of extensions but of the degree of control. *Network of Stoppages* is not quite definable in these terms. It would still seem to be more rhizome than network, its segmented lines still simply shooting away into the further territory of the painting. A more entrenched network structure is still to come in *The Large Glass*, where rhizomatic "segmentarity" may be dramatically visualized in that spreading tracery of cracks. Still, the notion of the rhizome as energetic lines flowing outward is contained within the deliberate circuit of its mechanical/organic elements, its subject of sexual concupiscence animated and controlled among the linkage of its parts.

Nonetheless, it's important to note that a network structure isn't necessarily tantamount to connection, and Duchamp's distributed figures in *The Large Glass* offer rules of governance that entail both working and derailed linkages, wryly schematized as opportunities for erotic (mis)connections. To increase the sense of ludic temptation, he conceives the Milky Way above his Virgin as a floating target with three portals—traps, nets, or draft pistons, as the artist variously called them. Their function is to capture the consummation, never gained, of the bachelors below. Those nine holes drilled in the glass are the missed "shots" of the bachelors, their seminal enterprise a roulette—only one of them grazing the Milky Way, as if this cosmic fabric were the bride's blowsy veil caught in an unfelt breeze. And why is it unfelt? Because time and action are bracketed in *The Large Glass* by the principle of the not-yet, of the sexual tease as model that bears down on every behavior with a final *"almost, but,"* a banner of delay in the land of the contingent. Wagner's use of delay in the form of endless melody intended to create a continuum, a projection of and aspiration for temporal totalism, but here the bride's love gas leaks like a trickling flow interrupted by parodic generality, the bride that's at once humankind and machine other, lacuna and link, suggesting an impossibly possible phylogenetic revision.

Below the interval of the split frame that acts as metaphorical prophylactic and signifier of deferral, our nine bachelors stand erect. They are "malic moulds"—malic, Duchamp's conflation of male and phallic. He designates their work specifically in his diagram: priest, delivery boy, guard, cavalry soldier, policeman, undertaker, liveried servant, busboy, and stationmaster. Their labors encompass transport and carriage of different kinds, security of different kinds, services rendered up to and including death. Yet their task in *The Large Glass* is the transmission of sheer unrequitedness, and their success at failure speaks to the particularly male need in what network theory calls the distribution of sovereignty, "the idea that control and organization are disseminated outward into a relatively large number of small, local decisions."[42] Their discharge of individual agency under various mantles of order—legal, spiritual, menial, military, ritualistic, and most importantly biological—is submitted to a system of desire whose code they share.

The malic moulds are actors within a mechanical travesty, their sputtering linkages serving as Duchamp's simile for the pathos of communal (dis)unity, the urge toward meaningful sociality and continuance rendered as a tireless, recursive consumption of energy accomplishing only disconnection with the bride. And, of course, the pathos lies in the underlying premise of bottomless subjectivity, of a fundamental perspectival shift à la Cézanne that's so Duchampian in his questioning of any system and that makes her unattractive to us, with her insect-like, machined body, while to the malic moulds she's all allure, of common kind under the protocol of a new machinic being. Her love gas penetrates them, and in this they present yet another of Duchamp's many inversions, another tilt toward the fertile potential of unreason: *they* are the ones impregnated by desire, not she. They hover in the glass as portents of the artist's own transgender fascination made manifest in his alternate identity, Rrose Sélavy, as we'll see soon enough.

They shoot their desire through a series of capillary tubes and sieves through which a "splash," in Duchamp's word, occurs and makes its way past a "Fate Machine," with its contraption of a water mill that drives an apparatus on runners with scissors atop a chocolate grinder. Other fantastic obstacles are contrived: a butterfly pump, a boxing match, a juggler juggling gravity. These heterogeneous components of his temporally chained network are precisely mapped, forming a topology of control, a sequence of events repeated, a clarity of rules as a platform to stage a plot. Yet within the frame of this topology, a mechanism of internal doubt is placed, a mechanism equally precise in its signification of imprecision. The events of these desiring-machines are observed by what Duchamp calls his "Oculist Witnesses," their line of sight forever fixed not on the bachelors or the bride, but instead on the malic moulds' poorly aimed shots—as if to say the Oculists' role as figures of empirical analysis is to witness how badly vision and calculation fare in this universe of contingency. They offer self-negation as an oneiric logic in a network of endless delays.

Along this sputtering path, Duchamp intensifies his notion of the regularly nonregular that underwrites an alternative category for the medium of *The Large Glass*. Rather than a picture, he notes to himself that the work could be called a "delay in glass," and clarifies that "delay in glass does not mean picture on glass—It's merely a way of succeeding in no longer thinking that the thing in question is a picture—to make a delay of it in the most general way possible, [. . .] a delay in glass as you would say a poem in prose or a spittoon in silver."[43] He imposes a hybridized, formal ambivalence, which he called an "indecisive reunion" of possible meanings or, as Joselit has aptly written, a "state of perpetual postponement," all the more appropriate in light of the aborted tryst between the suitors and their not-bride.[44] Postponement, like deferral and delay, is a crucial term here, and it's useful to call up the word as it appears as well in Deleuze's brief, prophetic essay "Postscript on the Societies of Control," where he writes of computer networks and their "limitless postponements" within a new order of social production, one that holds the implication of frustrated expression that's therefore also alive with restless energies waiting to find new embodiments, liberatory or recursively and infinitely spent.[45]

The Large Glass could be said to visualize its own machinery of bureaucracy, and these jolts to the system, these postponements and delays, are, in the Duchampian mode, means of undressing the body of control, seducing control, revealing a formlessness rising up from under the skin of form; an ecstasy, perhaps, of unburdening, frustration, freedom, and an existential taunt on the road from the symbolic to the real. Deleuze's delays are constituted within the organization of communities of things, human and nonhuman, and he speaks of these organizations in a way that mirrors the networked system of *The Large Glass* and its operational behavior.

Deleuze writes: "Enclosures are *molds*, distinct castings, but controls are a modulation, like a self-deforming cast that will continuously change from one moment to the other, or like a sieve whose mesh will transmute from point to point."[46] This is exactly the operative mode of *The Large Glass*, just as it can be theorized about discipline-objects within the network of interdisciplinary works that they constitute non-totalizable containers continually modulated, pregnant with mutability, latencies, vectors of nodal intensity revised by viewer-agents, the whole in a condition, as Deleuze puts it, of "perpetual metastability."

This is the status of desiring objects embodied by the malic moulds as insignia of male labor always in service to rules, codes of behavior, enforcers of law, yet ruefully under the swooning influence of the unreason of desire and its will to undo every administration of control. So we see in *The Large Glass*, and in networks generally, as Kai Eriksson writes, that "a whole set of heterogeneous forces [is] immanently involved in creating, re-interpreting, and cancelling out things in a continuous movement, and some forces are stronger than others."[47] Force is also a matter of delay and deferral as the artist strategically arranges and assembles, maps narratives and flows that viewer-agents follow, stop on, move along the routes of, with sensations and faltering meanings unfurling in, from, and around the work.

Within *The Large Glass*, suitors and bride have their own halting motions and narratives—latencies within its network of modulating mechanisms that offer a fructifying process within its circuit that (unlike Hegel's notion of truth and unity in the ineluctable unfolding of bud, blossom, and fruit) doesn't complete. Each node in the network is on the way to satisfying its function, which is also to say it's on the way to the next moment of engorged delay, of climactic congestion. Each delay can be said to be a distortion of the pure signal—data packets that go unreceived because of noise, of the too much that's never enough, and, by analogy in Duchamp's work, only accomplishes the ultimate postponement of fruition, the final deferral of connection, ejaculatory but unreceived.

If each mechanism is as necessary in the circuit as every other, their mutual necessity is, in the Duchampian weltanschauung, the accomplishment of unaccomplishment, of nodal dysfunction. This ceaseless play in *The Large Glass* with gendered power relations, as Amelia Jones remarks, "reveals the tenuousness of all subject-to-subject relationships, the interdependence of self and other, of masculine and feminine," and she quotes Duchamp stating that binary sexuality "can no longer be called left and right of an axis."[48] His administrative satire is one in which relations of germinating interdependency find themselves continually halted by cancellations of stability.

Duchamp follows Cézanne's final exhaustion of attempts to sex the cherry of his Cézannescape and be its fruit. Yet while Cézanne suffered a kind of latency that found him perpetually in a condition of unrequited anticipation, Duchamp built it into a machine of representation that sought a different wholeness and a frustration of wholeness always in a condition of opposition: interrupted, antinomic, sexually ambivalent; a burlesque of the real, and always open to the inscription of contrarian protocols of control that offered his ironic doubts of his own inventions' competencies. *The Large Glass* is a machine populated with mechanisms that cut through nature, that retract the power of painting and just as mordantly the authority of the self, a representation of the self and of art as systems rerouted and reversed.

If there is a link in lineage to Cézanne, there is one as well to Wagner and the Gesamtkunstwerk. While Wagner attempted the "convergence of function and representation," it is Duchamp's *Large Glass* that conjoins the programming of the work to its anti-authoritarian figuration and does so in a way unlike Badiou's description of Wagner's redistribution of discontinuity within continuity. No, Duchamp never seeks a totalist's wholeness, but prefers to disassemble that ambition, analytically distant in his mechanical remaking of human yearning given at once to inefficiency, indolence, haplessness, energy, command, and schematization.[49] He mates transparency with inscrutability, regulation with misdirection, transgressing the binary in his reformations of nominative identity.

Precisely these qualities of continual discontinuity signal Duchamp's predilection to leave finality aloft, and he found his catalytic source in

Raymond Roussel, the author of the prodigiously dreamlike, immensely visual novel *Impressions of Africa*, published in 1910 and then
rewritten for the stage. Duchamp saw the play in Paris in 1912 with
Picabia's wife, Gabrielle, and Apollinaire, just before he left for his trip
that year to Munich. He claimed the play gave him his general approach
to *The Bride Stripped Bare by Her Bachelors, Even.* "It was fundamentally Roussel who was responsible for my glass. [. . .] I saw at once I
could use Roussel as an influence. I felt that as a painter it was much
better to be influenced by a writer than by another painter. And Roussel
showed me the way."[50]

In fact, the carnal machines of bride and bachelors are animated
not only by the wild inventions in *Impressions of Africa* but also by
Roussel's subsequent novel of 1914, *Locus Solus*. There the impeccably
manicured landscape is populated with extraordinary revisions of convention: music made from chemistry and metallurgy, logical chain reactions brought on by illogical or magical means, people raised from
death, and inanimate objects willed to life. Implicit in these works is
what Maurice Blanchot noted as Roussel's sense of lack, citing Flaubert,
who spoke of "too many things" and "not enough forms."[51]

Duchamp's debt to Roussel springs from that appetite for shifting
definitions and functions, that need for more forms made manifest in
the novelist's prolific wordplay, in which homophonic words drawn together in single narratives require the invention of dreamland contor-
tions of physical law and daily logic. Roussel explained:

I chose two similar words. For example, billard and pillard
(looter). Then I added to it words similar but taken in two different directions, and I obtained two almost identical sentences
thus. The two sentences found, it was a question of writing a tale
which can start with the first and finish by the second. Amplifying the process then, I sought new words reporting itself to the
word billiards, always to take them in a different direction than
that which was presented first of all, and that provided me each
time a creation moreover. The process evolved/moved and I was
led to take an unspecified sentence, of which I drew from the
images by dislocating it, a little as if it had been a question of

extracting some from the drawings of a rebus. For example, *Les lettres du blanc sur les bandes du vieux billard/*The white letters on the cushions of the old billiard table . . . must somehow reach the phrase, . . . les lettres du blanc sur les bandes du vieux pillard/letters [written by] a white man about the hordes of the old plunderer.[52]

His linguistic universe of puns and palindromes goes to the mechanical heart of Duchamp's bride and bachelors, beginning with the conspicuously dangling "même" in *The* Large Glass's French title, *La Mariée mise à nu par ses célibataires, même. Même,* a word the artist cited as "an adverb in the most beautiful demonstration of adverbness" and that "makes no sense, since it relates to nothing in the picture or title."[53] *Même,* which means "even" in English and is an aural twin of *m'aime,* translated as "loves me." It elicits an alternate reading of the title: "The bride, stripped bare by her bachelors, loves me" (perhaps satisfying Duchamp's unrequited affections for Gabrielle).

But then, as Molly Nesbit and Naomi Sawelson-Gorse have noted, Duchamp and his prewar French friends' fascination with Jean-Pierre Brisset—whose philological writings proposed that language was "always already sexual"—also shadows this labile play with words, with both him and Roussel offering an engorgement of procedural thinking about language and writing so crucial to Duchamp's own note-taking, semantics, and construction of the components of *The Large Glass,* both realized and only conceptualized.[54] Brisset proposed that "sexual suffering first induced man to speak": a plaintive and fanciful idea that casts a certain dour aura around *The Large Glass.* As Duchamp said to James Johnson Sweeney, "Brisset and Roussel were the two men in those years whom I admired most for their delirium of imagination."[55] *The Large Glass*'s figures are founded on this tumultuous ground that is literally engendered by a semiotic agitation of puns, with his disorienting erotic evocations, his douse of mirth.

There is in this a kind of rough play. Just so, one derivation of the verb "to pun" is from the English "to pound," that is, to beat violently on a word until its mistreated arrangement of letters and meanings takes on the skin of another. Duchamp's puns, however humorous and sly, abuse language in the play of reforming its meanings, just as he mistreats the authority of gender to *pun*cture it, *pun*ish it, turn it lightly against itself, perhaps wryly, but nonetheless inviting a rougher sexual rendering of meaning that has the scent of the misogynistic. There is always this double: a touch almost of cruelty in Duchamp's renovations of things, at once suggesting their sovereignty while simultaneously acknowledging the social assignment of their identities and his manhandling of these identities in the name of his own desire, even (and often) for his own amusement. So it is that the malic moulds are hardly the only ones who go without satisfaction. The bride, as already suggested, maybe, even, loves *him*—an indifferent passion and a pun hidden in plain sight, hidden in the doubling of both affect and meaning. And, of course, the bride and her bachelors always return to their even score of 0 to 0, the degree zero of erotic satisfaction in Duchamp's imaginary. This, too, is a form of distributed sovereignty in which sovereignty is always itself approaching a temperature of zero degrees.

These instances of local actions laid out in *The Large Glass* are, as I've proposed, contrived within a larger consideration of control. In the broadest sense, Duchamp has pictured a universe of randomness that's also claustrophobic, always coming to the same end—decision-making turned in on itself, inverted so that will and contingency entangle and combust, just as the pun is the braiding of samenesses that explode into difference. This doubling of choices is in the thing as itself and as other, a multiplication seen again and again with these two bodies, Cézanne's and Duchamp's. Duchamp said:

> The word art, etymologically speaking, means making; quite simply "making." "Making with," if you wish, and so perhaps "making with the hands." So, art is everything that is made with the hands, and generally by an individual. What is making? Making something is choosing a tube of blue, a tube of red, and putting some of it on the palette, and always choosing the quality of the blue, the quality of the red, and always choosing the place to put it on the canvas, it is always choosing. So, in order to choose, one can use tubes of paints, one can use brushes, but one can also use a ready-made thing, something that has been made

either mechanically or by the hands of someone else and that you appropriate since it is you who choose it. Choice is the main thing, even in normal painting.[56]

Yet at the root of Duchamp's practice there is no single choice, nor a linear progression, but a protocological form that contains the contingency of inherently dynamic relations within his looped desiring system that has as its telos not success in any conventional sense, but success as the continuousness of its circuit of attempt and failure—always the delay, the indecisive reunion. Quentin Meillassoux notes this sort of formation when he writes, "Thus chance always presupposes some form of physical invariance—far from permitting us to think the contingency of physical laws, chance itself is nothing other than a certain type of physical law—one that is 'indeterministic.'"[57]

Indeterministic regulation is intrinsic to the constitution of a network's multiplicity of elements. It's what Galloway and Thacker call "contingency handling," which is "how a network is able to manage sudden, unplanned, or localized changes within itself."[58] Duchamp implicitly understood the comedic physics of this idea of a kind of system of management and its underlying philosophical gambit. He called it "canned chance," though his idea, in Rousselian fashion, accommodates an entirely invented physics—a mirrored idea of regulated deregulation, of controlled uncontrol and its opposite, that he worked out years before *The Large Glass* in the concentrated formulation of his *3 Standard Stoppages* (1913–14) that I've previously mentioned.

The work consists of a long wood box in which Duchamp stored three pieces of string, each glued to a painted canvas strip, each mounted on a glass panel, and three wood slats shaped along one edge to match the curves of the strings as they had originally fallen when he dropped them. The title is yet another paradoxical word game, a double identity. In French, *stoppage* means the seamless mending of a garment with thread—another thing hidden in plain sight, an invisible gathering together, a desire to make whole. Yet in English, a stoppage can refer to a halt in work, a strike, an eruptive break in labor. So it is that Duchamp's stoppage, captured in the resting form of three threads, is a form of repair and a strike of its own kind.

He let each of his strings—each of them exactly one meter in length—fall from the height of one meter onto a canvas. He marked the random lines they made and used these happenstance results as a "standard" for measurement. It was a choice woven to chance—an initial determination of the length of his "instruments" that seemed in its precision to embrace the methods of empirical science, though the operation's point was to doubt fact. At once ironic and earnest, Duchamp's double gesture activates the surfaces of empiricism and randomness, abstracting them, treating them as ideas, as re-presentations toward the ends of indeterministic regulation in the form of a Duchampian observation. He said to Pierre Cabanne:

> The idea of "chance," which many people were thinking about at the time, struck me, too. The intention consisted above all in forgetting the hand, since, fundamentally, even your hand is chance. Pure chance interested me as a way of going against logical reality: to put something on a canvas, one bit of paper, to associate the idea of a perpendicular thread a meter long falling from the height of one meter onto a horizontal plane, making its own deformation. This amused me. It's always the idea of "amusement" which causes me to do things, and repeated three times. [. . .] For me the number three is important, but simply from the numerical, not the esoteric, point of view: one is unity, two is double, and three is the rest. When you've come to the word three, you have three million—it's the same thing as three. I had decided that the things would be done three times to get what I wanted. My "Three Standard Stoppages" is produced by three separate experiments, and the form of each one is slightly different. I keep the line, and I have a deformed meter. It's a "canned meter," so to speak, canned chance; it's amusing to can chance.[59]

Chance is inverted, reversed, permeating the administrative membrane of what contains it, much as a network incorporates the potential of contingencies that could affect its code and just as we see in the hazardous clockworks of *The Large Glass*. Here the word "incorporates" holds the specific sense of taking into the body, into the operative platform whether of painting or not-painting, as is the case in

Cézanne's and Duchamp's contiguous enterprises, in which bodily and machinic forms are, as I've said, fluid, porous, open to the heterogeneous elements with which they combine. Deciding, which is never simple or whole for Duchamp, is the choice he imposes on chance. He chooses to drop three strings because for him three is the indecipherable number of everything as yet another expression of delay. He doesn't choose four or forty, he chooses his own fully defined and predetermined nomination of the infinitely variable quantity, the number 3. Then he makes his outcomes an irregularity *as* regulation, to deform regulation, the reason of unreason continually reflecting itself till the mind and eye no longer know if any statement of being can hold its ground.

In 1963, Duchamp summarized his oscillation: "If I do propose to strain a little bit the laws of physics and chemistry and so forth, it is because I would like you to think them unstable to a degree. Even gravity is a form of coincidence or politeness since it is only by condescension that a weight is heavier when it descends than when it rises."[60] He won't let go of his decades-old idea of the halting mechanism of contingency and its effects, still somehow mannered in its way within the breadth of the circuit of chance and order; a stoppage that, with seeming civility, offers the perpetual possibility of reconfiguration, the world as it is not and the not that is. In this, Duchamp is the consummate artist of re-placement, of placing again, first protesting the authority of a thing, the authority of any standard, in order to claim (with amusement) a self-determined counter-standard as a sign of the unrequitedness of deterministic reason. All redounds to difference reverberating within a semblance of wholeness, to canned chance as that infinite regression of assurance, which must, of course, include all materiality, of which the body itself, gendered and sexual, is a reconfigurable thread.

The double choice is an invitation not merely to negate, which is far too univocal for the Duchampian universe, but (in the manner of Roussel) to renegotiate the fixity of law. If the vertical, as Duchamp suggests in his reading of gravity, invites him to condescend, which means in the original Latin to "descend together," then the choice he proposes, as Cézanne did before him, triggers a horizontal slippage, an equalization, a network logic of nonlinear interaction that is as ludic as it is logical, pertaining to all things, including the self. Everything, even gravity, even physics, even the self, is a fund of potentiality because universal law as the presumption of nature's irrevocable truth—that Rilkean "*is*"—is replaced by the infinitely molten power of things made in the mind, of ideas themselves, of Meillassoux's principle of unreason.

What Duchamp intuits in advance of network society is a form of "free-floating control," to use Deleuze's phrase.[61] The deformation and reformation of the thread running through the conventions of the world are the triumph of a pluriversal openness in which, to return to *The Large Glass*, brides are wasp bodies filling courtly love canisters, while an invisible fourth dimension projects what we come to see as pictures that are not pictures. In Duchamp's endlessly chameleonlike playfulness of things and what constitutes them, network aesthetics finds a prototype: the inscription of nodal connections in his *Glass*'s eros of connectivity engenders unstable, dynamic relations that are nonetheless contained within a shared schema of addressable flows.

At the crux of Duchamp's ontological wobble is the nature of the phenomenological and cognitive interactivity of art-making, art reception, and the always imprecise experience of protean thingness. In this art, to be is to fidget with the furnishings of being, with standards, with material and immaterial properties, which are finally matters of impatience, even the notion of sight itself. When Duchamp talks to Cabanne about *The Large Glass*, there's a moment in which he's asked if the perspective in the piece was based on calculations, and he responds that he was mixing story with visual representation, while most crucially he was "giving less importance to visuality." And then he says: "Everything was becoming conceptual, that is, it depended on things other than the retina."[62] This simple statement is axiomatic; it's the bolt of lightning whose charge transfigures art practice in the latter half of the twentieth century and on into the twenty-first. Of course, the bridge from the retinal to the conceptual was hardly alien to Cézanne before him, from the painter's consciousness embedded in the landscape that thinks itself in him, of which he is its consciousness.

For both of them, the subject is displaced by the doubled subject-object, which is neither one nor the other but a fluctuating third term. Duchamp claimed his disdain for the merely retinal in the physical act of making *The Large Glass* when he said: "It was not an original work, it was copying an idea, execution, technical execution, like a pianist executes a piece of music that he has not composed. The same thing with that glass; it was a mere execution of an idea."[63] His use of glass is an acknowledgment of its retinal utility that, in celebrating transparency, reifies the idea of visuality itself and simultaneously puns on the Renaissance notion of the window/picture. We look through his not-picture to find a replication of the world. Yet this, too, has particular consequences due to Duchamp's impatience that sees in every thing a like unwillingness to sit still in its constituted being. Embedded in his remark about "things other than the retina" is the stubborn ghost of essences that are somehow always hovering, of the noumenal and an expressive causality that spills out in the flesh of the world.

So it is that Duchamp may seem to disdain the retinal, but that's hardly the case. The glass of *The Large Glass* is the sign of the retinal, of the retinal stripped bare. Like the bride, the retinal remains an inviolate presence; like the bachelors, the glass is a courtier. It seeks to seduce the pictorial if only to upend and transform its sanctity. There is, as always, the difficulty, the slipperiness of Duchamp's own limitations of habit. The rigid masculinity of the *Glass*, in its male/female binary, is not overwritten by a transformation of flesh to machinic construction. There is still the *stripping bare* in its plain inference of misogyny, despite the unsuccessful attempts of the suitors to consummate and attain their bride. If the sexual vectors of power are in play, they remain in the circuit of assumptive patriarchal aggression that is, at the same time, given over to cosmic-comic deconstruction. And so, there is a winnowing away, a seed of conceptual dematerialization implicit in his anti-retinal idea of execution, as Duchamp premised, yet one nonetheless enacted through visualization. Duchamp's ideas keep catching on habits, customs, on the materiality they want to evade. His production of meanings stutters, eludes, is in flux between convention and disregard, dressed in the real, dragging the burden of the routine with him as he makes his ironic way through pictorial, conceptual, and linguistic means—his delight in slippages, as well as stoppages, that are of multiple consequences in the development of interdisciplinary art.

Duchamp spoke of choice, yet in place of the single choice is the turning glance of the double choice. It offers a postulate of reversibility stating that there is no perfectibility, but only convertibility that's also always a willed perversity, amused by the transgression implicit in transformation. Plasticity is all. We've already seen the way language satisfies Duchamp's postulate: doubled choices embedded in the puns and palindromes he emits. Naming, as an operation of reversibility, transmits to its objects a permission to rescind their conventional assignments, their burden under the yoke of indexical authority, such as the license implied in *même/m'aime* for Duchamp to gratify himself, to complete a new linkage.

Those interlocking homophones are the potential source of another pun in Duchamp's purposefully reflexive and incomplete title for what was the last painting he made, with its sense of archival suspension. The work is an inventory, as he said, of all his preceding works—a completion by way of the title's incompleteness. This is his 1918 *Tu m'*, whose pronoun and incomplete verb offer various inflections of its author's engagement. Perhaps it can be completed to form the description or command *tu m'aimes*, you love me. Or perhaps the pun returns as *tu, même*, "you, even." Or perhaps, still more self-reflexive, *tu m'ennuies*: you bore me, pointing to his alleged resignation as a painter, his exit from the field— for *Tu m'* has within it a translingual aural pun as its pronunciation in English also unearths the word "tomb." No doubt, this is still more speculation, but a speculation in keeping with Duchampian amusement, to imagine the title as yet another inverted double, referring to the previous year's foundational readymade, *Fountain*, signed R. Mutt, with the letters of the painting's title (t, u, m) as Mutt's partial mirror.

Just so, the hand with its index finger extended from the center of *Tu m'* directs viewers' eyes away from the frame, out of the world of painting production—the work's title, whatever its referentiality might yield, presenting another provocation of delay. The painting's physical bottle brush pokes from the canvas, with its painted shadow below, leaving the viewer caught again in Duchamp's gaming of the retinal, splicing material fact and representation. The double take takes doubleness, as always, as its motive of instability, the postulate of reversibility in the air. Think of *L.H.O.O.Q.* (1919), Duchamp's mustached, masculinized Mona Lisa done the year after *Tu m'*, whose initials claim that s/he has a "hot ass," teasing the double agency of its gleeful inversion. We may be invited to enter the snare of the visual, to picture in our minds that unseen ass, but the figure runs back and forth over the bridge of the most mobile system of signs: language.

Duchamp's obsessive linguistic activity, haunted by antinomy and aporia, its Rousselian play, and its sleights of hand and logical stalemates, implies, as we've already seen, a paradoxical comfort taken in destabilization that establishes a unified model of non-unified identity. The word "palindrome" advertises its usefulness here, with its Greek origin that means "to run back, to recur." Consider Duchamp's "Precision Optics" pieces from the 1920s that populate his short film *Anemic Cinema* from 1926. The movie features motorized, rotating discs in two variations. The optical ones show hypnotic swirling lines that present a retinal display of reversibility in their duality of flatness and illusionistic depth. The language discs are filled with tongue-twisting, aurally reflective double entendres, as exemplified by one disc's compulsive, internally rhymed (and puerile) question, once again à la Roussel, *"Avez vous déja mis la moëlle de l'epée dans le poêle de l'aimée?"* (Have you ever put the marrow of the sword in the oven of your beloved?)[64]

Of course, the word "anemic" is palindromic, too, nearly mirroring "cinema," so that "Anemic Cinema," like the film's revolving discs, advertises its doubled signification that simultaneously swallows its tale and the tail of its medium. While still steadfastly and pruriently male, at stake is any solid claim on materiality and the indexical fix, as Duchamp's deracinated language and meanings radiate their latency, and with them a release into the vaporous condition of the spectral: a dematerialized materiality that hovers beneath, above, and in front of what was assumed to be stable. The goading of his postulate of reversibility draws us downward, spiraling like his discs into his own double state and double choice of liberation from the rigidity of form that brings both pleasure and unease.

Freud's thoughts about the uncanny are beneficial here, published in the same year that Duchamp regenders his Mona Lisa. Freud, too, takes up the theme of exposed oppositions and does so via a volte-face in language. He writes:

> In general we are reminded that the word *heimlich* is not unambiguous, but belongs to two sets of ideas, which, without being

contradictory, are yet very different: on the one hand it means what is familiar and agreeable, and on the other, what is concealed and kept out of sight. *Unheimlich* is customarily used, we are told, as the contrary only of the first signification of *heimlich*, and not of the second. [. . .] On the other hand, we notice that Schelling says something which throws quite a new light on the concept of the *unheimlich*, for which we were certainly not prepared. According to him, everything is *unheimlich* that ought to have remained secret and hidden but has come to light.[65]

The uncanny, the *heimlich*, or homely, becomes *unheimlich* when what is meant to be private becomes public, when a hidden state of burden is brought up to the surface of visuality, an idea that instantly connects with a crucial statement Duchamp makes about the readymade: "You see, I was already disgusted with my hands. I just wanted things to get to the surface on the canvas by themselves, from my subconscious if possible."[66]

This is the second time that disgust has been mentioned. First, Rilke commented that Baudelaire was willing to bring everything into the light, even the disgusting as equal to all else. In this, he made way for Cézanne. Now Duchamp makes his own claim for the equality of status among things by radically claiming that the hands of the painter proffer materiality to bring meanings to the surface, though instead they hide what only the non-retinal can produce as a means for revealing, even for revelation. The matter of what matters must be recalculated, recalibrated such that what is not matter is as important as what is. Or, perhaps yet more complexly, that the physical and the conceptual must both be equalized in a network of visualization. He is impatient to accomplish this horizontalizing of representational status, this new form of visual and immaterial immediacy. To touch, to use one's hands, in this masculinist sense is to soil, to pollute, just as the bachelors' failure to touch the bride enlarges her power.

The narrative of *The Large Glass* poignantly states that the act of transmission is to be repelled; the physical act is a complicated machine that ultimately goes awry. This weakness of the flesh signals Duchamp's predilections: manual work in the transport of representation is deemed awkward. It's not swift enough, and all the more so as the malic moulds' identities link their professions of labor to service of one kind or another, and with it a sense of obligation, of encumberment, just as they're chained in a temporal loop to their Sisyphean network that codes an instruction set of fleshly failure. Quicker means are required—lighter, less a product of the material labor of the body and more of one conceptually achieved. And yet, there's still a balance. Even disgust, as Rilke claims, is a way forward, a dilation of possibilities. To revoke the success of these awkward bodies isn't to dismiss them. Here they are, endlessly asserting the presence of their bodies, their *attempts*, their *repetitions*, the course of corporeal weight. Meanwhile, the dematerialization of making neither affirms nor denies what the state of the retinal might be, just as we can decode the tactical deployment of the bottle brush and its shadow in Duchamp's last painting as a statement of decided indecision that leaves its circuit of retinal equivalence open. In effect, the postulate of reversibility applies and includes the retinal/physical as an apparatus of exchange: every image can be a thing in the world, just as every thing (including Duchamp, including us) is always already a way toward the emergence of a (not-) picture.

In Freud's telling of the uncanny, the infection of the animate by the inanimate is central to the exposure of an anxiety of doubling through what might be called, in the context of Duchamp, retinal fusion that leads in this case to mortal confusion. Freud recounts E.T.A. Hoffmann's story "The Sand-Man," in which Nathaniel falls in love with Olympia, whom he spies through the precision optics of a wicked optician, the telescope of Giuseppe Coppola, whose true name is eventually revealed to be Coppelia. Already, doubles and double entendres are accumulating: falling in love with an Olympian height impossible to (b)reach, as with *The Large Glass*'s bride, through the services of a telescope offered by a man whose doubled name is too close to copula, copulate, and copy to ignore. Through his retinal machine, the uncovering of Olympia as an automaton is realized—a readymade that quickly gets Nathaniel to the unsatisfying surface of infatuation in the anguish of lack; an object animated solely through visuality, through its primary status as a picture that provokes love's confusion of the self with an other. The possibility of the fusion of the animate and inanimate is brought to life through the imposition of a visual mistake, a doubling that creates the double of desire.

Still, there is the Freudian reckoning between anxiety and repair. The fluctuation between the homely and unhomely and the road back to his predatory, male, Victorian notion of health that presents an unwilling choice by the patient under duress, brought into sight as a kind of disgust to be eradicated. The *unheimlich* is "cured"—though in Nathaniel's case, the cure is fatal—when the sight that isn't meant to be seen is seen again and a new choice is made. (It is pure coincidence that Coppola/Coppelia is also phonemically contiguous with the Italian "cupola," or dome, while evoking the copula, just as the name of Olympia's co-inventor, Professor Spalanzani, approaches "spalancati," which means "wide open," both names spilling over into intimations of female sexuality.) The picture is thought again, a double take made by the eyes of the patient and the observer, who are both agents within a network of local decisions regarding self and other, ego and super-ego, I and it, nodes within this network of complex and short-circuited transmissions, the *heimlich* and *unheimlich* enfolded in a narrative aporia of retinal confusion, of machinic collapse.

The uncanny animation of the object couldn't be more useful as a mirror of the Duchampian doubling of painting and its delay, the not-picture that also describes his readymades, and, in this context of authority and regulation, affects the regulatory binds of art to be punned, beaten into a new shape, revealing what was not meant, at least previously, to be brought into the light. If there is no reason that anything that is can't be something else, isn't it also possible that this release from the heaviness of the hands into the conceptual, demoting any obligation to the manual, is a way of thinking that there can be two bodies or more, that gender and sexuality, too, are rich with the plasticity of reasoned unreason? No less is the case for reviewing the premise of painting as picture-as-world, so that its inversion to transform into world-as-picture may emerge, and then logically go one step further to be conceived as world-as-not-picture, easing conceptually in and out of materiality, the retinal and the non-retinal shuttling between the burden and unburden of a diurnal physics of being, a recrossing of boundaries.

It isn't that the objects Duchamp famously revivified as readymades—
the bottle rack, the urinal, the comb, the shovel, the typewriter—
aren't still what they are: quotidian things made and assigned their
normative use. It's not that painting isn't what it is: a convention
of representation, a discipline-object with its internal properties and
long-held means and modes of execution. But it is also that Duchamp,
trained as a painter and perpetually seeing the world through a painter's
eyes, is scratching the skin of the seen in order to transmit differently
those objects rendered artistically within what can simply be called the
painting network, with its historical codes and protocols, and about
which Duchamp wriggles impatiently and amused inside the body of
painting, of pictures, just as he wriggles inside other bodies—language,
the sexual body, the gendered body. "I just wanted to get things to the
surface."

The bottle rack could easily be called a body rack with its ribs, or
the body racked as the torment of the object as representation, as picture. In the Duchampian pluriverse, the readymade is provided with
the nomination of "art," but as with his thoughts about physics and
chemistry, and even gravity, the laws are "a bit unstable" and are open
to indeterministic regulation. "Art," then, is a machine to be put into
reverse at any moment of amused choice, of canned chance, of the uncanny not as ill sight and malfunction but as another order of seeing
and function. What is imposed on the bottle rack is the canned chance
of its emergence as an inverted double. It's now a sameness that isn't,
that shakes loose its surface from its body, even while it doesn't, while
it presents its factuality and its alter-factual doppelgänger, matter and
ghost, a weightless image that disrupts the index of use, disrupting for
a moment of delay our understanding of what it is, of how we expect it
to be, and how it should to be activated. There's now a space between
the hand and the mind, a smiling alienation. This interstice causes a
state of oscillation and wry ambivalence, the blur of the double-choice
that erupts from the object in silence and echoes onward, such that the
world itself is an endless inventory of reskinned things, of pictures and
not-pictures, of readymades.

In this way, and keeping in mind Freud's determination of the uncanny as a site of trauma and revelation, then the inference that the

blur of the double-choice proposes—the nearly seamless seam between home and unhome, between the self in comfort and the self out of joint—is that there are potentially two selves, a pounding of the self beaten into the shape of a possibly discomfiting, possibly comic form of a pun. But isn't this deformation what Freud claims? "The word *heimlich* identifies one [meaning] which is identical with its opposite." Freud's text is filled with tales of the optical rendering of doubling fusions, of automata, visions of anxiety and horror about the home as the site/sight of maternal comfort and the sight/site of sex, of the "dread of the evil eye," of dead bodies that lead to the opticality of haunting. Each of these is troubled by the animistic, the dislocatedness of what Freud calls the "omnipotence of thoughts," a conceptualization that doesn't adhere to the comforting regulations of habit.[67]

The solving of the uncanny is, then, a triumph of normative conceptualization based on a second sighting, literally seeing twice to reconcile the problem of heterogeneities that appear as homogeneities. Freud's conceptualizing of these behaviors based on visual errors of similar dissimilars strategizes a mental hygiene through light, a recognition that cures when retinal clarity heals the confusion of doubling. Difference is neutralized not through a talking cure per se, but through a retinal one, when what is hidden in plain sight is clarified and the investment of pathos in Hoffmann's Olympia—that's to say in the machinic, the automaton, the it—is revealed to be at once the same and not the same: an object, not a subject, for copulation resolved in its irresolution as a delay in consummation, so resonant with Duchamp's bride and the doubled appearance and use-value of the readymade.

The troubling condition of the uncanny, with its features of doubling and reversal, may be antithetical to Freud's notion of cure, but for Duchamp those features offer the liberatory overcoding he needs. The readymade as a not-picture brought to the surface, as object and image in one, blurs its nominative identity and merges solid thing with semiotic slippage. It radiates the quizzical intermaterialization he inherits from Cézanne at the same time that it exemplifies his operative principle that to re-form what "art" is is not to repair it but to sublate it, to hold everything aloft, juggled, run through loops, run backwards, accumulated and levitated and fused, as if the processual development of bud, flower, and fruit were itself compressed and understood as a readymade, just as *The Large Glass* can be seen as an antic condensation of processes of desire—a network of desiring things.

A network is always on the cusp of slippage, of flux among its assembled parts such that its identity operates within an internal logic, yet vulnerable to what is outside, contingent, looking in. *The Large Glass* is a gathering of other works. It incorporates titles and images such as *The Passage from Virgin to Bride* and *The Bride Stripped Bare by the Bachelors*, both from 1912; the pictures of the chocolate grinder from 1913 and '14; and the *Glider Containing a Water Mill in Neighboring Metals* from 1913–15 (figs. 2.11 a–d); while the measurement of the malic moulds is derived from the *3 Standard Stoppages*. This self-referential assemblage continues discursively outside itself to complicate its engagement with a double sense of sight, meaning to be read as well as viewed—first in the *Box of 1914* and then in the more extensive *Green Box* of 1934, writing out the possible meanings, suggestions, sources, and incompletions of thought for *The Large Glass*. As with networks, *The Large Glass* is an archival modulation of its strings of code, its active and vestigial links, those connecting, those leading to dead ends, and pointing toward the hallucinations of artificial intelligence, to the curious existential blank of what will become the internet's Error 404 and, in the case of interdisciplinary works most generally, to the contingency that not every connection of one discipline-object with another functions as intended, if at all.

We think of the archive as a terminal enclosure, but of course the Duchampian taste for reversibility proves otherwise. His boxes of 1914 and 1934 are only other forms of slippage, of the tendency toward the centrifugal, spatially and temporally ramifying, uneasy with completion, or simply ludically so. *The Green Box* doesn't stop with discursive textual snippets, but extends into the aural with an unrealized musical imagining of what Duchamp called "the bottle of Benedictine" that "both sang and functioned as a lead weight."[68] In fact, he includes as well his composition *Erratum Musical*, written in Rouen in 1913 and meant to be performed by himself and his two sisters, Yvonne and Magdelaine.

No doubt, the drama and fatal musings that circulate through *The Large Glass* have an operatic air. Its chorus of bachelors is in full voice.

Its network contains the inscription of time, of a temporal score, of aural possibility, fluctuating between past and present. Still, unlike Wagner's glacial pace, Duchamp's work seems to operate at full speed, its parts evoking rattling and constant motion—not so different from Marinetti's race car, with its own pistons and wheel, while a premonition of the future lies there, too: a note in the *Green Box* writes out the title of Duchamp's final work, *Étant donnés: 1° la chute d'eau, 2° le gaz d'éclairage.*

These objects, ideas, sounds, and slips of paper—whether realized in the space of the glass or inscribed elsewhere—enter into a relation of minute differences, of spatial, visual, and intellectual location or some form of suspension, as Duchamp's notion of delay suggests. They are together and apart, peer-to-peer relationships linked and latent, like the bride and the bachelors, like the world and/of (not-)pictures, always in a condition of hesitancy, of which double choice, similar dissimilars, their continual reversibility seeming to metastasize, effectively off-register. Duchamp had a word for this condition of infinitely small yet complex divisions, which he thought of as spatially asymptotic, the nearly touching, nearly consummated, yet not. He called this the "infrathin"—in the original French, the *infra-mince*—*mince* connoting hunger, a waiting need. The infrathin, in keeping with so much of Duchamp's weltanschauung, denotes the particular state of the never-enough, of the uncompleted, unsatiated, or in the re/visionary sense of self and other, the thing that is another thing and in whose difference lies a recognition just out of reach, an echo of the chasm of the uncanny.

How apt that Duchamp, when asked to define the infrathin, answered: "One can hardly give examples. It's something that escapes even scientific definition." Though he gives an example, and one that reveals his fascination with the slip of resemblance: "Infra-thin separation. 2 forms cast in the same mold (?) differ from each other by an infra thin separative amount. All 'identicals' as identical as they may be, (and the more identical they are) move toward this infra thin separative difference."[69] This strikes at the undoing of the restrictively gendered body. This is the territory of the readymade and its retinal-cognitive-temporal delay. Its optical route travels not only from the subconscious to the surface but also in reverse, from surface to retina to the mind.

The infrathin provides Duchamp with the bio-technical fantasy of a spatial delay that allows a formal difference, a mechanical/organic or multigendered imagining within the double choice. This is implicitly a kind of hunger to which the answer is accumulation: of physical alternatives, of puzzles, re-formations, of measurement and the meta-presentation of representation as opportunities for multiple means to engender a protean and erotic questioning that touches everything that *is* as progenitive, mobile, indeterministic, a tongue of semantic puns. As we see this formal revisionism in *The Large Glass*, we see it in the visual and conceptual realizations of the readymade. They speak to the need for *more*, for forms that aren't sufficient in themselves but are always enchanted by a copulation, a link to an otherness that has a carnal underbelly of the carnivalesque, the overcoming of rule, such that the retinal (as with bodies and identities, objects and functions) isn't denied but is proposed to be joined by the supra-retinal, the *and also* of extended, elasticized, and recoded boundaries and modalities.

So it is for Duchamp that sex holds the antinomic impulse that intermittently engages gender difference as an amused reckoning with heterogeneities that might negotiate homogeneity, of the canned chance of sexual sameness and difference brought within his curious frame of unity, and in which subject and object, seen with the same eye that visualizes the readymades, are fused. What is brought into the light is the onanistic possibility that to satisfy oneself may be as good as satisfying oneself with another, or, ruefully, is the only means of satisfaction. It's all a matter of contingency, of the shifting economy and mechanical situations of desire. To return for a moment to *The Large Glass*, we are the chocolate grinder grinding our own chocolate—a machinic other that subsumes the bodily action of both him and her as one. The glass is both transparent and a mirror, and the desiring body is a surface of identity at once seen through and reflective, easily drawn on and revised to create a blur, an infrathin delay between sameness and difference. So it is as well with *L.H.O.O.Q.*, which typifies Duchamp's use of writing and sexuality, subject and object, as two forms of doubling animated by reversal, revision, derision, and risibility.

In the same vein of this investment in the trans nature of I and other, I and it libidinally encompassed and categorically doubled, there is Duchamp's alter-self to be reckoned with, captured in Man Ray's 1921 photograph of Rrose Sélavy, whose punning name translates as "Eros, that's life." Is this another instance of the infrathin? It would seem, in a way, an infrathin of an infrathin, not precisely a delay, as the visual consummation of male and female is already accomplished, but *perhaps* a delay in the obvious recognition that the figure hesitates on the border of gendered difference. Of course, the title lures us into difference as well. Its wordplay goes beyond foreplay for Duchamp, as the impatience to get past the weight of the hands is to get past the weight of the body, the form of the body, and so to re-render the constructedness of gender, just as everything else is re-rendered, at once invaginated and exvaginated. The Duchampian self and body are clearly not static frames of identity but events in which, as Michel Callon says in another context, "a clear boundary between an actor and the network is dissolved, as 'the actor is both the network and a point therein.'"[70] The re-rendering of the body that is he and she seeks its own unity, an eventfulness of the dynamic networked body that invites the glitch while nonetheless reminding us constantly of order, mechanism, and repetition.

The Large Glass's glass is one catalyst of this kind of eventfulness: an optical presence whose transparency, reflectivity, and content provoke us to shuttle between stripping it of its materiality and acknowledging it as boundary and container. And while the figures on the glass are still vertically segregated along gender lines, Man Ray once again offers a Duchampian inversion. His 1920 photograph, *Dust Breeding*, shows *The Large Glass* covered with dust during a time of abandonment by Duchamp, laid down horizontally like a runway, as if the divide between bachelors and bride (though they aren't shown, only the chocolate grinder and glider are) were the shallowest hurdle for desire's intimacy and union that form this geographic writing of the body in transit, and yet one in which delay has taken hold.

Both the objects of *The Large Glass* and the readymades, however industrial they may appear to be, exist within the particular ambience of intimacy and suspension, hesitancy and the desire to locate and quiet that hesitancy, the domestic scene of the homely and uncanny unsettled. When we think of the readymades, each is opened by the space of the infrathin, each forming a contiguity between the body and something else, something machinic and projecting an other, each therefore sub-jected to re-objectification and doubled. So, Duchamp stated that his readymade comb, functionally linked to the body, could be imagined as a "generator of space," adding,

> the axis would be at the edge of the comb on the other side from the teeth, and the teeth would describe a series of circles which would be nothing at all in fact but a comb with different curves. It would no longer be a flat comb, but rather a curved comb. All these things never went further than the remark I made here in writing [in the *Green Box*]. But there is a possibility, as I said, of generating space from a flat surface. You can do it with any surface.[71]

The surface he wants to get to as quickly as possible is one of lubri-cated misregistration, the infrathin that facilitates visualized alteration and alterity, including the gendered body that isn't flat but curved, in Duchamp's imagining, and is same and opposite, functions inverted, another type of readymade, another type of object/subject/not-picture that is nonetheless an emanation of the visual, of the nomination of "art" as such revised. We are in proximity to the Deleuzian evocation of the schizo body, of William Burroughs's imagining quoted ear-lier with respect to Cézanne's need, "No organ is constant as regards either function or position."[72] The body as a network of interoperable, changing nodes—the body as a concatenation of modularly declined tenses of form: past, present, future, but always conditional—is the body of uncanny animation, Marcel/Rrose's two bodies in one, and to which we should add to he/she, the object that contains the image, an it that is the spatial generator of image and idea, an it that is, therefore, a concentration of human and nonhuman, subject and object, not so unlike Hoffmann's Olympia who was at first a visual doubling over of the idea of the human, a superimposition of elements contained in an energetically invested object form. These doubled subjects/objects are "hot" and indifferent, amused and urgently at work, bracketed by the canned chance that is decisive, contingent, decidable, and not. Marcel/Rrose's transvestism announces the plasticity of a charged erotic signal analogous to the plasticity of the painting/readymade, a coupling that decouples regulation, "a genital field of discontinuous grammatical delights," as Molly Nesbit and Naomi Sawelson-Gorse have written.[73]

In the complexity of this delight, with its irony of law and counter-law, its similar dissimilars and just plain disjunctions, its lurking subjectivity among objectified beings, there would seem to be no real sense of social obligation in Duchamp's work, no moral imperative underwriting Duchampian doubling. Hegel speaks of the *Aufhebung*, the concept of sublation that holds the twofold character "to preserve, to maintain" and "to cause to cease, to put an end to."[74] Cézanne's desire to transform painting and himself in an idealized intermateriality of the self and nature is a specimen of *Aufhebung* that's answered in turn by Duchamp, who proposes the infinite playfulness of a fatalism in which there is no self indexed to irrevocable rules; there is no thing that isn't already free for new entanglements and recoding, that is and is not, simultaneously ceasing and maintained.

Just so, we see this liberatory impulse in the image capture of Rrose Sélavy, in *L.H.O.O.Q.*, and can say as well that the emancipatory gesture of the readymade proposes its doubling as the transvestism of painting, of the picture as not-picture, just as gender fluidity for Duchamp traffics between conceptual insurgence, physical fantasy of misrule and desire, and retinal fact impregnated with a content given over to hesitation and doubletake. Even his urinal—an apparatus designed specifically for phallic use—becomes an inverted conjugation, another slippage in the coding of gender, and so of coding (and life) itself as both regulatory and seeping willfully into deregulation, re-regulation, double and doubt. Gender inversion and re-regulation are at work when he remarks with a strange and vivid insistence that "one only has: for *female* the urinal and one *lives* by it."[75] But it should also be said that his conception of the female is hardly a leap from Wagner's objectifications of women.

In *The Large Glass*, despite her evasions or because of them, the bride is a mechanized thing hung perpetually in place in a routinized ritual of defense and a defense of ritual, while Rrose is a lampoon of the feminine as much as the masculine, nonetheless a transcription of male will that has an earnestness in keeping with Duchamp's desire in all things for two-at-once or three. Still—as there's always a "still," a delay and reversal—the artist's *never enough*, like love gasoline, prefers that there be a constant hiss of intoxicating influence between subjectivity and objectification that allows Rousselian flights of revision. These lines of flight imply that we are all spatial projectors like the *Comb*, all (marble) sugar cubes whose temperatures need to be taken to measure the state of health of the real in *Why Not Sneeze, Rose Sélavy?* (1921), all apparatuses that mark the doubleness of sameness and difference because every individual thing, every instance of doubt in essence and doubt in completion, lies on the cusp of intermaterialization or slips over its edge.

Duchamp returns to the trans-self hidden in plain sight in his final work that, as previously mentioned, appeared by name in the notes for *The Large Glass*: *Étant donnés: 1° la chute d'eau, 2° le gaz d'éclairage* (*Given: 1. The Waterfall, 2. The Illuminating Gas*) (1946–66). The work is a deconstruction of painting that replays the Renaissance invention of recessional perspective, thinking again of the "window" of the picture, yet not enlarged by the transparency and all-in-the-round of *The Large Glass*, but now in reverse, as a form of immobilizing constraint. Duchamp hid the making of the work over the last decades of his life, claiming to have given up art entirely for the strategic pleasures of chess, while in fact plotting and making with immense deliberateness his last artistic move.

In its final resting place at the Philadelphia Museum of Art, *Étant donnés* resides in an adjoining gallery to *The Large Glass*. The viewer approaches a heavy wood door through which there is no access, only two small peepholes that limit the body and eyes to a fixed confrontation with a scene whose three-dimensional and two-dimensional components create a shallow depth like a diorama's, both sculptural and pictorial, a painting that is not a painting, an installation of the infra-thin, a nodal constellation of networked object-images posing narrative questions while summarizing the dynamic, vectored forces of instability and reversibility at the heart of the Duchampian body and art.

In the foreground, through the rough framing of a broken brick wall, the artist lays out a female nude seen from the neck down, only a trace of blond hair visible. Her legs are splayed, her sex shaved and misshapen, perhaps suggesting mutilation, and in any case fully exposed.

She lies on a bed of leaves and twigs, her left hand holding aloft a small, lit gas lantern. The body, a parchment-covered armature, is highly realistic and meticulously made, throwing into reverse Duchamp's insistence on an art free of the hands. To her right, where the viewer's eyes are led behind the lantern, is a sylvan landscape, photographed and hand-painted, in which a waterfall nestles, based on the Forestay Waterfall in Chexbres, Switzerland, hard by Lake Geneva, where Duchamp spent five days in August 1946 at the nearby Hotel Bellevue. The tiny waterfall, rigged with a little motor driving a rotating disc, seems to pour.

Of course, whatever repudiation of prior Duchampian principles *Étant donnés* may seem, his antinomic reflex and super-cooled ambivalence are fully present. The components of the work fulfill Eriksson's description of networks as actualized multiplicities whose interstices among parts are a latency in semiotic space, a delay in the relation of elements that offers a suspense of meaning. The naked figure is literally one of delay, permanently so, known to be based on Duchamp's lover Maria Martins, a liaison begun the year of his trip to Switzerland and ended in 1951, when Martins refused to leave her husband and returned with him to Brazil—the source of another consummation left ultimately unconsummated. In the larger context of Duchamp's career, the network of his carefully self-referential production that continued to re-form itself while linking objects, images, and ideas, found a final transformative eventfulness in the recapitulation of reversal and doubling, sublative to the end.

Marcel doubled as Rrose is also the bride wedded only to him/herself. Still deeply entrenched in the masculine, he is now reversed, from clothed to unclothed, stripped bare, head out of view, body gaping, supine, almost as if dead, with the visual suggestion of decapitation, yet also reversed from death to life. That hand held high is a Rousselian gesture, as the novelist once wrote of the Lazarus-inspired potion, Resurrectine, and so this Marcel as Rrose is a bride who shifts between ruin and hope, the lantern bright. And here, too, is a possibility of reversal: a lantern's function is to make visible what darkness hides, and the intimation of *Étant donnés* is that while this upheld light could be fueled by love gasoline, it also illuminates what isn't meant to be seen:

the most violent of consummations; the bride in a condition not of love but of brutal transgression by the bachelors.

Duchamp reinstates painterly representation with his bucolic scenery as a backdrop to the figure that is itself a mordant visual pun, for it's impossible not to see floating before his splayed nude one of the nineteenth century's most infamous paintings, Gustave Courbet's *Origin of the World* (1866), a work that underscores the restrictiveness of the male gaze in its evocation of life-giving fertility. Courbet's picture constrains the eye by its brusque cropping that removes its figure's head and shows only a pulled-up gown, breasts, soft belly, pubic hair and pudenda, fleshy thighs. Through the same apparent optics in his final work, Duchamp proposes a sublation, an infinitely repeated and ghostly loop of life and death and life again, of coterminous origin and destruction, preservation and cessation that is so wholly male at the same time that it encompasses the unstable status of his own identity, the twice-gendered body, the twinned bodies of painting and the readymade, the representation of self and of representation itself, also transmogrifying Cézanne's lifelong project.

With its recessional layering of visual data, its toylike novelties, its constricted view and potentially brutal scene, *Étant donnés* characteristically offers a doubling: the rough play of ludic semblance between "ravishment" and "ravishing" in the figure of Marcel/Rrose who is here conflated with the arousal of painting, the mobilization of the painting network, the life and death and life again of painting, even preceding Cézanne's desire for the mobility and reconfiguration of his own body with the landscape, for his own picture-making and nature generatively reformatted as a new networked form. The punishing playfulness of Duchamp's final act in which he undoes the body of his work as he undoes the body of the one who makes now displays a forensic reconstruction in which the perspectival realism of miniature, right-sized objects painstakingly reproduced is represented narratively as a stake in pain, so to speak, which, with typical sardonic humor, is also an echo of *L.H.O.O.Q.*'s unseen but signified ass, now (almost) made visible, while suggesting in the broadest sense that "art" in all of its potentiality, in all of its precision and seductiveness and blur, over which so much labor and ardor are expended, is also a nuisance, even to the point of pain—unstable, deserving of its devastation, and is as well a testimony to the devastation of love, though love nonetheless persists, is illuminated.

Of course, *Étant donnés* isn't offering an ultimacy, any terminal decidability in itself. That would be counter to Duchamp's career-long gambit, his gnomic affection for aporia. As Amelia Jones has observed, "The viewer takes the position of 'mastery' offered by this machine of perspective but at enormous cost: The very subjectivity that she or he hoped to confirm through this action is undermined by the 'gaze' of the figure's cunt. As Jean-François Lyotard has written vis-à-vis this dynamic of viewing in *Étant donnés*, 'Con celui qui voit' (He who sees is a cunt)."[76] That's to say, as we look into the work, it looks back at us as if it's a reversed camera obscura in which we are the figures in the room. We are Marcel/Rrose ourselves, the doubled self now tripled. And if this is so, we are now zombie-like formations of personhood that are also overcoded as objects, which suggests as well that we are at once enlivened and entombed in the act of looking at art, and that art, then, in this Duchampian construction, is itself a tomb in which we are laid down, a light to see with in hand.

Here is *Étant donnés*'s palindrome, a sublation and terminus, both final and not allowing finality, its waterfall running on a hidden rotating disc, a cycle endlessly repeating, its synthetic flow of a piece with the synthetic image of passion that is also an image, potentially, of death. The work marks time, is its looping counter-sign, and marks time again. Its claustrophobic geography is all control, a closed network of command gathering all into one, and yet whose meanings remain, as always, only on the edge of clarity, a multiplicity. Duchamp's he/she/it/us is half-buried in the earth, half-buried in the body of otherness per se, of otherness beyond human otherness, of picture and not-picture in the circulation of the painting network, and, in the trembling of being, is a *tu m'* and tomb of self-reflective and interdependent parts, of unconsummated ending and continual transmogrification, after Cézanne, an untotalizable totality held aloft.

The Senses

TOUCH

• • • But every thing that can be touched has first found other form among the senses. Didn't we hear things first or see them, smell them? We felt in the dark. Taste comes at the service of touch. Nipple. The turning head, the mouth latching on. Inside, outside. Or later, Lacan's infant at the mirror, pressed up against the glass, touch as the author of knowing lack and, on the other side, the self of my untouched completion.

I'm in my bed in the dark. A *you* is here, your smell in the bedsheets, outline of your side, your warmth—lures, sovereignty of the fingers, hand. A moment. The word "purchase" has the double meaning of acquisition through the abstraction of money and a second meaning: to have a physical hold. My purchase on the surface of you, the textures, roughness, the slip of fine hairs, pliant denseness underneath, wetness, an astonishment of inside, touch the intensifier of location.

What Merleau-Ponty wrote is true: when I lean on the hard surface of a desk, my existence is in the palms of my hands, and more precisely in the feel of my flesh against the bones of my knuckles, finger bones, the bunchy tendons in the pads of my palms. The rest of me disappears like the tail of a comet. It's difficult to turn this into sociality, into a sense *for* others. I'm wholly engulfed by the lack of the otherness of the tactile. What I touch is in the province of the I. (Touch is elementally self-determination.) The exception is the laying on of hands to heal, a word whose origin is a derivative of "whole," so that touch is a gathering of parts backward through time and brought forward, a reversal of lost. Touch as a felt meaningfulness of similar and different in the language of electrical impulses, links flowing outward: motion, acquisition, safety. Pressing my hands to the desk is to know what isn't me and ties my material to other materials, so that touch calls forward in the speech of the commensurate.

If this first premise of touch is a mechanism to preserve the I, then: the texture of textures, the layered complexities, temperatures, pliancy, hardness. The immense vocabularies of coarse, smooth, soft, crumbly, loose and solid, slick and dry, fluttery, empty, tingling, moist are the acquired inventory leading us from ourselves-in-ourselves to expression—social regime of touch, political regime, the gainliness of the aesthetic. And all the functions, from punishment to art, rise in the air of human competencies and learned practices with touch. Touch, the prime teacher and instrument of making and the made until, and almost instantly, sight, too, becomes a maker, an agent of production. (Even digitization, the production of the immaterial, is a word invoking *digit*, finger, the realm of touch.) After the I-ness that deploys touch to affirm its wholeness, touch reaches through every body to spread the form and formlessness of self, catalyst of the aggregation and dispersal of materials, labor, divisions, destructions, societies of surfaces toward the ends of rituals and commerce, of dominance or ruin. The wheel, the Catherine Wheel, the hammer, the awl and nail and bullet and instruments in the catalogue of scrape, mark, penetrate, seal, and finish are projections of the knowing of touch.

Is there anywhere where touch isn't the sovereign of the senses? If it isn't always first in every moment of experience, it is always the urge in us to seal, to be the action of closure. As I turn my gaze in a gallery from one artwork to another, where I'm forbidden by custom to place my hand because of the power of touch to change materials, I *want* to touch the painting, the sculpture, even the surface of the paper (though I'm afraid to smudge the pencil line), even to make the sensual-spatial leap and know each thing I see in the video by remembering what it feels like against my hand, the air on me, the sun.

All law, all judgment begins with touch, ends with it.

Four

THING-THINGNESS AND HOW SPACE MEANS

• • • As it turned out, Rilke's "*is*" was an opening onto the artistic possibilities of equivalence and autonomy, of the Adornoesque conflict and Duchampian comedy of identity and alterity. This wasn't the sole province of *is*, but of *it* as well. The co-relation of things has been at the heart of this thinking about interdisciplinary art's urge toward wholeness in its production and our experience of it, in its systematization in different hands—its different thinking toward relation, transmission, and distribution coterminous with networks and network aesthetics. Essence and outward projection, the in-itself and the for-us, communality, the *society* of these particular things called discipline-objects are inextricably bound together in their becoming, their being, and the dynamism of their links to one another. Having argued for the structural and operational construct of network aesthetics as a means to understand the interactions between discipline-objects in interdisciplinary works, it seems a parenthesis is necessary, an excursus to examine thingness itself and space and how space means for these works. Every interdisciplinary example looked at in this narrative points toward the future of installation and performance art, demanding our phenomenological understanding of objects in concatenation.

As we've seen many times already, these assembled objects constitute a living together. This is the lot given to them by their creator, the
interdisciplinary artist, installation artist, performance artist, the artist
collective. This is also the lot given by their environments, by design
and chance. But the production of meaning doesn't terminate there.
We, the viewer-agents, the rogue nodes, generate, refract, and combine significances projected onto the surfaces of discipline-objects in
a continual process of nomadic interpretation. Their sociality assumes
three defining characteristics at least: first, they are things; second, as
things, discipline-objects have spatial presence; and third, as things,
they exist in a continuum of temporal states, a declamation of times:
was, is, will be.

We come to this point in the history of the interdisciplinary and
network aesthetics having looked with extended scrutiny at Cézanne's
and Duchamp's nascent interdisciplinary practices, as well as Wagner's
founding concept of the Gesamtkunstwerk. Each inspection attends
to these artists' particular things and environments, their tendency
toward wholenesses of different kinds, wholenesses including differ-
ence(s), and charged relations to notions of totality. What becomes
clear is that an essentializing vision of a totalizing total—of stability,
homogeneous identity, and hegemony—is eroded by multiplicity and
hybridity, by ego, doubt, and will.

In light of the imposing artistic and political demands made by
Wagner, Adorno argued that the very sanctity of identity is a wound
that can only be repaired through the declaration of its opposite and
the fundamental instability and dangers of sameness. In the case of
Cézanne, his struggles to overcome the formal boundaries of Being,
filtered through his anxious consciousness, upended any notion of a
unified self. While for Duchamp, through the complex aporias he
created, the deconstruction of fact and the slipperiness of desire and
personhood revoked assertions of totality in the same breath that he
constructed systems of intricate and pliable relations.

Of course, all of these immense and extraordinary efforts to encompass what it is and how it is to be in the world redound, as I've said, to
questions of control, to ways that the fragmentation of social existence

can be transferred to and be overcome in the act of artistic making—
parts and wholes. And so, issues of the spatio-temporal call: space as
representation and space as event, space as a plurality of significances,
as established and leaking boundary, as the condition of interrelations
that engender place. These spatialities take in the qualities of fixity and
simultaneity, the smoothing of time and its stubborn unevenness, and
uneven space. They encompass a topological space of haptic encounter,
a space in which discipline-objects form communities that we *enter*,
which is a verb of spatial action. We walk among them, sense them,
cognize. As Maurice Merleau-Ponty's metaphorical encounter says,
we rest our hands on them figuratively, our minds are engaged, we're
pulled into this constellation of nodal things, and the rest of our bodies
recede momentarily.

Two phrases set us on this course. The first is from the philosophical
geographer Doreen Massey, who writes simply, "for there to be difference, for there to be time [. . .] at least a few things must be given at
once."[1] And then the second, dependent on the first, a phrase that Steve
Hinchliffe, another geographer, writes in an essay honoring Massey—a
cogent expression to describe an interdisciplinary artwork: "a social yet
thing-filled world."[2] Of primary concern for us in this phenomenological unpacking of interdisciplinary art is the vitality of things in their
population of being together and an understanding that any quality of
immanent life within discipline-objects gives an extra vivacity to them
as we perceive their material, haptic qualities as objects that produce
meanings.

Whatever the inner necessity of the discipline-object, it is ultimately
toward the realization of micrototalities that draw us in, draw us
forward—the materializations, interfaces, and instruction sets that define
the painting, sculpture, video, and so on. These properties and actions
inscribe their individuated protocols within and alongside the overde-
termining protocol of the interdisciplinary whole. While our reception
is typically the trajectory of the work, it's worth turning for a moment
to ideas explored in recent years concerning the metaphysical character of objects, their internal lives that possibly have an ulterior vivacity not visible to us. Consider, for example, Ortega y Gasset's thinking
about this independent existence, cited by Graham Harman, that "just

as there is an I-John Doe, there is also an I-red, an I-water, and an I-star. . . . Everything, from a point of view within itself, is an 'I.'"[3]

Relevant to this, Quentin Meillassoux critiques, with reference to Hegel, what he calls correlationism: "We cannot represent the 'in itself' without it becoming 'for us,' or as Hegel amusingly put it, we cannot 'creep up on' the object 'from behind' so as to find out what it is in itself— which means that we cannot know anything that would be beyond our relation to the world."[4] By correlationism, Meillassoux argues that this proposal of what seems an inextricable relation between objectivity and subjectivity isn't inextricable at all. He speaks of the mathematizable details of things and the difference between this operation of understanding and representing things and qualities understood through the subjectivity of our perceptions of objects. Of course, in the realm of art, discipline-objects and their gathered properties are, as I've said, typically with and toward subjective reception.

Meillassoux writes: "Would there not be more modesty, then, in considering that the Universe has nothing to do with our subjective qualities, that it could very well do without them at any degree whatsoever, and to say, more soberly, that there is no absolute scale that makes our properties superior (because more intense) to those of nonhuman living creatures or inorganic beings?"[5] This modesty, this distribution of existential priority, suggests the executant force of being contained within objects themselves.

Yet in contrast to Meillassoux's argument, what I've noted are discipline-objects' materials, techniques of production, histories, styles, and temporalities as intrinsic (though not necessarily accompanied by internal sentience), while the point of the objects' essential being is their outward projection, their presence for us singly and in the ensemble of an interdisciplinary artwork. Meillassoux's correlationism, despite his critical refusal of it, is useful precisely in coming to this opposite understanding, to an appreciation of correlationism in the specific case of art objects in their reception by subjective beings. This correlationism is always already inclusive of contingency, whose origin in the Latin *contingere* means "to be with touch," to be touched by, one thing moving another, causing the contiguity among things to ripple, affecting one another as lines and edges whose intensities connect, ramify, and change.

This co-relational thingness of discipline-objects in an interdisciplinary work, as I've said, is finally brought before the viewer-agent, the
rogue node among all the nodes of the work's network such that they
indubitably enter into correlation among parts and whole physically
and in human thought through human and nonhuman contingencies
and interactions—a trembling alive to the perturbations of the world
sensed and cognized in individual and group experience. Tristan
Garcia argues in his broad philosophical work *Form and Object: A
Treatise on Things,* "To try to be in-itself is to attempt to remain outside
the world. And indeed, to try to be in-itself is only a path of entry into
the world."[6] To this, Slavoj Žižek adds that the outward projection and
consequent reception of objects constitute "consciousness external to
the thing-in-itself."

In this sense, the thingness of things comes to us as a projection of
layers, a semantic construction that we read from the objects in front
of us and that we move among, a "here" that Massey argues "is where
spatial narratives meet up or form configurations, conjunctures of
trajectories which have their own temporalities (so 'now' is as prob-
lematical as 'here')." She thinks of these layers as accumulations,
weavings, and encounters over time, as accretions that offer histories,
and that this deep intertwining of physical things, of site and sediments
of receptions, narratives, interpretations, and revisions of meaning
must include "there and then" as "implicated in the here and now."[7]

What needs to be underscored in this is the specific application of
thingness as a correlationist reciprocity between the interdisciplinary artwork and its viewers, as it's this correlationism that operates
within a network scheme and takes its part in network aesthetics.
In this pragmatic description, the internal properties of discipline-
objects are understood in correlation with those who receive them: the
phenomenological gathering in our consciousness of those properties
and objects as they emerge as situated layerings of feelings, thoughts,
influences, and histories that, in terms of a network conception of
interdisciplinary works, present a spatial co-figuring of nodal protocols
and network protocols. True, there's still something enticingly mystical,
something metaphysically animated, that insinuates itself among
these layers—the I-red of a red thing speaking in some unseen way to

the I-water. Merleau-Ponty got at this spatial quality of layered thing-ness in what was quoted partially before: "The thin pellicle of the *quale*, the surface of the visible, is doubled up over its whole extension with an invisible reserve."[8]

Yet in that sense of the internal layering of the thing's assembly of materials, techniques, and methods toward subjective reception, and the external layer of the network's communicative necessity for us, there is again that unevenness of flows to be recognized: the always open character of the spatial and temporal that places the metaphysi-cal dimension of the discipline-object's thingness alongside the expe-riential, and alongside this network aesthetics of dynamic, relational meaning production and distribution conveyed by the linkage of the interdisciplinary work's componential things.

Heidegger's definition of "thing" is in keeping with this notion of the discipline-objects internal assembly of properties, as he thinks of a thing as a gathering of qualities. He notes the origin of "thing," signifying in Old Norse and a handful of other Northern European languages a governing assembly, a meeting, while Proto-Germanic's *thinga* designated an appointment in time, possibly tied to the proto-Indo-European *ten*, which means "stretch," perhaps as in a stretch of time for an assembly. And so, in relation to Meillassoux's querying of correlationism, the argument can be made that if a thing is a gathering of qualities, then the assembly of these qualities, say, in our art things, our discipline-objects, is precisely for the act of gathering meanings in place and time as they pool in and around these individual and concat-enated objects in the network of the interdisciplinary work.

In turn, "meaning" finds its own origin in the Old English *gemǣne*, cognate with the Dutch *gemeen* and the German *gemein*, translated as "common." But then farther back in this etymology lies the Latin word *medius*, "middle," pertaining to the middle of the body, of arteries, veins, nerves, and which relates to the Proto-Indo-European *medhjo*, "between," so that meaning is what sits in the body and is something shared between bodies. It's a center that has in common its center with the center of the bodies of others, a form of our commonality grounded in the fiber of our blood, our nerves, our senses. A thing's gathering of qualities is assembled so that its meaning is absorbed by our bodies and shared, *medhjo*, between bodies. And yet this "between" also suggests a carrying, so that what is at the center moves to the *periphéreia*, the Greek for circumference, and *periphérein*, to carry around, to bear. Meaning is borne from one thing to another, an assembly of multiplicities—all bodies and all meanings not being the same but having a co-presence. This *medhjo* of meanings, this between, is a linking of links, a legibility of what lies in the center and moves the center of knowing between us, among us, centrifugally, asymmetrically, gathering and moving. This is the schema of networks.

With this sense of meaning's potential between-ness and carriage among bodies, we return to the shine of the nonhuman. If we were to entertain the idea that things have some form of self-awareness, of I-ness in relation to other I-nesses and their network of meanings, then we have to ask how is it, for example, that the sui generis character of a urinal turned upside down somehow confers a sense of autonomous being? Or we build a table, and that table commands our attention as if it were itself sensing, extending a communicative *cogito*. Did this energy exist already, this self-executing self-meaning, which would suggest that before the table was assembled, each of its components— mahogany, nails, glue, metal brackets, felt pads, mother of pearl inlays— already had autonomous life within, down to the scale of neutrons, of quarks? Or inexplicably in their gathering, in the invisible alchemy of Being, the being of Being emerges as an I-ness in otherness.

At this point, we could return to a consideration of Meillassoux's proposal of mathematizable detail, antithetical though it is to the case of the fundamental subjectivity inherent in the artistic production of discipline-objects and their correlationist reception by viewers. Still, the question must be raised that if this dark energy, this ether, is everywhere already, then should we really be discussing the nonhuman in this way as an *I*-red, an *I*-water? Why give priority to an anthropocentric weight in the analytical examination of all things? Jorie Graham's lines from her early poem, "The Way Things Work," come to mind, in which she states, "This is the simplest form / of current: Blue / moving through blue; / blue through purple; / the objects of desire / opening upon themselves/ without us."[9]

Desire ascribed to the nonhuman is itself an anthropocentrism that returns us to an antagonism between ground and condition, the thing in itself and our reckoning of it. We are talking, then, about a thing-consciousness understood again and always in relation to self-consciousness, which Hegel, in *Phenomenology of Spirit*, called "Desire in general," and in which he defined self-consciousness as "a return from otherness." By this he means a reflection of one's own I in the mirror of another's to overcome what he deemed, in a wonderful phrase, "motionless tautology."[10] In this reciprocity, the otherness of the other is the otherness of the self; an owning of the self in which object and subject are joined inextricably, in which desire is a structural condition of existence, and other and self are individually and reciprocally executants of an I predicated on the other to know one's self. And so, we return to the society of objects, to the network of relations among discipline-objects in relation to our cognizance as viewer-agents, which is emphatically a correlationism alive within the nodal arrangement of interdisciplinary artworks and crucial to network aesthetics.

As we walk among the related artworks within an interdisciplinary installation, every discipline-object has its own life, its own properties, its own shape and projection of its particular expressiveness, but it has as well the relationship of its present being to the otherness of the other things in its network that form a second and simultaneous presence. Then there is a third presence that accounts for each of us, such that we can never grasp ourselves as subjects in the contemplation of the work without also being related to each discipline-object and to all of them within the community of the interdisciplinary work and the shine of its meaningfulness.

Experiencing the work in this condition of mutuality offers up its phenomenological vitality, its combinatorial blossoming that seems to invoke the active will of its components in their orchestration. We may agree or disagree with Jorie Graham, when she writes of objects opening upon themselves without us, or when Wallace Stevens speaks of an eschatological condition of things "without human meaning, without human feeling" in his poem "Of Mere Being." We may or may not agree that the world of things is inhabited by fields of nonhuman consciousness, of uttering I-reds and I-waters unheard by us. They may or may not look at us, in whatever attendant sense perception might be, as we look at them.

Nonetheless, in our specific experiential reckoning with the thing-ness of interdisciplinary artworks, it's our own reception and interpre-tation of the work's components and whole that we cognize. Each of us projects onto the seen in order to produce a feltness and meaningfulness that rises from the sphere of the work's sociality and, therefore, that also implicitly contains an ethics. For the gathering of qualities is finally, as I've argued, *toward* gathering—gathering as the *ten* and *thinga*, gath-ering toward the socius of meaning-making and the centrifugal *periphérein*, which is what the network in its distributive nature offers as a structural accommodation to otherness and the answer to Adorno's trauma of homogeneous identity. Inscribed in network aesthetics is this ethics of things in their individual resonance and in the chorus of their conjunction—which is to say, an ethics bound up in spatial relations.

There is at least one more consideration of this aspiration and strug-gle toward being together and the thingness of things as they enter the spatial realm of the interdisciplinary artwork's sociality. We can think of this as the reciprocity between the centripetal action implicit in the work's internal structure of gathered nodes and their individual prop-erties devised by the artist and the artist's desire to reach outward, to harness a means of centrifugal distribution, to affect an audience of viewers, each of whom, too, is part of an operative network of connec-tive interactions.

The quality of *address and invitation* is always already present in the interdisciplinary work, both among its discipline-objects and with its viewer-agents. The outreach of the work, the extensibility of its network, is a form of hospitality. Hospitality, with its obligations and generosity, its protocols and legitimacy, its gathering toward reception, of making audible what is unspoken toward the communication of things making meanings together, calls to the work's viewers just as it contractualizes them. Jacques Derrida writes in his first text on hospitality, delivered as a paper in Istanbul in 1997:

> What we call hospitality maintains an essential relation with the opening of what is called to come [*à venir*]. When we say that "We do not yet know what hospitality is," we also imply that we do not yet know who or what will come, nor what is called

hospitality and what is called in hospitality, knowing that hospitality, in the first place, is called [ça s'appelle], even if this call does not take shape in human language. Calling the other, calling the one the other, inviting, inviting oneself, ingratiating oneself, having or letting oneself come, coming well, welcoming [se faire ou se laisser venir, bien venir], greeting, greeting one another as a sign of welcome—these are so many experiences which come from the future, which come from seeing [something] come or from allowing [something] to come without seeing it come, no less than the "not [pas]," and hence the "not yet," the past "not yet" of the step [pas] that crosses the threshold. What is called hospitality, which we do not yet know, is what is called.[11]

What we do know of hospitality is that it engenders the dynamics of exchange in which the rights of host and guest—who may well be strangers to one another and beings, therefore, of Adornoesque non-identity—are rendered through gestures of offering and receiving in a customary ritual, a protocol of reciprocity. The legalistic aspect of hospitality follows cultural variations, but they're always the same in the conventional obligation of the host to the one who is hosted and of the guest who entreats, but in doing so is also demanding. Demanding what? Time. Food. Attention. Care. Shelter. Listening. Understanding. Patience. The purest form of hospitality doesn't require the quid pro quo of repayment in kind. Nonetheless, the inference is that a bond has been made in giving and receiving, a link of understanding between nodes of sociality that performs a mirroring of selves, from one to the other, from the other to the one. Derrida notes at the very start of his talk that

> it is a human right, this right to hospitality—and for us it already broaches an important question, that of the anthropological dimension of hospitality or the right to hospitality: what can be said of, indeed can one speak of, hospitality toward the non-human, the divine, for example, or the animal or vegetable; does one owe hospitality, and is that the right word when it is a question of welcoming—or being made welcome by—the other or the stranger [l'étranger] as god, animal or plant.[12]

The space of hospitality in a world of heterogeneous things encompasses this coming toward, of arriving at the threshold, of stepping into the place and gestures of exchange where things foreground their differences; of receiving, entreating, and offering the status of their non-identicality toward an implicit community, a code to be shared, an acknowledgment of the contract of self-consciousness in its obligatory reciprocity and circulation. It is the step (*pas*) into this space, in which host and guest are always projecting onto one another their self- meanings and their otherness as other. And here, at the same time, as Derrida says, the host is also the hostage, the guest's requirements presented as both request and demand, an act of subjugation.

It's like this, too, in our scheme of interdisciplinary art and network aesthetics. The artwork is host and each visitor is guest, the rogue node who enters the social world of things, demanding that discipline-objects individually and in their communal gathering offer their meanings in exchange for attention as a form of care. Each step into the space of the work is one in which the visitor is offered the network of links and in turn augments its meanings, shifts them, disputes them, distributes them, presenting the meaning of others. This act of entrance and exchange, of supplication and offering brings with it—surely, in the best of works—a condition of immersion, of a quickening. The objects themselves seem to intensify.

As I've proposed before, their material shells seem to shimmy between physicality and the immaterial—an extrusion of internal being, a flame-ness, if you will, a vitality inside. Loosened from their casings of wood, paint, film, time-based narrative, polymer, whatever their carapace, they seem to disclose a purer giving. It's a matter of moments, the tiniest leap. The thing figuratively emulsifies: it becomes the liquid of itself, an openness of form, a generosity and demand implicit in the production and reception of meaning. Of course, we are talking about many objects, multiplicities, unfoldings. In this process of hospitality, the space of the work is enlarged. It's as if in this act of attention and care, of query, hesitation, and engagement, we swallow these meaninged things as pieces of the world.

In turn, a space of relations opens inside us, just as space itself, as Massey says, can be thought of "as an emergent product of relations."[13]

Every discipline-object in its nodal relationships acquires relationships of position, of intersection, and so, every position is already a relation. These things in their thingness speak to one another as relational entities in their outwardness, radiating meaning production, whether hospitable or in contest, landscape and consciousness, bride and bachelors, a *Gebrauchsmusik* of collective use. "Space does not exist prior to identities/entities and their relations," Massey notes, adding, "More generally I would argue that identities/entities, the relations 'between' them, and the spatiality which is part of them, are all co-constitutive."[14]

In this reciprocity of offering, accepting, and demanding, these identities/entities disclose their relations always as a communal enterprise, a for-us. We swallow some of the world's scale and bear meanings from the middle of one body to another. But if there is always already a *between*, always relations as such, there must first be the *medius* of the self, the originating relational point, the point from which space begins.

Henri Lefebvre writes in *The Production of Space* that space is "first of all *my* body, and then it is my body counterpart or 'other,' its mirror-image or shadow: it is the shifting intersection between that which touches, penetrates, threatens or benefits my body on the one hand, and all other bodies on the other."[15] My own body is the invariable element among all variable elements that come into the presence of my body or that my body comes into the presence of. My body is reactive to the thingness of things around it, including all the inhabitations of spaces we consider: sensorial space, temporal space, political space, economic space, racial space, gendered space, psychological space, ontological space, epistemological space, spiritual space, participatory space, memory space, the technical non-space space of digital representation, the space of rhetorics, the space of the imagination. All the layerings of interiorization and empathic projection, of semantic flows in spatial encounters with objects and, in our case, with discipline-objects, are the product of sensual and then cognitive hospitalities, a gathering as the eventfulness of space carried by and through our bodies in the production of networked relations. Merleau-Ponty writes in *Phenomenology of Perception*:

> It is clearly in action that the spatiality of our body is brought into being. [. . .] By considering the body in movement, we can

see better how it inhabits space (and moreover, time) because movement is not limited to submitting passively to space and time, it actively assumes them, it takes them up in their basic significance which is obscured in the commonplaceness of established situations.[16]

He proposes the body's experience of space as "a sort of co-existence" with the objects inhabiting whatever space the body is in. He calls this "the spatiality of situation," which can be thought of as the emplacement of meaning markers around me so that my I recognizes itself in relation and reaction to all that's also reflected in a cognizance of otherness. In this way, the spatiality of situation is also the partiality of my body in space bound up in otherness. My I activates the power-geometries of its spatiality and enters into the sociality of being. In the most plainly operational sense, space is all that is filled in, a vessel for the gathering of thingness as it becomes manifest to us, cognized, which is to think of space as a process of semantic inscription, and among the things it is inscribed on is my body.

To think of the body as one form of the indexicality of meaning, we can say that it is bound up with its linguistic identity, even if we accept Henri Lefebvre's pronouncement of the body as an organic primacy, a quiddity.[17] The linguistic I stands in reference to an ontological emergence at the same time that it is a means of performing social inscription, a means of bringing that primacy with others into relations, "recognizing one's place *within* continuous and multiple processes of emergence," as Massey says.[18] Meaning is also influenced by the physicality of the body in relation to other bodies and other things—space, volume, weight, forces of resistance against the boundary of the body, as well as that interface of physicality and sociality that I've spoken of as hospitality.

In relation to interdisciplinary works, our bodies are involved in the haptic and cognitive choreography of feeling and meaning-making in which the human and the nonhuman are joined in a continuum of difference as we move among the particular discipline-objects of the work, apprehending them, finding both their hospitable and resistant moments. We test their space, their sensual and semantic connections, we assimilate their co- and counter-meanings, their points of coordination and asymmetries within the work's data stream. Though the work stays within the physical boundaries of its room, its stage, its installation, the artist hopes that the viewer has taken its significances in, that they inhabit our bodies such that, in our movement outward and away from the work, our subjectivities as viewer-agents continue the work's development, that it continues to influence us as if in chemical reaction, so that psychologically, intellectually, socially, politically, spiritually, perhaps even physically, it moves us as we move beyond it.

In this hoped-for carrying forward, the process of the interdisciplinary work's continued emergence is marked in an expanded sense of a network that ramifies beyond its internal codes, and in doing so only amplifies an ethics of difference and the flow of potentiality. This is the transformational possibility not only for the work itself, but for the way we understand our own transformations in and through it. If the primacy of the body begins within the location of the bodily self as a still point in the turning world, and then as a point within the work, we are also, like all objects within the work, nodes containing instability, oscillation, receivers of contingency that act on us, while space itself as co-constitutive with the body encompasses us in its shifting shapefulness, so rich with semantic density.

Is it enough to say that space is that which fills in? What are the interrogatives that space introduces into the production of meaning? So we return to the taxonomy of space in order to unfold the production of meaning and networked meanings in interdisciplinary works. We begin with the fundamental ontological space, a space we can't creep up on (in Hegel's phrase) since we insert meanings into it, and yet that may have its own internal quiddity—something that Heidegger proposes as an active immanence, a presencing, something that operates in a realm of energy, whether of physics or spirit. Then there is the manifestation, the physical space, the space sensed in and by bodies, physically affected as well as ratiocinated. And in this sensing, both felt and thought, we come to a third category of space in this triad, which is the resultant space of what I'll call existential eventfulness: the space of all interactions, holding both commensurateness and division—communal, aggressive, negotiated—and, therefore, is the space of the agora of our living with others, human and nonhuman, the space of sociality per se, and which is also, therefore, the space of creation and destruction.

The way that the body situates itself within this triad of spaces is something that Gaston Bachelard ruminates on in *The Poetics of Space*. At one point in his text, Bachelard quotes Rilke, who has already proven so invaluable in the genesis of interdisciplinary art in his thinking about the ontological sense of equivalence among things. Rilke writes of the bodily self:

> [But within you. . .] there is almost no space here; and you feel almost calm at the thought that it is impossible for anything very large to hold in this narrowness. But outside, everything is immeasurable. And when the level rises outside, it also rises in you, not in the vessels that are partially controlled by you, or in the phlegm of your most unimpressionable organs: but it grows in the capillary veins, drawn upward into the furthermost branches of your infinitely ramified existence. This is where it rises, where it overflows from you, higher than your respiration, and, as a final resort, you take refuge, as though on the tip of your breath. Ah! where, where next? Your heart banishes you from yourself, your heart pursues you, and you are already almost beside yourself, and you can't stand it any longer. Like a beetle that has been stepped on, you flow from yourself, and your lack of hardness or elasticity means nothing any more.[19]

The *between* of the body Rilke imagines is intuited; meaning carried in its middle of blood and veins, then borne outward. The "heart" in the poet's words is an evocation not singly of feeling, of the perceived thing as sensually felt, but as the translation point of communicable data, of the understanding that issues from intellection, of meanings gathered from networks of things working on us, working in us. In the scope of interdisciplinary art, from our correlationist vantage, discipline-objects, if not actually coursing with felt organs, take on for the viewer-agent the palpitating and connective sense of communicative relations thickening space, this becoming of the multiplicity of things assembled by the artist in the surround of our experience. And we, as the perceivers of these discipline-objects, may go about our taxonomic task and topographical routines, analyzing what's there in front of us, around us, but always, as Rilke suggests, lit by the tissue of inward feeling and external conditions, cognized and linked to the world. Nodes, transfers of data, latency perhaps, reception, exchange.

When we experience the interdisciplinary work, we ask what elements it marshals into coexistence so that a space is marked off, boundaried (though we may violate those boundaries), and how do these elements coexist? How does the artwork organize its haptic spaces, so that we as viewers insert ourselves into this grid, and then process, produce, and distribute meanings? How does the work take up space, annex it, distribute it, so that we react to its areas and volumes, its lightness or dark, its cold or warmth, its wetness or dryness, its smells and sounds? This inside and outside are made present in the body as ontological, epistemological, and phenomenological spaces in conversation with the physicality of things, but there is also the *illusion* of space, the representations of inside and outside that artists incorporate into images—time-based, still, made with the hand, made mechanically, appropriated, digitized.

Rilke's "infinitely ramified existence" implicitly includes allusions drawn from one spatial image toward the remembrance of others. Time inhabits the space of memory, and memory's space is a component of many of these spaces—economic, psychological, social, spiritual—certainly of each of our image repertoires. Our genetic code itself informs the way we are historically inscribed as creatures equipped with the memories of biological predecessors. Memories are produced as temporal artifacts of individual experience and group experience. And here what we seek is an encompassment of action, memory, and image in the experience of space. What we seek is the total spatial fact of an artwork, what the anthropologist Marcel Mauss called in terms of ethnography the total social fact and that I carry over into the spatial consideration of interdisciplinary art's heterogeneous things and their nodal arrangements. What is the total spatial fact of each interdisciplinary work? Or more precisely, invoking the network's dynamic asymmetries and its non-totalizing total, the *almost* total but never total spatial fact of the work.

To seek totality of any kind is to seek a picture, a schema, all elements captured, frozen or seen from above—not that verticality is necessarily truth, but for a moment, at least, encapsulable. The act of spatial reconstitution through memory and intellection is described in a useful way by Michel de Certeau in *The Practice of Everyday Life*, where he distinguishes between tour and map. An installation is the most applicable form of an interdisciplinary artwork in this schema. When viewers make their way around an installation, their bodies move forward, backward, from one side of the space to the other. They stop, move on to some other element of the work, reverse course, turn. They make their tour, and de Certeau defines a tour as a discursive itinerary through place, moving among things in a narrative action of mobility. He opposes this to the map, which he considers a totalizing of knowledge. It's the tour seen from above, a topography of the entire place, which is a static description of what has come into appearance as a fixed state of knowledge.[20] The map is a representation of space imagined as seen and finished.

All spaces might be imagined this way, since theoretically when our bodies leave a space, this resides in our minds as a finished encounter. In this moment, all types of physical space are representations. Administrative space and labor space. Carceral space and leisure space. Landscape, office, factory, hospital, school, museum, home. But this is an incomplete concept, an unrealistic finitude. Memory is never done with space. We're always re- and misremembering the spaces we've visited. Each thing in its thingness, as Merleau-Ponty says, is "treated as representative of its previous appearances in me, and of its simultaneous appearances in others."[21] So it is that each space within the domain of experience is given to recollection, change, antagonisms and agreements among constituents, and therefore a politicized space of beings within spatial proximity and habitual behaviors who must test and attempt resolutions of their relations. Simultaneously memorial and negotiable in nature, these spaces as political representations speak of individual identity, group identity, local identity, national, international, and transnational identities, and of Adorno's specter of the trauma of identity that demands the word and concept of non-identity as pertinent to mourning and deterrence. For Adorno, even the nonhuman enters into the politicized representation of space—implicit in his remark in *Negative Dialectics* that "things congeal as fragments of that which was subjugated."[22]

A coupling of representation and immobility lurks in Adorno's words, of things whose vitality is drained. But the intention of his remark is toward the mobility of recuperation, reinstating the ethical right of non-identity as an existential tour precisely against the static representation of being as a consequence of suppression and enslavement. We can think of this prospect of mobility in relation to the interdisciplinary work, to this sociality that must continually negotiate fixity and motion, boundary and leakage, objects physically set in place and set into semantic motion. Artists and viewer-agents are each set in their roles within the network: enforcers and revisionists of protocols, tyrants and tricksters, turning and turned by things in the "distinctiveness of their constructed relatedness," to borrow a phrase from Massey. The platform of the interdisciplinary work makes, in this sense, as Benjamin Bratton says of platforms generally, "multiple jurisdictional claims," which means in the actions of viewer-agents that the spatial and temporal are joined in agonistic travel, at once vessels and engines that contain, distort, assert, vary, dissolve, and reassert the relations of the objects within, always weighing, suppressing, unleashing, and leaking difference.

Network aesthetics shows itself to be in a state of restive hospitality, wrestling with and accommodating the disruptive, the chaotic, the spatio-temporal exchange of control and boundary inflection—the installation work and the performance work as clearings in which these inflections gather and glint. So Ernesto Laclau writes: "It is in our pure condition of event, which is shown at the edges of all representation and in the traces of temporality corrupting all space, where we find our most essential being, which is our contingency and the intrinsic dignity of our transitory nature."[23] Immobility as a form of oppressive temporal compression that chains us, that corrupts spatial freedom, is condemned as antithetical to the dignity of dynamic social relations and the implication of negotiation and improvisation. This, too, is the condition of discipline-objects marking differences and transacting contingencies within their networks. Space without time to alter it, to undo stability and by extension stasis, is a perilous picture-thinking of totalization, a will to subjugation. Ilya Prigogine remarks that were the world based on stability, it would be entirely different than it is. "It would be a static, predictable world, but we would not be here to make the predictions."[24]

If we're to seek the spatial fact of the work, the conceptualization of space needs, in any case, to overcome symmetry. Victor Burgin argues in his essay "Geometry and Abjection" that our reception of representation, in fact our understanding of space itself, remains bound to Euclidean geometry and its child of the Renaissance, the anthropocentrism of symmetrical two-point perspective. The human body is in the middle. Its two eyes look out to the horizon, and everything on either side of the central axis of this immaculate perception falls incrementally away, while affirming a fixed point of infinity.

Space does not shift here, and it isn't corrupted by time. In this understanding, space is pure recession, recession from the center perceived by those Renaissance eyes, the center an imperturbable identity, identity a pure space in relation to other identities of equal Euclidean purity and assurance, each person a pillar among like pillars, a verticality of meaning, a mathematical proof of unmoving stability. Burgin argues that Euclid's space, formulated on the basis of his geometry and optics circa 300 BCE, remains the model of the representation of space even centuries later, in the time of high modernism and its art of fragmentation, with Cubism and Russian Futurism always in a state of return to the Euclidean source. "The mirror of perspectival representation was broken only in order that its fragments, each representing a distinct point of view," he writes, "be reassembled according to classic geometric principles—to be returned, finally, to the frame and the proscenium arch."[25]

This is intriguing for the very reason that it is historically wrong. The moment of European modernism to which Burgin refers is not an inverted *corso e ricorso*, from order to anarchy to order's revanche. The fragmented structures inimical to this dominant strain in modernist art weren't intended to recuperate a classical wholeness and stability, but rather to mimetically express the destruction of a past society swept up and wrecked; to find artistic equivalents for the technologically advanced machinery of the First World War that atomized the architectures of bodies and buildings, detonating the givens of what had been and proffering imbalance, asymmetry, and radical dispersion. Reassembly not required.

To say there is a genetic strain of Raphael in Braque or Mozart in Stravinsky may hold some essentialist logic of progression, but it says nothing of historically local intentions or of modernism's wrecking ball of invention, with its heft of both mourning and promise.[26] Nonetheless, Burgin points to the breaking of Euclidean-based symmetrical representations of space and their concomitant stasis, and this resonates paradoxically with so much of the counter-tendency we see from Wagner on of the will to the unseparate, to the organizational rationale of interdisciplinary practices and network aesthetics and their uneven spatial relations.

Burgin highlights the renunciation of the Euclidean in his observation of a contemporary condition of multiple actions seen simultaneously (or nearly simultaneously) by the viewer, which is of crucial concern to network aesthetics. His writing precedes by nearly thirty years the advances in technological mobility that smartphones and wearable computing offer, but he intuits it in earlier computational technologies. He notes that computers allow the comprehension of space as dispersal, an etherization of physical space and its redistribution. He quotes Paul Virilio, who writes that "technological space [. . .] is not a geographical space, but a space of time." Of course, as Tung-Hui Hu points out in his *A Prehistory of the Cloud*, our etherized world of planetary computation is physically based on older networks, such as nineteenth-century railroad tracks along whose lines terrestrial cables have been run to carry digital data streams.[27] Spatio-temporal conditions can't truly be untwined, but we can say that space is as vulnerable to time-shifting as it is to place-shifting, and spatial relations between things, both heterogeneous and homogeneous, live fully in a meshwork.

We can say for our purposes that network spatiality is transfigurable and transformative space, modular and rewritable. So Burgin writes, in what already feels antiquated, though still of essential relevance: "Spaces once conceived of as separated, segregated, now overlap: live pictures from Voyager II, as it passes through the rings of Saturn, may appear on television sandwiched between equally 'live' pictures of internal organs, transmitted by surgical probes, and footage from Soweto."[28] He calls these "fold-over spaces." Similarly, Marc Augé speaks in his book

Non-Places: Introduction to an Anthropology of Supermodernity of the "spatial overabundance" that television, for example, creates.[29] Newer platforms, such as TikTok, only exponentialize the potency of spatial overabundance—and that, too, will no doubt be a technology that will seem antiquated soon enough.

Space becomes a bombardment of clustered knowledges, experiences, bound practices, aleatory events, and epistemologies that abut and give entrance to one another in a temporal sluice. The perspectival delineation of space is given over to an architecture of contingency, of constant reconstruction that's even Cézannesque in its imbricated bits, evocative of Borgesian simultaneities, twins, and vertigo. The body as the ground zero of spatial production is entered into the matrix of fold-over spaces encompassing myriad types that it passes through, pushes against, and holds traces of, as Michel Serres writes in his essay, "Language and Space: From Oedipus to Zola":

> My body, therefore, is not plunged into a single space, but into the difficult intersection of this numerous family, into the set of connections and junctions to be established between these varieties. This is not simply given or is not *always already* there, as the saying goes. This intersection, these junctions, always need to be constructed. And in general whoever is unsuccessful in this undertaking is considered sick. His body explodes from the disconnection of spaces. My body lives in as many spaces as the society, the group, or the collectivity have formed: the Euclidean house, the street and its network, the open and closed garden, the church or the enclosed spaces of the sacred, the school and its spatial varieties containing fixed points, and the complex ensemble of flow-charts, those of language, of the factory, of the family, of the political party, and so forth. Consequently, my body is not plunged into one space but into the intersection or the junctions of this multiplicity.[30]

To these spaces, as I've noted, must be added that spatial overabundance of the digital, which offers fold-overs in extremis. The devices we use and wear contain their own techniques for representing spaces and attaching us to forms of action and experience that present elongated and truncated spatialities fused with instant and archival temporalities. In the expansiveness of the internet and of apps on digital devices, all the more so with the technologies of augmented and virtual reality, we can speak of the instrumentalization of space as an execution of tasks in time. This is a technical species of fold-over space that appears endless, decentered, unmoored, time-shifting but no less time-exacting, and incorporates graphical signs of instrumentalized space that register for the user as the particularity of place.

Place is the result of the ways in which things in spaces, nonhuman and human alike, physical and etherized, engender meanings, coming into relation with our bodies and cognition. Though this may seem to suggest coherence, even a linearity of decoded or revealed significances, asymmetries and asynchronicities so common to the challenge of networked systems add further complexity to our apprehension of contemporary space. The intensification and density of all the fold-over spaces of contemporary life that help us understand interdisciplinary works, as they help us understand our lives today, include the intricacy of their placefulness, the congestion and flows of meanings, even the sense of what Massey has called place's "throwntogetherness," which demands negotiation and necessitates invention.[31]

Discipline-objects and rogue nodes exist in this colliding, interleaved, porous condition of place whose components produce the lapidary and wandering situation of meaning. They invite hospitality yet are always pressing at individual boundaries, generating the allure, the intrigue and promise for viewer-agents that "a boundary," as Heidegger proposed, "is not that at which something stops but, as the Greeks recognized, the boundary is that from which something *begins its presencing.*"[32] This presencing of space becoming place is the action that transpires among the interdisciplinary work's network of things. It elicits the excitement of emergent meanings for viewer-agents—an experience of materials in their concentration and arrangement appearing to blossom before us as they project their properties, and we, in the correlationist mode, project onto them the assignment of particular significances. As we move among the work's parts, space unfolds into the specificity of place for each of us, and what was emergent, what was becoming, shuttles between tour and map, a settling on the disposition of elements and meanings that may take hold or shift again either as we move or in retrospection.

For viewer-agents, the activity of being within the work is one of re-constitution, the process of re-cognizing the schema of the work—and potentially, in some way, oneself—through interaction; that the interdisciplinary work and its viewers joined together in the network of the work, composed of interface, content, address, and user, embody Merleau-Ponty's summation that space is about seeing, while place is about doing. It can be said that in this activation, viewers situate their agency, note their relationship to the nodes alive in the work they've entered, discern transitions among them, and interpret and judge them at the crossroads of individual subjectivities and sociality, of peer relations, politics, of all manner of framing, positioning, and decision-making.

And here, Adorno's scourge of identity weighs; as does Édouard Glissant's thinking about opacity as a political tool of resistance to oppressive administrative overlords; as does Fred Moten's attention to identity in *The Universal Machine,* where he speaks of Hegel's "being for others" as twisted within the binds of colonialist rule and asks who has the possibility and will to invent an emancipatory impurity of prior systemic laws, "the ensemble of political, aesthetic, and philosophical derangements that compose the being that is neither for itself nor for the other?"[33] This question bears on the framing of the interdisciplinary work in its ethics of difference. In fact, it could be said that while Lefebvre's proposition that our own body is always at the center, I want to reiterate that, just as the body enters many spaces simultaneously in the way that Serres describes, our own bodies, as they enter the interdisciplinary work as rogue nodes, become an/other body that reconstitutes the work and is reconstituted by it, become an/other thing, which also touches on the potential implicit in Moten's question.

What lies before the viewer is a problem-set concerning the underlying meanings of the work's identity, interrogating what is intended by the artist, what is inflected by viewer-agents, what is influenced by various external forces, layer upon layer. Within the problem-set, then, is the richness of each problem to be solved, its difficulty and the fecund potentiality, prodigal and lapidary. An energy is present that, as I've said in various ways, seems to emerge at once from each discipline-object in its thingness and from the vectors of dynamic relations in the whole of the assemblage, an unfolding material being *with* the viewer, its networked spatiality and time of becoming tied to vitality, contingency, containment, and ramification.

In the lapidary unfolding of the interdisciplinary work's structure, there is a likeness to what Gilles Deleuze describes in *The Fold: Leibniz and the Baroque*, where he writes: "If the world is infinitely cavernous, if worlds exist in the tiniest bodies, it is because everywhere there can be found 'a spirit in matter.'" He goes on to say that this internal energy, so much like the essence, the in-itself, the internal properties and necessity of art objects I've spoken of so many times, lies within matter's "infinite division of parts," each one containing "a world pierced with irregular paths," and that a "conservation of force" resides within matter's porous and spongy texture that is "without emptiness."[34]

The nodal intricacy of nodes and vectored paths of the interdisciplinary work add this notion of the Baroque to Burgin's fold-over spaces and Serres's junction of multiplicity; energies generated from within discipline-objects in their networked interactions among themselves and with viewers to produce the oscillations witnessed in engaging the work—taking their tour, stopping to formulate a map of its topography, shifting again, finding ways through the work's irregular paths, its "pleats of matter," as Deleuze puts it. Of course, these paths are not only irregular but may not seem obvious to viewers at all, their pleats folding over and interrupting clear lines of meaning. Inherent in network aesthetics, inherent in the historical works we've already examined, is the struggle to accomplish and maintain connection. The interdependence of things in contiguous and continual spatial relations are always caught up by imperfections within the system, contingencies, latencies in network structures, the links sometimes failing. So Bruno Latour writes, "nets, networks, and 'worknets' leave everything they don't connect simply unconnected."[35]

Yet we can also say that it's precisely the asymmetries, the irregular flows of energy, the links between individual art objects that are (at least at first) too difficult to grasp that make the whole of the work compelling. It's the sense of chunked energy that disturbs and enthralls—that refractive spatiality that touches the way *we* mean in the correlation of agency between ourselves and the components of the work—"a system of constantly changing relationships in which action and the conditions of action are mutually constituted during the same process," as Kai Eriksson has written.[36]

In this sense, all artists of interdisciplinary works, whether they want to control every aspect of the work or welcome the inevitability of change, are animated by the same liveness of desire: desire for situatedness, for meaning as place, for collectivity as a plenitude, drawing audiences into the epistemological and experiential complexities of the work so that they parse the eventfulness the artist seeks and the way that it ramifies for them among the nodes and edges of linked discipline-objects, losing and gaining connection—a chorus, a cabaret, a curriculum, detunings and retunings, a network aesthetics.

This is the dynamic space inbuilt in the interdisciplinary work's society of things, folded over, baroque, multiplicitous. Its network is always the agora I've spoken of—a place of disputation, improvisation, iconoclasm, and mutable consensus. As we saw with Wagner and will see with the Cabaret Voltaire and the Bauhaus, the Althusserian notion of expressive causality, "the existence of the structure in its effects," indicates the internal combustion and renovating power of discord and negotiation, the record of old bodies of regulation bridled at and broken. What these artists and their works embraced is summarized in Yuk Hui's phrase "the normativity of laws is replaced by the performativity of procedures."[37] What they ignited were radical revisions of procedure. What boundaries they merged, mutated, and revised asked what unity and wholeness might look like and feel like, answered in their moment at a cost, and left to posterity to question.

The Senses

TASTE

• • • Doesn't it come last on the ladder of Necessity? Taste is the sensory terminus when proximity is already breached. Whatever the foreignness is, the lips have felt it, and now, as my tongue opens like a palm at the end of waiting, here the very strangeness of chemical facts comes to make their argument and the tongue judges, because taste is a seat of decision— sweet, salt, bitter, sour, savory. The neither-heat-nor-cold of milk from the first breast is accepted, a medial place of safety, which is what savory is. As with Proust's madeleine, crumbling time like small cake on his tongue with that sweetness, time as a fume lifting from taste, always a before, the five receptors in the meat of my mouth like nodes linked to memory. And also after, which is taste in two ways, that branching judgment, either on the tongue as round, sharp, rough, silken, smooth, or with law and against it—disgust, approval, bridged to the look of things, the scent.

Taste is the taste of I, though equity wishes us to sense in ourselves the sense of other. But always first, if it is a seeing on my tongue, its shapeliness in knowing goes down a hole under my I-ness that becomes my I-ness, and changeable, like me, each thing a piece of time swallowed. Time as meat and taste as its carriage. The tongue that shapes the light, like Adam, into sound and words that first had the taste of the world on it, like sea, like flower, green and meat again, the taste of burned, the taste of is and, quickly, was. Which is to say that part of survival is to recognize similarity, so that the tongue is an instrument for tasting likenesses and of translation, a knitting of the world, inside moving to the surface, to others, a chemistry of forms. And yet as likeness is a tyranny of sameness, taste in all ways tingles with regulation. Flesh knowledge is a locksmith's trade.

I imagine the first pineapple brought to the tongue to taste its strange armor and shape, its juice an amalgam of mineral and sudden sweetness, a world still readying itself, but already unable to untaste what it knows.

Five

A WALTZ BEFORE HITLER/HUGO BALL AND THE DICTATORSHIP OF UNREASON

• • • Yet there is another body in the founding practices of the interdisciplinary. The body into which the political will is cut, an inscription with no postulate of reversibility incised. The militant will of reason, this he hates. "Reason" as the pretense of governmental rule, *rationality*—they're almost a form of mutilation, of mortification; traumas twisted in the carnage of the war he briefly witnessed, with inklings of religious fervor never too far away. And so, after the long flares of disaster rise over Liège, Mons, over Ypres, 1914, 1915, another escape to Zurich, sixty-six years after the flight of Wagner. Under false papers, destitute, with his lover Emmy Hennings beside him, Hugo Ball arrives. And then, after nine months' gestation, so does the Cabaret Voltaire.

A tie beyond the geographical already exists between Ball and Wagner, a calling backward and forward to the Gesamtkunstwerk and the dream of wholeness. In 1914, the year before his flight to Switzerland, Ball gives a talk at the Ostasiatische Gesellschaft in Munich. His subject is his vision for a truly modern theater, which he later summarized: "My thesis went like this: that the purpose of the expressionist theater is the festival play; it contains a new conception of the total work of art."[1] *Eine neue Auffassung des Gesamtkunstwerks.*

Here was the total work of art and festival play again (Wagner had called the Ring cycle a *Bühnenfestspiel*, a stage-festival play), yet inflected differently, refracted through the ideas of the Russian artist, poet, and teacher Wassily Kandinsky. Ball met Kandinsky in 1912 in Munich, where they planned a second volume of Kandinsky's hymn to a new totalism, the *Blaue Reiter Almanach*, the first of which was published the year they met. Kandinsky, rethinking Wagner's failed unity in his music-dramas, sought a union at once more integrated and more modular. This Ball recalled in the document through which we know him best—his diary, aptly titled for the restlessness that impelled him from one fundamental concern to another over his short life of forty-one years, from art to political struggle to deliverance beyond the rooted, warring nature of worldliness. He called his diary *Flight Out of Time*.

Kandinsky named his own form of unity the "monumental" work of art, and Ball, in a lecture he gave on the Russian's creative practice in Zurich on April 7, 1917, remarked that the "externalization" of the disciplines in Wagner's conception was insufficient for Kandinsky. Externalization meant suppression of the properties of each artistic form under the regimenting surface, the endless melody that engendered a false, inorganic unity. Not enough in-itself, so to speak—or what Ball argued, recapitulating Kandinsky, "contradicted the intrinsic laws of the arts involved." He goes on admiringly, saying that Kandinsky

> envisages a counterpositioning of the individual arts, a symphonic composition in which every art, reduced to its essentials, provides as an elementary form no more than the score for a construction of composition on the stage. Such a composition would allow each individual art its own material mode of operation, and it would create the future monumental work of art from a blend of the refined materials.[2]

For them, every art form held within it an inner necessity, a notion that elided material properties and spiritual essence. Between these two lay both aesthetic and existential identity, a transformational reciprocity subtending a profound opening of materiality, an ultimately eschatological ambition underwritten by a belief in a fundamentally palpable world lifting into the fugitive nature of each mortal body and, even more, the fugitive boundaries of all things. For Ball, the total work of art as a monumental composition has an extra-musicality, a body beyond the body that, as he wrote in his diary the week before, "insists on the inherent, unifying life nerve."[3] His source of inspiration may have been his Russian émigré friend, but this musicality was for Ball particularly sown in the German spirit, the aesthetic and the social already conjoined, already for him a rustling of *Heimat*, of an inward, exclusive, and ascendant Germanity. So, he claims in another diary entry, on October 22, 1915: "We Germans are a nation of musicians, full of an unbounded faith in the omnipotence of harmony. [. . .] Harmony is the Germans' Messiah; it will come to deliver its people from the multiplicity of resounding contradiction."[4]

Yet what was rooted in that soil of both Germany and harmony was entirely riven by contradiction as he wrote those words, now in self-imposed exile in Zurich. Walter Benjamin, a friend for a time of Ball's, captured the techno-historical moment ruefully, writing:

> For never has experience been contradicted more thoroughly than strategic experience by tactical warfare, economic experience by inflation, bodily experience by mechanical warfare, moral experience by those in power. A generation that had gone to school on a horse-drawn streetcar now stood under the open sky in a countryside in which nothing remained unchanged but the clouds, and beneath these clouds, in a field of force of destructive torrents and explosions, was the tiny, fragile human body.[5]

This was the European chaos from which Ball took flight—a world in which time, landscape, borders, and the theaters of the First World War's battles were so vastly fractured and compressed by technologies of communication and weaponry that it came to be called, as I've noted, the Cubist war.[6] He tried three times to enlist and was rejected, and then, having briefly toured Belgium's battlefields as a civilian, his shock at the carnage fit Benjamin's description all too well. It led Ball not only into exile but also to envision a very different Germany: nostalgic and fiercely aspirational, with its harmony rising from ruined land. In that same lecture on Kandinsky, he professes a fascination and dedication to something we've read before in a Rilkean register. He speaks of Kandinsky's vision, in which "evil is put beside good, good beside evil. Tranquility, peace, equality come to be equality, freedom, fraternity of forms. [. . .] Nothing is suppressed. Everything is allowed to flower, to float, exist."[7] Ball's version of Rilke's "*is*" also accommodates beauty and the vile in a continuum of felt perceptions that result in equivalences, in a fraternity of forms as points of intersection, contagion, and transfer that we know already as the lingua franca of network aesthetics and interdisciplinary art.

Yet Ball's *is* is weighted inevitably less toward wonder than disgust, shaken by the destructive torrents of the war, even at a distance in Zurich. Fraternity of form is not, as in Rilke, a polite gloss on artistic matters in the past but an answer to his current, ruinous Germany, corroded and broken by the collapse of its moral authority. In his diary entry on June 16, 1916, Ball writes about what he calls a variety show that he has recently begun with Hennings and friends. It's a realization of that earlier notion of the festival play, now deconstructed and become a new form—in fact, a multiplicity that relies on contradiction as its mode of discourse and operation. It is a "*Candide* against the times," Ball writes, noting that the war's slaughter, despite calls of European glory, "cannot force our quivering nostrils to admire the smell of corpses."[8] And so Voltaire, who wrote *Candide*'s raking satire of European optimism and religious faith while himself a Swiss expatriate in the 1750s, is the nominal angel of that little variety show, opened on February 5, 1916, at the address of Spiegelgasse 1, where its eccentric performers unleashed their tiny thunder. They called it the Cabaret Voltaire.

Ball speaks of his times as "godless"; he cites descriptions of Germany as "savage and barbaric"; he writes of the "demoralization of Germany."[9] Yet, as it was with Wagner in the midst of societal violence and change, and his escape from it, this breaking down is a breaking up, a dilation signaling a redistribution of powers forced by necessity to revile and revise, to claim a new nomos for a collective contemporaneity of expressive means. The cabaret's intentionally aleatory and chaotic structure works mimetically to reflect unshapeliness and ungainliness, the thrum of interference on the line of a desecrated order, while holding to an assumption of ethical clarity, of long-held rectitude.

Along with Ball and Hennings, the original agents of the cabaret's willful turbulence were Jean (Hans) Arp and Sophie Taeuber-Arp, Richard Huelsenbeck, Marcel Janco, Hans Richter, Walter Serner, and Tristan Tzara (born Samuel Rosenstock), along with more temporary participants. The founders recited and displayed their works alongside contributions from Giorgio de Chirico, Robert Delaunay, Max Ernst, Kurt Schwitters, and from Kandinsky and Paul Klee, who became early faculty members of the Bauhaus, with its very different experiment in systematic interdisciplinary production.

"Systematic" could not be farther from Ball's initial response to the European debacle. Or so it seemed. In fact, he operated on two fronts. In his diary and the texts he was at work on, Ball railed against the war and its destruction of the homeland, ranging over the German Idealist tradition in philosophy, over ethics and theology, over art, literature, and political theories. He was already deep in thought about his scathing *Critique of the German Intelligentsia*, published in 1919, having written a decade earlier an unsubmitted dissertation on Nietzsche at the University of Munich. Its subtitle, "A Contribution Toward the Renewal of Germany," already placed him in a lineage of contrarian diagnostic thought, with a particular incipient attraction to the Nietzschean notion of the transvaluation of all values and a rejection of Kantian reason. In the very first daily entry in *Flight Out of Time*, Ball writes: "Kant—he is the archenemy; he started it all. With his theory of cognition he has turned all objects of the visible world over to understanding and to control."[10] His journal may flit from subject to subject, day to day, as diaries do, but his thinking through subjects was methodical.

Cabaret Voltaire is the other front, Ball's co-invention of a participatory platform, a performativity of procedures seeking in practice what the stagecraft of his previous work and outrage could produce. It would seem topologically inverted, apparently devoted not to repair and unity but to artistic bedlam; not cultivating reason but protesting its ferocious travesties. His first announcement of the cabaret, three days before its opening, seemed decorous enough, simply stating that "guest artists will come and give musical performances at the daily meetings." Yet the next sentence includes a single phrase quietly indicating that strain of the Rilkean *is* against the grain of hierarchy, proposing an implicitly horizontal network of artistic transmission, a receptivity to Zurich's young denizens to perform, "whatever their [disciplinary] orientation."[11] The still unfurled possibility of equivalence is revealed in this format for the cabaret's performative space, and with it a circuit opened that did not close with the shuttering of the cabaret in early July (just six months after it began) and hasn't closed since.

What was unleashed was a new stigmergic formation for artistic practice. As with other forms of stigmergy, openness and collaboration are the underlying characteristics of organization among a diverse network of actors drawn to a site and who begin to cross-fertilize ideas, means, and practices in variations that invite contingency and voluntarily coalesce into a new system of connections.[12] Cabaret Voltaire exemplifies this networked openness, whose formation of alignments emerges in situ as an environmental cascade of actions that accumulate a distributed yet systemic affect, at once apparently desultory and yet within a structure, a complexly self-reflexive, self-organizing one. It is a platform, in Benjamin Bratton's term, for "generative mechanisms" that mediate "unplanned and even unplannable interactions," and the performers thrive on their own outrage, as well as their audience's.[13] As Georges Hugnet, the noted Dada historian in the 1930s, records:

> A trusting and hopeful audience, gathered together for an art exhibit or a poetry recital, was insulted beyond endurance. On the stage of the cabaret tin cans and keys were jangled as music until the enraged audience protested. Instead of reciting his poems, Serner placed a bunch of flowers at the feet of a dressmaker's dummy. Arp's poems were recited by a hidden voice in an enormous hat shaped like a sugar-loaf. Huelsenbeck roared his poems in a mighty *crescendo*, while Tzara beat time on a large packing case. Huelsenbeck and Tzara danced, yapping like bear cubs, or, in an exercise called "noir cacadou," they waddled about in a sack with their heads thrust in a pipe.
>
> Tzara invented static and chemical poems. A static poem consisted of chairs on which placards were placed with a word written on each, and the sequence was altered each time the curtain was lowered. For these acts, Janco designed costumes of paper,

cardboard and rags of every color, and the costumes were held together with pins, so that anybody might "do as well"; not only were the costumes without artistry, they battled against all semblance of any established art and all the formal rules it implied. Perishable, deliberately ugly and absurd, these materials, chosen at the whim of eye and mind, provided magnificent tatters, symbolizing perpetual revolt, despair that refuses to descend to despair.[14]

Disgust and humiliation were sentiments much in the air at the time. Tzara famously said in a 1922 lecture, looking back at earlier days, that what they made was not "the beginnings of art, but of disgust"—a lecture in which he uses the word "disgust" nine times in a single paragraph.[15] Meanwhile, Ball remarked, "Our cabaret is a gesture. Every word that is spoken and sung here says at least this one thing: that this humiliating age has not succeeded in winning our respect."[16] The random, heterogeneous, and irrational destructuring of convention becomes the mimetic bulwark against this humiliation by swallowing it whole, tactically embodied in the transactional expressive mode of the cabaret, coherent mostly in its taste for the ad hoc and appearance of incoherence, or at least what they perceived as the symbolic capital of illogic. These performances, recitations, and displays, willfully against established aesthetic standards and practices, offered what Hal Foster has in another context called an anti-aesthetic, an anti-normative posture as a spectacular norm on the stage of the cabaret.[17]

In its original Greek, *anti* means "against," "opposite" or, in a confrontational direction, "toward." Each performance at the cabaret, each radically disorienting poem, each yapping musicale, each combatively collaged artwork displayed as a negation of tradition, lunged toward opposition, linking one anti-aesthetic effect to another, the discipline of discipline-objects turned on, revoked, and revamped. The cabaret's deconstructed *Festspiel* advertised its chaos as precisely an *is* in which everything that could disgust could flower. Its ethics hewed to the labor of undoing the commonness of common sense, though it did so by offering its public a common interface that did what all compelling interfaces do: It drew its users, or more precisely provoked them, to interact in predicted behaviors and patterns, opening and closing pathways of reaction. That's to say, there was a style to the cabaret's user interface based on its protocol of indignation, engendering its participants to co-react within its makeshift system of wildly decentered and nonlinear nodal interdependencies, linked together by a performative violence of spirit.

What took place at the cabaret predicated the modification of artistic precepts, each work a local component of the Voltaire network upending the past in light of the present's trauma in order to reform the audience as well as the art, to create a collectivity based on that sense of life itself as "insulted beyond endurance." The cabaret's tactical mode of risible, incendiary non-sense taunted its viewers with riotous disjunctures that followed the distinct strategy to create (in contrast to Wagner's captive audiences in the dark) viewer-agents who would mirror its own aggressiveness. Hans Richter described the transformation succinctly. The audience, he wrote, "had begun by sitting impassively behind its beer-mugs. From this state of immobility, it was roused into frenzied involvement with what was going on."[18]

Ball never asked the main contributors to the cabaret to cohere as a group. Richter recalled that each member "sang his own song with all his might." Yet there was a unity of affect, "how one movement could unite within itself such heterogeneous elements. But in the Cabaret Voltaire these individuals shone like the colors of the rainbow, as if they had been produced by the same process of refraction."[19] For Ball, of course, Kandinsky's vision of the monumental artwork lay on his mind as a premonitory guide, an artistic polity represented by that inner necessity of individual disciplines in conjunction. The cabaret's discipline-objects act as overlapping sovereignties, staking autonomous jurisdictional claims within a collaborative artifice.

In these terms, the audience, these newly minted, outraged, energized, and random viewer-agents are precisely rogue nodes, interjecting, interfering, and so revising each nodal interaction, each performance, as its dynamics alter in the rowdiness of action and reaction. The lines between these performances impose their asymmetrical power relations equally among themselves and their viewers. The reciprocity becomes a melding; a sense, once again, of the Hegelian *Umschlag*, an inversion, in which the interaction within the performative system of the cabaret presents what Bratton calls a "symbiotic recursion," which he notes is "not just the negotiation among actors within the *User* position; it is a durable interpenetration of actors, mutually embedded one within the other."[20] So, as Richter describes, performers and audience are mutually caught in the meaning-net of the event. They ensnare one another, forming an interpenetrant, transitory sense of collective wholeness driven by the scattershot display of rapid-fire yet linked differences.

> Readings of modern French poetry alternated with recitals by German, Russian and Swiss poets. Old music was played as well as new. This produced some unlikely combinations: Cendrars and von Hoddis, Hardekopf and Aristide Bruant, a balalaika orchestra and Werfel. Delaunay's pictures were exhibited and Eric Mühsam's poems performed. Rubenstein played Saint-Saens. There were readings of Kandinsky and Lasker-Schüler, as well as Max Jacob and André Salmon. [. . .] Imagine the combination of Ball's piano improvisations, Emmy Hennings' thin, unrefined, youthful voice (which was heard alternately in folk-songs and brothel songs) and the abstract Negro masks of Janco, which carried the audience from the primeval language of the new poems into the primeval forests of the artistic imagination. [. . .] Bells, drums, cow-bells, blows on the table or empty boxes, all enlivened the already wild accents of the new poetic language.[21]

How far this is from Wagner's mode of control in which all is plotted and, despite claims to the contrary, hierarchy reigns. Instead, Cabaret Voltaire's relations between actors and agents intermixing, these rogues and rogue nodes, these discipline-objects pressed by contiguity to speak to one another, afford a porousness and elasticity of intersubjectivities that shape a distributed form of network, at once formally inventive and socially informal—given to the collision and levitation of difference that brothel songs, heads in a pipe, Saint-Saëns, and cowbells cumulatively insisted on. Kris Cohen, writing of our contemporary context of distributed networks, groups, and memes, remarks that "the gathering of people around things becomes less a world-building activity than an inflection, a survival instinct, an adaptation to the population form, a 'way of life.'"[22] This resonates with the moment of the cabaret, for if its bubble proscribes a temporary hothouse of world-building, its aspiration was to mimic the tumult of life in wartime and then to shake life further and instigate a new way to live in a future yet unseen.

At the core of this cacophony was the abiding spirit of the poetic voice. An aporia is at work. In his diary, Ball ruminates on the need to lose ego, to renounce vanity and greed, the sullen weights of personhood. But simultaneously he's caught in the heat of his cabaret, caught in the explosive renunciation by his group of *the* group, meaning the powers that brought the catastrophe of the war. He approaches this opposition in the structural organization of individual voices that remain so in the format of the cabaret, while presenting a unified expression of anti-art in the upheaval of poetry as a medium for his message. He writes, "The poem tries to elucidate the fact that man is swallowed up in the mechanistic process. In a typically compressed way it shows the conflict of the *vox humana* with a world that threatens, ensnares, and destroys it, a world whose rhythm and noise are ineluctable."[23]

A poetic structure based on the musical operation of recitative and that seems like an acceleration and collapse of traditional antiphony mirrors the shattering theater of the war. His poetry's upheaval both occludes and promotes the individual, forcing individuality into the operation of *against*, *opposite*, and *toward* by multiplying subjectivities to the point of density as noise—a noise as loud and rapid as munitions—and blurring the line between individual and group, difference and inclusiveness, all ego and no particular ego, the one-in-the-many and the many-in-the-one. Ball finds words for this in his diary on March 30, 1916, when he describes one of the central inventions at the cabaret: the "simultaneous poem," most famously the poem "L'amiral cherche une maison à louer" (The Admiral Looks for a House to Rent), collectively written and performed by Tzara, Huelsenbeck, and Janco.

"All the styles of the last twenty years came together yesterday," Ball writes that day, and then explains the *poème simultan*'s totalizing method as "a contrapuntal recitative in which three or more voices speak, sing, whistle, etc., at the same time in such a way that the elegiac, humorous, or bizarre content of the piece is brought out by these combinations."[24] How different this simultaneity is from Cézanne's, and yet the radical desire to cross over into a controlled yet liberating hybridity of forms resonates as an intrinsic impulse in the war on convention. "The Admiral Looks for a House to Rent" is shouted out in overlapping French, German, and English, voice over voice in a concentrated din, with sound effects of different kinds: a combustion of multiplicative effects and, once again, a violence of compression that elicits the shock of the war's multiple, simultaneous, and looped operations of aggression and communication.

So, for example, on August 23, 1914, in the first year of the war, during the battle of the Marne, the vastness of the battle theater allowed the French to be winning attacks in one place, holding their own in others, and retreating before the German advance in others—and all of this communicated instantly by telephonics engulfing and collapsing space, never before used in battle. In that single month of August, more than 2 million Frenchmen were deployed on 4,278 trains, while on the first day of the battle of the Somme, July 1, 1916, the British had more than 57,000 casualties and 19,000 dead—most of them, it was speculated, in the first minutes of the battle.[25]

The simultaneous poem is an aestheticization of the war's own combinatorial dynamics, which serve as precedent, but there were formal poetic precedents, as well as musical ones, as I've written. The spatial configuration of "The Admiral Looks for a House to Rent," with its range of lines in blocks and rows, has the appearance of a musical score, while it evokes the visual structure and oral sense of slippage, elision, and overlap, of discontinuity and flow, of fold-over space, of Futurist verse, of the work of Blaise Cendrars, and before them of Stéphane Mallarmé's lines carefully strewn across the pages of his most celebrated poem, "A Throw of the Dice Will Never Abolish Chance" from 1897—all the more fitting, as contingency and simultaneity were essential to the operative network structure of Cabaret Voltaire. It serves as an apparatus of textual, aural, and performative actions in an evental sense: dense, simultaneous, shrill, irrational, and all of a piece as the representation of the woven presence of immediacy.

Henri Bergson's ideas about simultaneity were important to the members of the cabaret, which led, in Ball's words, to a "purely associative art," its links forming a "grammar of connection."[26] In his 1889 treatise *Time and Free Will: An Essay on the Immediate Data of Consciousness,* Bergson had already theorized consciousness as a mechanism of temporal association and coalescence:

> While I am writing these lines, the hour strikes on a neighboring clock, but my inattentive ear does not perceive it until several strokes have made themselves heard. Hence, I have not counted them; and yet I only have to turn my attention backwards to count up the four strokes which have already sounded and add them to those which I hear. If, then, I question myself carefully on what has just taken place, I perceive that the first four sounds had struck my ear and even affected my consciousness, but that the sensations produced by each one of them, instead of being set side by side, had melted into one another in such a way to give the whole a peculiar quality. [. . .] In a word, the number of strokes was perceived as a quality and not as a quantity; it is thus that duration is presented to immediate consciousness.[27]

Bergson follows this notion with an idea of aggregation and unity, of succession that calls to mind the unifying spirit Richter invoked when speaking of the heterogeneous acts of the cabaret as much as the staggering range of events and actors on battlefields yet to come, and which Bergson calls "the multiplicity of conscious life": "below the numerical multiplicity of conscious states, a qualitative multiplicity; below the self with well-defined states, a self in which succeeding each other means melting into one another and forming an organic whole."[28]

The typographic line of Tzara, Huelsenbeck, and Janco's collective poem suggests this multiplicity and formation, though it seems visually to represent mechanical force rather than organic flow. Its chunked sections appear like units shuttling, mobile—an unsettledness of the image and the voices rising from it. The poem's spatial configuration and sense of sped-up, congested time, both in print and performance, signal its tactical aggression, its intensification of noise as a provocation underwritten by existential disruption embodied by its military protagonist, a homeless admiral in search of rootedness and shelter.

The poem begins with a twice-repeated word, *Ahoi ahoi*—a call for attention and a prospect of landfall. Its phrases are honeyed nonsense,

Janco singing, for example, "She said the raising her heart oh dwelling oh yes yes yes yes yes . . ." Or Huelsenbeck simply following that inaugural "Ahoi" with grinding sounds, "przza chrrza prrrza": its totalizing cacophonous effect, once again representing the velocity of the war's chaos and its destructive technologies whose logic was to sow illogic, to bring victory through disorder, dislocation, and ruin.[29]

The complexly overlapping nodal activity and contingencies devised for the poem—so much in the spirit of a network's "ambient field of systematic intercommunication and assembly"—suggest the simultaneous experience of non-integrated and integrated being.[30] This is the admiral's condition of homelessness and desire to settle, so resonant with the cabaret members' state of exile. Homelessness is to be without dwelling—the middle term of Heidegger's essay, "Building Dwelling Thinking." He traces the German word for building, *Bauen*, to the Old English *buan*, which means to dwell. *Buan* is linked through a series of variables to the German conjugation of the verb "to be," as in *ich bin*, I am, and makes a bridge between I am and I dwell.

Dwelling, then, is to reside in the place of being, in the place of origin. To dwell is a construction of the self, a building of the self. To be without dwelling is to be without the roots of origin, to be without the home in which the self sits. Heidegger goes on to correlate this being-in-dwelling with preserving the self. And here, in the performance of the simultaneous poem, as in its contents, there is the trauma done to origin. The self isn't preserved in its status as being-in-dwelling's stability of place, but instead through its counter-action of a counter-self—stripped away, blown across the plain of being at once crowded with the density of sensations and needs while overcome by a devastating sense of emptiness.

The cabaret is the *un*-building of dwelling. Its artifice of language, of I, of us, of the admiral as avatar, points toward a multiplicity of consciousness that seeks wholeness in the face of negativity and through negativity, through acts of artistic undoing. This is the acknowledgment of the exile's unwanted yet unalterable swerve into transience, through which an otherness is imposed among all the uprooted others—a multiplication of the self amid the pile of catastrophes. The *poème simultan* represents this pluralization in the tripled voices through which understandable strands of phrases are caught fleetingly, a nostalgia possibly for the purity of a signal that is still remembered in its vanishing.

Matthew S. Witkovsky speaks of Tzara's use of "media interference," of noise as productive resistance in the name of new production. "The Admiral Looks for a House to Rent" can then be read and heard as a form of confrontation through latency, by which meaning is jammed by the equivalent of a denial-of-service attack on the network, with a torrent of data being projected at the audience, too much to process. Latency is enforced: whatever packets of meaning are sent are piled up, slowed, or lost through congestion—a true denial of service, order lost to bellicose tumult, facilitated by ruthless technologies. The poem's competing voices are crossed signals, Witkovsky says, as "a poor man's spoof of communication in wartime," and he invokes the media theorist Friedrich Kittler to propose that what happens in the simultaneous poem is a message sent and transposed as willful disharmony, which is Tzara's strategy.[31] Yet Ball is after something else, something of an entirely different order of juridical ambition: the rebuilding, the re-dwelling of being in the world.

Nineteen days after the performance of the poem, whose admiral never finds a new home, who searches a world no longer indexical and is caught in the shattered landscape of non-sense, comes another entry by Ball, April 18: "Tzara keeps on worrying about the periodical. My proposal to call it 'Dada' is accepted."[32] The word, as Huelsenbeck recalled in his history of Dada from 1920, was "accidentally discovered in a German-French dictionary. [. . .] Dada is French for a wooden horse. It is impressive in its brevity and suggestiveness. Soon Dada became the signboard for all the art that we launched in the Cabaret Voltaire."[33]

Only one issue of the periodical *Cabaret Voltaire* was published, in June 1916, with contributions from Apollinaire, Arp, Ball, Cendrars, Hennings, Huelsenbeck, Janco, Kandinsky, Marinetti, Picasso, and Tzara, among others. Subsequently, Tzara launched a series of publications under the titles *Collection Dada* and simply *Dada* that spawned a global avalanche of Dada-ized journals. Tzara attempted to claim the word's discovery, but historical evidence seems to hold that this was Ball and Huelsenbeck's contribution. Their paternity battle only underscores the cleaving of intentions between Ball and Tzara.[34]

For Ball, the event of the cabaret was on the road to a specific form of wholeness—the tutelary vision of Kandinsky's idea of monumental art hovering amid the smoke and beer at Spiegelgasse 1. For Tzara, there was the chance to make something monumental in the very different sense of a movement, as Dada became internationally—a new empire of permanent misrule with him as self-anointed Sun King around whom the artistic precincts of Zurich, Paris, Berlin, Hannover, New York, and elsewhere would boil.

Ball read his "Dada Manifesto" on the fourteenth of July, 1916, at the first public Dada gathering. Cabaret Voltaire had closed by then, with Huelsenbeck claiming it had gone broke because, in true chaotic fashion or administrative revolt, they never bothered to collect entry fees from the audience. Ball's manifesto is a declaration of subtraction, a repudiation of the Dada group in six brief paragraphs. On April 11 he had already written in his diary that he and Huelsenbeck were against "organization," which was the very basis of their anti-art, and "one should not turn a whim into an artistic school." Ten days later, he said outright, "I am anxious to support the cabaret and then to leave it."[35] Within two weeks of proclaiming his manifesto, he and Hennings quit Zurich, moving to the Swiss village of Vira-Magadino.

His manifesto argues first that the word "Dada" is a universal nominalism to be applied to everything. In his citation of its meaning as a "hobby horse," he attracts the word to the flame of general fixation, as well as to its meaning as a toy. He affixes Dada to the names of artistic disciplines, to social class, war, revolution, and to people—Dada Tzara, Dada Huelsenbeck, "Dada Dalai Lama, Buddha, Bible, and Nietzsche." He turns it into mere sounds and half-signifiers, "dada m'dada, dada m'dada dada mhm, dada dera dada, dada Hue, dada Tza." In all, he loosens and distributes the term's addressees and semantic ownership. Its universality is its inappropriateness to property claims. And then Ball offers a clarifying statement, suggesting his private trajectory toward what totalism might mean and what his approach to it will be. He writes: "If this pulsation is seven yards long, I want words for it that are seven yards long."[36]

Ball's desire for unalloyed rendering, a directness of committed expression, reveals what purity will ultimately mean for him. Here in his manifesto, in any case, it means an intention to gain mimetic purity—what Michel Foucault describes in *The Order of Things*, when he writes, "In its original form, when it was given to men by God himself, language was an absolutely certain and transparent sign for things, because it resembled them."[37] Before Foucault, Walter Benjamin proposes what happened to that purity. In his essay "On Language as Such and on the Language of Man," written the same year as the Cabaret Voltaire's florescence, Benjamin contends that God "set" language in Man, that "God's linguistic being is the word," that "all language communicates itself," and that in the fallenness of Man, language becomes confused, a multiplicity, a prior originality in God at once lost and to be hankered for. It is a secret, a healing magic hidden in plain sight in nature's own grammar of connection that must be recovered in order for humankind to find itself again.[38]

The theological implications are entirely apposite for Ball. The material thingness of language strips away its mundanity. It is a total object, an absolute, an essentializing sign of Being made manifest, the networking of networks, the Logos as godly transmission, the Word as the true dwelling that Ball seeks not as latency, noise or chaos, which he has grown weary of as mere hobby horse and toy, but as a direct connection to retrieve a fundamental order. So he reports in his diary the month before his manifesto that the writing of non-sense at the cabaret has "helped us to rediscover the evangelical concept of the 'word' (logos) as a magical complex image." He speaks of a "new" sentence: "Touching lightly on a hundred ideas at the same time without naming them, this sentence made it possible to hear the innately playful, but hidden, irrational character of the listener; it wakened and strengthened the lowest strata of memory."[39] The mystical omphalos of language in things and things in language exist beyond the reductive limits of reason. Lashing out in his final lines of the manifesto, he lectures his fellow Dadaists as he exits: "[. . .] your stupendous smugness, outside all the parrotry of your self-evident limitedness. The word, gentlemen, is a public concern of the first importance."[40]

The Logos, the Word, is a theological prime, but "public" is also of a crucial urgency to Ball. "Public" signals a mandate under the aegis of the highest authority, tying him to a hunger both for the divine and for Germany's recuperated wholeness. He writes that same year, "I cannot live without the conviction that my personal destiny represents an abbreviation of that of the people as a whole." "Public," then, is his repudiation of anti-art and the Voltaire ethos, a contradiction to contradiction, musing: "I can imagine a time when I will seek obedience as much as I have disobedience: to the full."[41]

Ball had already attempted this sense of a new harmony with God and public through radical artistic means in the most famous performance at Cabaret Voltaire and his last. The performance was of his own poetic composition, inspired by Kandinsky's 1913 volume *Klänge* (Sounds), an artist's book combining prose-poems and woodcuts, some of which were recited at the cabaret. Ball called his friend's poetic experiment a "daring purification of language" and added: "In poetry too he is the first to present purely spiritual processes."[42]

The performance took place at Cabaret Voltaire on June 23, 1916, and later that night he wrote this entry in his diary, quoted in full:

> I have invented a new genre of poems, "Verse ohne Worte'" [verses without words] or *Lautgedichte* [sound poems], in which the balance of the vowels is weighed and distributed solely according to the values of the beginning sequence. I gave a reading of the first one of these poems this evening. I had made myself a special costume for it. My legs were in a cylinder of shiny blue cardboard, which came up to my hips so that I looked like an obelisk. Over it I wore a huge coat collar cut out of cardboard, scarlet inside and gold outside. It was fastened at the neck in such a way that I could give the impression of winglike movement by raising and lowering my elbows. I also wore a high, blue-and-white-striped witch doctor's hat.
>
> On all three sides of the stage I had set up music stands facing the audience, and I put my red-penciled manuscript on them; I officiated at one stand after another. Tzara knew about my preparations, so there was a real little premiere. Everyone was curious. I could not walk inside the cylinder so I was carried onto the stage in the dark and began slowly and solemnly:
>
> gadji beri bimba

glandridi lauli lonni cadori gadjama bim beri glassala

glandridi glassala tuffm i zimbrabim blassa galassasa tuffrn i zimbrabim . . .

The stresses became heavier, the emphasis was increased as the sound of the consonants became sharper. Soon I realized that, if I wanted to remain serious (and I wanted to at all costs), my method of expression would not be equal to the pomp of my staging. I saw Brupbacher, Jelmoli, Laban, Mrs. Wigman in the audience. I feared a disgrace and pulled myself together. I had now completed "Labadas Gesang an die Wolken" ["Labada's Song to the Clouds"] at the music stand on the right and the "Elefantenkarawane" ["Elephant Caravan"] on the left and turned back to the middle one, flapping my wings energetically. The heavy vowel sequences and the plodding rhythm of the elephants had given me one last crescendo. But how was I to get to the end? Then I noticed that my voice had no choice but to take on the ancient cadence of priestly lamentation, that style of liturgical singing that wails in all the Catholic churches of East and West.

I do not know what gave me the idea of this music, but I began to chant my vowel sequences in a church style like a recitative, and tried not only to look serious but to force myself to be serious. For a moment it seemed as if there were a pale, bewildered face in my cubist mask, that half-frightened, half-curious face of a ten-year-old boy, trembling and hanging avidly on the priest's words in the requiems and high masses in his home parish. Then the lights went out, as I had ordered, and bathed in sweat, I was carried down off the stage like a magical bishop.[43]

As opposed to the creation and performance of a *poème simultan*, which could have many performers speaking in various languages at once to evoke a radical universality, Ball enfolds universality in his own body in a sanctified form, with language that, too, after Kandinsky, is meant to express a prelapsarian condition of abstract, purified utterance. The sounds he makes are meant to represent all sounds of all bodies—guttural, rasping, sibilant, emphatic, intoned, appearing to form words, appearing to speak in languages known and foreign—an internalization and expression of difference. T. J. Demos notes this localized convergence in Ball's costume and performance as an assemblage of heterogeneous, hybridized things. "In costume, Ball became 'like' other objects, animals and people, [. . .] his torso was 'like an obelisk'; he wore a 'cubist mask'; his arms gave the impression of winglike movement'; he sang in the 'ancient cadence of priestly lamentation.'"[44]

In this way, Ball performs becoming. He embodies a symbiotic recursion within himself: *he* is the collectivity; *he* is the discipline-object that exemplifies what Demos calls "identity-as-difference," taking into himself "collaborative articulations"; *he* is the Gesamtkunstwerk; and *he* personifies all of these acts of synthesizing will in a condition of politico-theological distress. For as Ball writes in his diary on June 12, 1916, some seven weeks after the word "Dada" first entered the world's artistic terminology, those who joined him in initiating the Cabaret Voltaire are conjoined as a single being, the Dadaist, who "is still so convinced of the unity of all beings, of the totality of all things, that he suffers from the dissonances to the point of self-disintegration."[45]

This embodied assemblage of heterogeneous entities is a very different case than that notion of Cézanne's own form of distress and aspiration to meld himself with what Merleau-Ponty called "the fleshness of the world." That merger, as I've proposed, goes at re-formation through an immersion in the phenomenological condition of things, an urge to become that Deleuzian Body without Organs imagined as a nodal unit among all the others that fill the natural world, linked in a network of networks in which fluid dematerialization offers a zenith of liberation beyond the burdened social world of the human. Ball's incorporation of difference has an entirely opposite trajectory that is one and the same with his attack on the problem of Germany's fallenness.

Sovereignty is the issue that claws at the reality of integration, both personal and national, here expressed by Ball through performance. His dramatic recitation of his sound poem as a combinatory mechanism for heterogeneous elements, for difference and thingness as a multiplicity that gestures toward totality, is a matter of jurisdictional claims made by him for the repair and assertion of his self and "for the people." For Ball, this is a matter of making his way toward a recalibration of things and actions, reaching into the primacy of the Logos and the dwelling of the self toward the reconstruction of a sovereign wholeness under theological auspices.

His sound poems, which advertise their abstraction as the rediscovery of an ontological essence, are a form of displacement by which language disorients the constrictions of mundane power. They suggest a new net of relationships initiated in this representation of becoming, a stepped disarticulation of conventional speech toward a renewed meaningfulness in which his valedictory performance at the cabaret is intended as an event of language's literal opening, the mouth as assembler of order, and his auditors, the audience as viewer-agents, receiving these mutations, cognizing them, and ultimately distributing them in turn by word of mouth—an act that is simultaneously aesthetic and political, stylistic and material, and so invokes this mobilizing action as a particular kind of network thinking, "an assemblage of enunciation [that] does not speak 'of' things; it speaks *on the same level as* the states of things and the states of content," in Deleuze's phrase.[46]

At stake for Ball is the diremption and reassembly of language, leading away from one sovereignty toward an evangelism for another. The cabaret's incipient form of wholeness for Ball was in the spirit of Kandinsky, yes. But more than might at first seem apparent, a lingering Wagnerian strain of totalization is there, too; a yearning for an overarching will that lived sub rosa in the cabaret's pitched political anti-aesthetics and its caustic rejection of what, years later, in a 1924 review of Carl Schmitt's *Political Theology* (1922), Ball called "the dictatorship of reason."[47] Schmitt, the political theorist and Catholic who came to the apex of his prominence in the Nazi putsch of the Weimar constitution, underwritten by his theory of the state and rationale for dictatorship in its technical juridical totalism, was a profound influence on Ball—all the more so because Ball and Cabaret Voltaire would seem to mirror Schmitt, would seem in some sense an aesthetico-political representation of Schmitt's thinking *avant la lettre*.

Schmitt begins *Political Theology* with a declaration (in)famous in modern jurist thought: "Sovereign is he who decides on the exception." Some pages later, after proposing that the very notion of sovereignty has to be considered within the framework of what he called a *Grenzbegriff*, a limit or borderline concept that makes legible the state of exception, Schmitt continues his definition of the sovereign leader: "He decides whether there is an extreme emergency as well as what must be done to eliminate it. Although he stands outside the normally valid legal system, he nevertheless belongs to it, for it is he who must decide whether the constitution needs to be suspended in its entirety."[48] The previous year, Schmitt published *Die Diktatur*, in which he wrote that "sovereign dictatorship utilizes a crisis to abrogate the existing constitution in order to bring about a 'condition whereby a constitution [that the sovereign dictator] considers to be a true constitution will become possible."[49]

The means of extreme power were not novel at the time in Europe. Nearly a decade before Schmitt's theorization of dictatorship, Ball arrived in Zurich at a time when Switzerland's Federal Assembly proclaimed "the unlimited power to take all measures necessary to guarantee the security, integrity, and neutrality of Switzerland." But it is Schmitt's proposed renovation of constitutional law by diktat that has consequential impact on Ball's rethinking of himself, of his cultural and political place and purpose. Schmitt claims:

> All law is "situational law." The sovereign produces and guarantees the situation in its totality. He has the monopoly over this last decision. Therein resides the essence of the state's sovereignty, which must be juristically defined correctly, not as the monopoly to coerce or to rule, but as the monopoly to decide. The exception reveals most clearly the essence of the state's authority. The decision parts here from the legal norm, and (to formulate it paradoxically) authority proves that to produce law it need not be based on law.[50]

Schmitt derides liberalism's degenerative condition, stating that negotiation is a "cautious half measure," turning every definitive dispute into parliamentary debate, permitting decisions "to be suspended forever in an everlasting discussion."[51] The decisiveness of individual authorial vision in place and time is at the base of Schmitt's theorizing, going so far as to say in the preface to the second edition of *Political Theology* in 1934, after Hitler abolished the office of the German presidency and held total power, that "the decisionist implements the good law of the correctly recognized political situation by means of a personal decision."[52] It is he who decides the exception as a law outside of law and yet within its basis of enforcement—or what Giorgio Agamben, in his contemplation of Schmitt's theory of sovereignty and exception, calls "force-of-~~law~~." The strikethrough could as well fit as the emblem of Cabaret Voltaire and Ball: the sign of negation that maintains the visibility of what lies beneath and marks its authors' obloquy. Agamben's strikethrough signifies exception, standing outside of while also belonging to "a power that neither makes nor preserves law, but suspends it."[53]

At first, the cabaret that Ball imagined and brought to life was meant to interrupt and suspend the laws governing society and art, its *Festspiel* itself a *Grenzbegriff,* an aesthetico-political state of exception whose force-of-~~law~~ was its own miniature polity that decided that nothing should be decided. But if the cabaret meant to produce representations of power's corruption and demise, how could its state of exception be other than the mimetic spark and hiss of its own dissipation? It's relevant to note Bratton's observation that platforms produce "new strata of jurisdiction where none existed before," and yet they cause "any particular site [. . .] to be so layered with jurisdictional image systems that no one of these can ever really resolve into a single consensual sovereign geography."[54]

Ball's performative sound poems are, in their own form of theological searching, their own ground zero, a procedure to neutralize the project of the cabaret. Its hothouse aesthetic, though it started in protest, began to only mirror itself in his eyes. It seemed a rowdy spell, a thinness in the face of the war's calamitous depths, which for him were ultimately a question concerning the spirit of Germany and German-ness. For Ball, the cabaret's realization as a Gesamtkunstwerk was finally mere novelty, its network of heterogeneous discipline-objects a technical system that had already exhausted its initial incendiary meaning. With the sound poems, he willfully cut the transmission lines not only to the ruined present—much as Germany cut transmission lines from Britain, France, and Russia in the first months of the war—but to the routinized artifice of lawlessness that he felt the cabaret and Dada had become.[55]

It should be noted that for Tzara, the cabaret as a platform and na-scent network was entirely different. Far from politically and artisti-cally entropic, the cabaret launches his expansionist, cosmopolitan ambitions for Dada. His hunger for scale reconsiders the political ur-gencies of Ball's vision and the cabaret's local audience with what Leah Dickerman calls "a new form of media network," a "proto-globalized identity" that's essentially corporate. What could be more fitting than Tzara printing stationery for the "Mouvement Dada," with Paris as its HQ and a list of its Swiss, German, and American branches, implying its structure and stature as an international business? As Dickerman notes, "there were activities conducted under the banner of Dada in places as far-flung as Romania and Japan."[56] Tzara wrote in his book, *La première Aventure celeste de Mr. Antipyrine*, brought out in July 1916, that Dada is "shit after all but from now on we mean to shit in assorted colors and bedeck the artistic zoo with the flags of every consulate."[57] Dada in Tzara's formulation is a strategic geographical apparatus that replaces its initial impulse with a totality of networked interfaces that continuously generates its pan-anti-authoritarian exceptionalism to become its own centripetal mechanism of authority.

Walter Benjamin described Dada as "an instrument of ballistics" that "struck the spectator like a bullet."[58] Yet for Ball, the bullet had strayed too far from its target. Within months of castigating his friends at the cabaret in the reading of his manifesto, and after his fateful per-formance as a magical bishop seeking a fresh Logos to lead him toward a new obedience, Ball expresses in his diary entry of November 21, 1916, that Germany's demoralization was "a result of the lack of an unequiv-ocal model on which to base one's life."[59] This would be the trajectory of his interests, and in it the longing of the exile speaks.

Dissensus and the suspension of conventional political power were giving way within him to his growing urgency to engage more directly with the nation he has left behind. After all, he hadn't been away for so long. And though it seemed that he decamped intellectually, emotion-ally, and geographically, the German question was insistent, already posed in his diary in 1915, hardly a moment after arriving in Zurich. There was his comment about harmony as essential to what being German is in October of that year, and before that, on June 15, 1915, he wrote: "I am not an anarchist. The longer and farther I am away from Germany, the less I am likely to be one."[60]

And yet both he and Schmitt were intrigued by Bakunin's anarchist ideas. As T. J. Demos notes, "Ball easily chose Bakunin's anarchism over [Georges] Sorel's nationalism. For instance, he noted in his journal one of many 'important points' gleaned from Bakunin's *The Paris Commune and the Idea of the State*: 'The state is like a gigantic slaughterhouse or a cemetery; there, in the shadow and on the pretext of representing the general interest, all the real aspirations, all the living forces of a country give themselves willingly to the slaughter.'"[61] Yet Trevor Stark, in his own remarkable thinking about Ball, argues that both Ball and Schmitt were taken by Sorel in his *Réflexions sur la violence* (1908) as the prodigal of Bakunin's anarchism and a true danger, with Schmitt acknowledging Sorel's notions about proletarian violence as "a theory of direct, active decision."[62]

Certainly, at Cabaret Voltaire, the potency of anarchic actions are on stage in a continuous carnival of force-of-~~law~~. Yet we see within the cabaret's brief lifespan that it isn't the artistic mirror of insurrection that Ball turns away from. It's what he turns toward in its place. In his entreaties to himself, the whisper of supplication, of a desire for order in place of aesthetic refutation, continues to press on him. His fascination with power and rule only intensifies. Germany's spirit and spirituality, hierarchy and devotion, the beckoning of higher authority, keep echoing, even years later. So he writes on May 25, 1921: "Obedience is renunciation of belongings. Only the one who does not listen to himself can hear."[63]

Ball lives in this sequence of cascading impulses. He wants to create a new form of Gesamtkunstwerk in the shape of a cabaret at the same time that he wants to stand apart from it. Then, he wants all of Germany to be unified in a single identity, a monolith of obedience. He transfers this urgency, this anxiety for wholeness. The artistic state of exception that remains the hallmark of his contribution to what became Dada is over for Ball, or almost over—he and Hennings return briefly to Zurich from their home in Vira-Magadino to join Tzara in the creation of the short-lived Galerie Dada, whose exhibitions run from March to May of 1917—and it leads to a new, more provocative ideology of the totalizing impulse.

The great irony is that what Ball didn't want for the cabaret, as it became the Dada of Tzara's evolving corporate ambitions, is what he wanted more extremely and completely in other realms of authority. The language of his *Lautgedichte* offered this prospect of a liberating non-sense. Yet it was inchoate, just as the happenings at Spiegelgasse 1 were for Ball finally too weak a refutation and only pointed him toward a more directly authoritarian urge in his political evolution. He sought to find himself within a larger scheme than the cabaret's artistic state of exception made space for. To know the truth about oneself, to tell it, is to understand not only its cost but also its source and how to produce it in others.

Cabaret Voltaire was one such expression, though insufficient toward that more messianic reflection, seeing himself as an "abbreviation" of the German people as a whole. What follows in Ball's life has the character of a nonfiction *Bildungsroman*. His route leads along a peripatetic path literally and philosophically, shuttling from Zurich to Vira-Magadino, Bern, Agnuzzo, Munich, Rome, Vietri-Marina, Lugano, and Sant'Abbondio over his last decade; moving from the cabaret to social formations that entwine the directly political and the ecstatically theological, advancing toward prospects of the most absolutist totalism.

Ball's history with Schmitt, begun in 1919 and culminating in rupture in 1924 over the reception of Ball's revised version of *Critique of the German Intelligentsia*, published as *The Consequences of the Reformation*,[64] encapsulates his search for a self that can be rid of the world while living in it, that can recognize an ultimate truth that exceeds the aesthetic in an ascetism that he can embrace. The integers of the political and theological were already combined in the suffering ambition of Ball's calculus—witness his unpublished dissertation tying Nietzsche to the renewal of the nation, his constant calls for a purified Germanity, his attempts in his sound poems to perform a purified language intoned as a magical bishop, his reversal of disobedience into obedience, all with a dire weight so heavy that he writes in a diary entry on October 6, 1916: "The false structure is collapsing. Move away as far as possible, into tradition, into strangeness, into the supernatural; then you will not get hit."[65]

The power of Schmitt for Ball, the seduction of his ideology, is his conception of the hierarchical place of the political within a greater form of authority that underwrites, deepens, and sanctifies what the cabaret in its refusals, which were always a form of mourning, could never bring about. In his analysis of Ball's relationship with Schmitt, Stark adroitly summarizes:

> The groundlessness of the law, Ball asserted, did not have "just a juristic significance, but a universal one." "What is demonstrated" in Schmitt's theory of the exception, Ball wrote [in his 1924 review of Schmitt's *Political Theology*], is the "spontaneous emergence of the divine into the chaos of history, one could say: the political miracle." Indeed, Schmitt insisted that the exception was the structural correlate within the political sphere to the concept of the miracle in theology. Further, in opposition to the secularizing drive of the legal positivists, Schmitt famously claimed, "All significant concepts of the modern theory of the state are secularized theological concepts."[66]

Ball had written in his diary on June 12, 1916, that Dada was "a farce of nothingness in which all higher questions are involved: a gladiator's gesture, a play with shabby leftovers, the death warrant of posturing morality and abundance."[67] His complaint of moral failing underlines his longing for morality to be resurrected. This is the ground of Schmitt's turn of the political toward an immutability rigid with decisionism that shifts Ball from what he once considered the potency of mimetic irrationality toward what Schmitt, in an argument that aligns with sovereign dictatorship, calls the supremacy of Catholicism's "supra-rational" authority.

A curious nominalism is embedded in this for Ball, whose own reconversion to Catholicism in 1920 is of a piece with his magical bishop and, not coincidentally, with his rampant antisemitism, his imaginings of the *Blut und Ehre* of a revived and cleansed Catholic Germany.[68] It would even seem, according to the anecdotal remembrances of both Huelsenbeck and Ball, that "Dada," as the term of this simultaneously liberating and punitive irrationality, is the progeny of D.A.D.A.—the emphatically doubled double entendre of the name for this art with the initials for "Dionysius the Areopagite." Ball wrote in his diary entry of June 18, 1921, "When I came across the word 'dada' I was called upon twice by Dionysius. D.A.—D.A. (H—k [Huelsenbeck] wrote about this mystical birth; I did too in earlier notes. At that time I was interested in the alchemy of letters and words.)"[69] Huelsenbeck, in his own reminiscences, spoke of the nomination of the term as "selective-metaphysical," which had associations both for him and Ball "far different from the 'nonsensical' ones commonly ascribed to it."[70]

In fact, Ball was actually referring to the late fifth-century philosopher known as the Pseudo-Dionysius, who wrote works on celestial and ecclesiastical hierarchies and was one of the subjects of Ball's book *Byzantine Christianity*, the first draft of which he announces in his diary was completed just eighteen days after this mention of "D.A.—D.A." This is all the more intriguing for the unifying principle that Agamben has noted in the Pseudo-Dionysius's works, which he claims binds the power of the Church to the putative power of angelic order in the scheme of heavenly choirs. Agamben calls this the "sacralization of power" and goes on to say, "Hugo Ball was the first to grasp the true nature of the Pseudo-Dionysian angelology."[71] Was it the case, then, at least for Ball, that Dada and the cabaret from which it rose always bore a trace of unity whose origins lay in theological sovereignty, a foundation harking back to that trembling child hanging on the priest's words? After all, as already noted, Ball bemoaned the plight of Germany's indirection and weakness precisely in such terms, writing, "The demoralization in Germany is a result of the lack of dogma and of canonical individuals, a result of the lack of an unequivocal model on which to base one's life."[72]

Ball's predilections had evidently long run in this direction, and with the opening of the last decade of his life, he rethinks himself, traveling from the incorporation of difference coequal with anti-rationality in the cabaret to his entire submission to the monolithic, to the suprarationality of the Church. He had claimed already in his diary entry of May 24, 1919, that he was "thoroughly cured of politics," yet that was still far from the truth of his fervent and ongoing considerations of politics in relation to faith and authority.[73] In his review of Schmitt's *Political Theology*, Ball seems utterly immersed and merged with the author's reasoning of unreason:

> In fact, the irrational can mean two things: the non-rational and the suprarational. In the state, the opposition of ratio to

the irrational always relates to the ordering of the unpredictable material out of which the state is made [Staatsmateriel], which must be handled with great care. It relates to the masses of people abandoned to their own intuitions, which are predominantly spontaneous impulses of the will, most often material in their origins and in their aims. In theology, this opposition points to the relation of the legal and the institutional to the inspirations of a superior, creative, spiritual order; it denotes their relation to the numinous, holy, and miraculous, to revelation.[74]

At another point in the review, Ball wrote about the "artificial irrationalism" that marks and mars Romanticism and its cult of heightened individualism, which "lays claim to an identity with the Creator" that can't be sustained. In the face of this is the "true irrationality" linked to Roman Catholicism as a "strict realization of the principle of representation," tying the earthly to the divine in a manifest and sacred hierarchy, as told in the writings of the Pseudo-Dionysius. Ball cites Pseudo-Dionysius in the review and writes that the "Pope is not the supreme prophet, but rather the deputy, the Vicar of Christ; he represents the absent, ecstatic, irrational person of Christ; he represents the community of saints (absent in ecstasy), the body of Christ, the Church."[75] How understandable, having put the fever dream of Cabaret Voltaire and Dada behind him, that Ball then states that representation "originates in the aspiration towards permanence and finality."[76]

He has traded the cabaret's artificially irrational artistic representations of a world of impermanence, in which the cabaret itself was transient, for an institutionalized irrationalism of ecstatic permanence—and one that will, after Ball's death, devolve in the form of the Third Reich to the vulgarization of ascendant power in the state itself. He finds in Schmitt and his politicization of theology a severe illumination. He assents, for example, to Schmitt's admiration for the French conservative polemicist Joseph de Maistre: "For de Maistre, the Church's value lies in its final decision without appeal. The words 'infallibility' and 'sovereignty' are for him *parfaitement synonymes* [perfectly synonymous]."[77] So Stark notes that "Schmitt's own moments of political decision revealed that while he conceived of political theology as a means to protect the law and the state from illegitimate existential

threats, in practice it provided the transcendental ground of legitimation for the boundless exercise of power in a total state."[78]

This is the permanent state of exception that the juridical order,
descended from divinity's law-above-law, now embodies—and Ball
notes this when he writes in his review that Schmitt's conception of
Roman Catholicism has "that pathos of decision that [he] described in
his earlier writings as 'sovereign dictatorship.'" It is in the next sentence
that we read the conclusion of Ball's own path, citing a quotation from
Schmitt's 1923 book *Roman Catholicism and Political Form*: "This world
of the representative is what gives the Church its power in three major
respects: 'the aesthetic form of art; the juridical form of law; finally, the
glorious achievement of a world-historical form of power.'"[79]

Ball's yearning for unity; his contempt for the Jewish Other, which
was a contempt for difference counter to what he embraced for the cabaret; his desire for a Germanity of homogeneous *Volk* and for sovereign decisionism . . . all of this was underwritten by his enchantment
not with reason but with a transcendent dictatorship of unreason that
ultimately yields to divine obedience. He wrote in his *Critique of the
German Intelligentsia*, "Knowledge multiplies problems, but rapture
resolves and simplifies them. Knowledge cripples and confuses; rapture strengthens and liberates."[80] Earthly politics must give way, and
he claimed in his critique of Schmitt's *Political Theology* that "the
sacrificium intellectus [sacrifice of the intellect] that the Church
demands for its dogmas, miracles, and sacraments marks the point
where, at all times, there appears postulated the inferiority of the
powers of reason in the face of the incomprehensible."[81]

This is where the last pages of Ball's diary take us. He is so enlisted
in prayerful thought, so removed from what had driven him previously,
that the world of the cabaret couldn't have been more distant, more the
work of another body in another time left unbidden. And yet at almost
the same moment that Ball is drawn to Schmitt, after the brief flowering
of Cabaret Voltaire when he warns against turning its anti-aesthetic
into a school, other ideas of how to create unity, other notions of a network aesthetics, are emerging from the zeitgeist. In fact, a new school is
emerging, its teachings offering another way to braid artistic practices
(and far more), another way to assemble wholeness.

The Senses

SMELL

••• And then smell, the sister of forgiveness. We remember through smell the *once*, the what was, and now as we pass a scent on a street or happen on it in a room, we're suddenly filled. I'm a boy again in summer in a Maine motel with my parents, with my sister still alive, because a small pine pillow in a shop on a rainy day in Manhattan forty years later, and which I've absent-mindedly picked up and held to my nose, brings her to me here, impossibly, but. To smell: a gathering of data, an apparatus of retrieval, finding place in time. We find likenesses, eyes shut, pictures of what we knew, know again, so that time is a scent of wholeness and scent is a navigator of days. Along with taste, it's the most intimate of reminders, invented to acknowledge and unveil, invented, too, to nod toward the mystery of things without the abstractions of philosophy. Invasive, pungent, direct, so that revulsion or drawing toward are involuntary signs of an Edenic *firstness*.

Even in sleep and surely in dreams, smell is everywhere with us, and yet in control societies, contemporary societies of technology, the potency of scent is so little used, yes, exploited for commerce, but as a political instrument useless because it's always the specificity of the autobiographical self that's burned into us like ROM. The political is the space of selves together and smell is a weak spatial sensor—odor, the poor traveler.

Through sight, through hearing, the body understands the measured distances of the knowable, while scent, even lingering, is best understood through closeness and density, just as it is with the tongue. All I remember in that flash of pine comes to me now: my sister whose large eyes, whose voice are barely a trace in the air, the slightest opacity of white without heat, yet still here, if only a surplus spaceless enlivened relic.

So unlike Heraclitus's river, smell stores replica after replica of moments, so that suddenly I return to a moment out of time, in time, to sew myself to another world. Isn't that what desire seeks, the scent of things in some way remembered to come again? *Quick now, here, now*, T. S. Eliot's spectral children call, half-images of leaf and shadow, disappearing into the woods. He must have remembered the smell of leaves there, too, dust moving in a shaft of light. The smell of dust, what is it, teaching us its *always*, though I know it, *say it*, its sense of end.

Six

LIQUEFYING THE BAUHAUS

• • • If you teach in an art school, if you administer one, if you're planning one, if you dream of being a student in one, look across your global map of art schools and their curricula. This is the twenty-first century, and yet an odd thing. . . . It looks more than a little, in fact quite a lot, like an earlier time, and a figure comes to mind who has just lived through the First World War—a disillusioned German, politically agitated, looking for the next thing. His thoughts run to a revolution in education in the midst of continual political upheavals. The year is 1919. There's much to be done, days of organizing funding, faculty, curriculum, spaces, but it is evening. Perhaps he's listening to *Tannhäuser* on the gramophone, imagining Venusberg—or, with more than a touch of private irony, he's listening to Mahler, something sonorously mournful, but of course uplifting.[1]

Here is a brochure—a manifesto, really—and on the cover is a stylized Cubo-Futurist woodcut. A Gothic cathedral and a trinity of stars suggest something almost hymnal, an illustrative doxology that looks forward as much as back. The brochure proclaims: "The Bauhaus strives to bring together all creative effort into one whole, to reunify all these disciplines of practical art—sculpture, painting, handicrafts, and the crafts—as inseparable components of a new architecture. The ultimate, if distant, aim of the Bauhaus is the unified work of art [*Einheitskunstwerk*]—the great structure—in which there is no distinction between monumental and decorative art."[2] (Already, eight years earlier, his Russian compatriots in the avant-garde, turning to old folk art for their new work, proclaimed, "Our future is behind us!"[3])

So it was for Walter Gropius, architect and pedagogue, who founded the Bauhaus in Weimar, the most influential art school of the modernist period (and still is today), whose doors opened on March 21, 1919, and who made a curricular solid-state circuit out of noise, as we will see.[4] As early as 1916, the idea of a new system to teach communication, imagining the equivalent of nodes of integrated production, of closing the spaces of technē between the handicrafts and fine arts, was fixed in his mind. That year, he sends a proposal to the Grand-Ducal Saxon Ministry in Weimar. The title: "Recommendations for the Founding of an Educational Institution as an Artistic Counseling Service for Industry, the Trades, and the Crafts":

> For the artist possesses the ability to breathe soul into the lifeless product of the machine, and his creative powers continue to live within it as a living ferment. [. . .] It cannot be denied that a gap exists in the communication between these two groups of vocations—the technological and the artistic—which must be bridged from both sides with a reasonable approach and much good will. [. . .] Where the clear foresight of some individuals has nevertheless led to partnership, unmistakable attainments prove that this approach promises a fortunate solution.[5]

There is the smallest strain of happenstance that the following year finds Gropius teaching communications in an abandoned Belgian castle, then decamping to Italy to instruct Austrian soldiers in the use of dogs to send messages behind enemy lines.[6] The arts, as he would come to reimagine their pedagogy, were a network of transferred messages across fields of disciplinary difference. The interdisciplinary curriculum soon to form and rapidly (if often painfully) morph during the episodic life of the Bauhaus invites network thinking. The linkages are not superficial. The lines between technologies and art at the Bauhaus are heavily drawn, with thorough studies of materials and techniques that comprise a nodal reciprocity, heralding what we've been speaking about all along: a network aesthetics of dynamic relations between multiple expressive disciplines. Gropius signals this in the 1919 brochure with a word and principle for instruction that speak of systematic integration and wholeness. He deploys the term *Einheitskunstwerk*, the unified work of art, and it is instantly clear that the long shadow of Wagner's "The Art-Work of the Future" has barely faded seventy years after its first publication.

Still, Wagner served an entirely different regime of politics and sinecure. When Gropius proclaims in the brochure, "The ultimate aim of all visual arts is the complete building!" he doesn't simply trade the music-drama for architectural production. No, he is actually expressing common cause with far more recent sentiments. His words echo those of Bruno Taut, his fellow architect-in-arms on the radical left. Already in 1914, Taut wrote in the house organ of the German Expressionists, *Der Sturm*:

> Let us build together a magnificent building! A building which
> will not be architecture alone, but in which everything—painting,
> sculpture, everything together—will create a grand architecture,
> and in which architecture will once again merge with the other
> arts. Architecture will here be frame and content all at once.[7]

In fact, such notions were in the air, filling the discourse of art school reform. As Rainer K. Wick notes in his history of the Bauhaus, "The *academy was outmoded*; it was 'finished as a vocational school'; that is, it was no longer in a position to fulfill its duty to society, to educate the future generation of artists in a manner keeping with the times (i.e., true to life)."[8] In the very year of the Bauhaus's inauguration, Gropius's own mentor, the influential architect Peter Behrens, for whom he and Mies van der Rohe both worked as young practitioners, wrote:

> The first priority is to consolidate all branches of artistic activ-
> ity that belong to the visual arts into a single pedagogical entity
> and to keep the various fields within an internal coherence from
> the shared starting level onward. [. . .] In this way, the future
> advanced school of art would strive for an intimate fusion and

intellectual interpenetration of the three main areas: architecture, the fine arts, and the building technology of the engineers. But there is yet another area to be counted among the visual arts, the so-called arts and crafts.[9]

Architecture is imagined afresh as an assemblage machine, a totalizing force to counter the roar and stench of the war's trauma and its uprooted wholeness with a call to return to the interior necessity of form and to outward functionality, to order. With Gropius, these ideas lay the foundation of a curriculum. The interdisciplinary finds a new site of development, a new relational space. This is my central focus here: not an analytical tour of the Bauhaus's products, which has been done so often and so thoroughly, but an inquiry into the idealization and actualization of its interdisciplinarity, of its curricular invention. Gropius, like Taut, Behrens, and other peers, envisioned architecture in the most fundamental sense of formalism: a supra-disciplinary structure built from artistic and technical means in the face of national dissolution; and with this structure, a reclaiming of social form, of unified community, extending from this model of cooperative coordination.

Industrial technology had long been seen as the engine of social fragmentation, certainly in the influential ideas of John Ruskin and his Oxford student, William Morris, both of whose writings and practices were closely followed in Germany. Famously, Ruskin wrote of the deadening impact of industrialism in Victorian England: "We have much studied and much perfected, of late, the great civilized invention of the division of labor; only we give it a false name. It is not, truly speaking, the labor that it divided; but the men:—Divided into mere segments of men—broken into small fragments and crumbs of life."[10] Instead, he, and Morris after him, as I'll soon elaborate, sought to revive the communitarian practices of medieval monastic life in which craftsmen of complementary handicrafts worked together. Ruskin's views of technological change were understood differently by the Germans, who saw them as advances and were intent on catching up with them, along with English training.

So, at the turn of the century, the architect Hermann Muthesius was embedded in London at the German embassy to follow British town-planning and architectural practices, which led him to investi-gate handicrafts and machine production as well. His 1904 book *Das englische Haus* praised functionalism over ornament, and on his return to Germany he was named the superintendent of schools of arts and crafts by the Prussian Board of Trade. The links between what Ruskin and Morris established and what the Germans sought in adapting their concepts and practices are a basis from which the plans for the Bauhaus rise.[11]

Indeed, in 1916 Gropius writes: "We could again establish a prosper-ous working community similar to those medieval builders' workshops we so fondly long for, where architects, sculptors, all sorts of artisans be-longing to many guilds—would coexist, autonomously accomplishing their portion of the common task."[12] Looking backward is to look for-ward. The arts, handicrafts, and technology must be joined to achieve a renewed totality, and as Jeffrey T. Schnapp notes, "Metaphors of totality permeate 1920s culture, whether at the revolutionary vanguard, where they are associated with technological utopias, or at the conservative rear guard, where they are associated instead with the restoration of nature, nationhood, and tradition."[13]

We've already seen this latter form of totalism unfold for Hugo Ball on his journey from Cabaret Voltaire to the outright order of the Church and his cries for a purified Germanity. But for Gropius, who regularly visited the same galleries in Berlin that were frequented by the found-ing members of the Cabaret and Dada,[14] neither the anti-aesthetics of Dada nor the levitating phantasia of technological utopias fit. His notion of unity and revival were shaped by an almost dire pragmatism. At the time of the political upheavals in 1918 and '19 that brought the Weimar Republic into being, Gropius wrote to the American architec-tural preservationist James Marston Fitch: "This is more than just a lost war. A world has come to an end. We must seek a radical solution to our problems."[15]

Years later, he would write, "I felt that the art of building is contin-gent upon the co-ordinated teamwork of a band of active collabora-tors whose co-operation symbolizes the co-operative organism of what we call society."[16] Yet at the moment of Germany's reconstruction after the devastations of the war, cooperation and antagonism are in deep contention. Just as Gropius is bringing out his brochure for his new vision of unity, Carl Schmitt is making his case against the Weimar Constitution as a corruption of Teutonic authority. Schmitt, whose writings were for a time so influential on Ball, as we've seen, publishes his *Romantic Politics* in 1919. He equates Romanticism with contemporary liberalism's failure to be decisive in matters of state and goes on to elaborate in a barrage of works in the early 1920s, such as *Dictatorship* (1921), *Political Theology* (1922), and *The Crisis of Parliamentary Democracy* (1923), that liberalism restricts the state to the rule of law and ethics in place of the political will to do whatever is required to assert its sovereign might.

Germany's direction is ridden with warring ideologies of democracy, capitalism, socialism, and communism that were playing out in the very year of the Bauhaus's inception in a morass of murders, riots, strikes, exponential inflation, and broken alliances. The state's administrative and political agency in relation to its citizens was brutally contested: what rights and whose rights were protected; what did liberal jurisprudence allow that should be tolerated in the interests of the individual versus the interests of the state; what was the state of exception by which national leadership could disregard the ethics underlying the liberal conception of society; and who had the rightful place to make decisions that would bear fundamentally and finally on the conduct of the state.

Schmitt's conclusion that the social contract must be revised in the name of state expression over private interests comes with his infamous calculation that to a degree underwrites Hitler's evisceration of Weimar liberalism and his establishment of dictatorship: the punitive political binary of friend/enemy. He argues for the unequivocal right of the state's political will to decide who the enemy is and the coeval imprimatur of authority to destroy it. Unity is to be understood positively only in terms of a ruthless enforcement of homogeneity, counter to what Schmitt euphemistically called "anthropological optimism":

> Because the sphere of the political is in the final analysis determined by the real possibility of enmity, political conceptions and ideas cannot very well start with an anthropological optimism.

This would dissolve the possibility of enmity and, thereby, every specific political consequence.[17]

The spatial imaginary that Gropius invokes is charismatically opposite to Schmitt's vision of a violent suppression of difference. Here is an open space to accommodate the unformatted imaginations of students, inviting a linkage of process and effect based on the contiguity of relational difference, of heterogeneous elements united exactly in "anthropological optimism." The assertion of Gropius's evolutionary material pedagogy, interdisciplinary to the core, is stated in that single sentence in his 1919 brochure already quoted: "The Bauhaus strives to bring together all creative effort into one whole."[18] Though Gropius is replacing Wagner's music-drama with architecture, Wagner is on his tongue when he addresses his very first cohort at the Bauhaus's inaugural exhibition of student work in July 1919. He speaks of unity as a "spiritual-religious idea" that will find through the reformation of teaching at the Bauhaus a "crystalline expression in a great Gesamtkunstwerk. And this great total work of art, this cathedral of the future, will then shine with its abundance of light into the smallest objects of everyday life."[19]

What's imagined is a world of relations among things: things talking to things, things spatially associated in a network of things, a hospitality among things in ways I've proposed earlier. What is essential in a thing—its internal properties, its materials, its craft, its style—is, in Gropius's initial formation, imbued with an immaterial *Geist*, a somehow spiritual internal life that enunciates alongside the techno-logical an orthodoxy of communion circulating among persons and products. The structural logic of Gropius's pedagogy embeds within all bodies, human and subsequently nonhuman, an anti-conflictual wholeness, a getting-along, a working-together.

No more succinct summary of his educational project exists than the Bauhaus schematic of 1922, originally sketched by Paul Klee and then formalized by Gropius, that pictures knowledge acquisition in four nested circular sections of the school curriculum. Its outer ring is devoted to preliminary learning about materials and forms. Next comes coursework covering the study of nature, spatial and color com-position, principles of construction and representation, and the study of materials and tools. Now the curriculum lays the students' hands more fully on the materials that constitute buildings, with workshops devoted to wood, metal, textiles, glass, clay, and stone; with another course focused on the application of color. At the center of these circles within circles is *Bau*, the total object of building as noun and verb, and here the teaching is about site, testing, design, engineering—the architect's craft. The students are not students but "apprentices," while professors are instead called "masters," just as the Latin *apprehendere* means to take hold of, to grasp, as the apprentice does the master's teachings.[20]

So the Bauhaus's courses begin. One hundred fifty students enroll. A hope of and for the new shines in Weimar, a new code, beginning with the *Vorlehre*, later called the *Vorkurs* (preliminary or basic course), invented by the cultic teacher and painter Johannes Itten. "The aim of the preliminary course," Itten wrote,

> is to unleash the creative powers of the students, to teach them to understand the materials of nature and to recognize the principles of creation. [. . . The students] must combine and arrange the different materials in such a way as to make their relationship visible through *intimate* connections. [. . .] Every object has a more or less obvious property as its main characteristic [. . .] linear or planar, bulky, voluminous, [. . .] colored, uncolored, rhythmic, non-rhythmic, structural. [. . .] But always, for *psycho-physiological* reasons [of perception], this main characteristic must be clear. [. . .] While teaching forms of artistic representation, what was important for me was that the various *temperaments and gifts* [of the apprentices] felt *individually* addressed.[21] (Emphasis added.)

After visiting Itten's class, Paul Klee writes to his wife Lily on January 16, 1921:

> After walking to and fro several times Itten approaches the easel with a drawing board and scribbling pad. He picks up a piece of charcoal, his body tenses up as if becoming charged with energy, and then, suddenly goes into action—once, twice. One sees the form of two forceful lines, vertical and parallel on the top sheet of

the pad; the students are asked to repeat this. The master checks their work, asks some of them to demonstrate it individually, corrects their posture. He then, beating time, orders them to do it rhythmically, and then has them carry out the same exercise standing up. What is intended seems to be a kind of body massage, to train the body machine to function sensitively. Similarly, new elementary forms [. . .] are demonstrated and copied [. . .] with several explanations of the why and wherefore and the mode of expression. He then talks about the wind and asks some of the students to stand up and express their feelings in the guise of wind and storm. Then he sets the task: Represent the storm. He allows ten minutes to do it in, then inspects the results. This is followed by critical assessment. Thereafter work continues. One sheet after another is torn off, flutters to the ground. Some students work with such élan that they use up several sheets at a time. In the end they all become a little tired, and he sets his Basic Course students the same task as homework for further practice.[22]

Other painters on the new faculty, notably Klee and Wassily Kandinsky (who had long championed his own notions of the Gesamtkunstwerk, the "monumental" work of art, as I've previously noted), spoke to the same essentialist psychological intentions in their teaching. Theirs was an envisioned peeling away, a revealing of the internal and unique self to be developed through programmatic expressiveness, producing sui generis things animated by spiritual energies. At the moment of the apprentice's initiation, a paradox is presented: systematic, scientific, procedural methods to produce the unsystematic, anti-scientific, pre-industrially crafted expression not of society as a whole, but of the epiphanic strivings and psycho-physiological intimacy of an individually gifted maker; each an isolated figure in the spirit of Romantic genius, whether a genius or not. They were, after all, in Weimar.

For German national identity, Weimar was a cultural home. After the ruin of the Great War and the political mayhem that followed, Weimar gave an ennobled spirit of legitimacy to the new constitution from that *annus mirabilis* of 1919 until the National Socialist German

Workers' Party usurped it in 1933. Weimar held up its historic citizens as luminous household gods for the German people: Goethe, Schiller, Bach. There in 1850 Liszt premiered Wagner's *Lohengrin*. A decade later the Weimar Grand-Ducal Saxon Art School was established; and in 1902 the architect Henry van de Velde founded the precursor to the Bauhaus, the Weimar School of Arts and Crafts, two years after Nietzsche died in Weimar. Creative genius par excellence was embedded in Weimar's sense of legacy. What Gropius found there—or better, heard—were two forms of noise that competed to overwhelm his concentration on a radical and totalizing interdisciplinary education: political and pedagogical.

Noise, which I've considered in discussing the *poème simultan* unveiled at Cabaret Voltaire, is the entire environment of data, events, entities, and sensations, of cognitive traffic brought to a point of dissonant congestion. And yet, as Michel Serres writes, noise is "our perennial sustenance, the element of the software of all our logic, [. . .] no logos without noise."[23] Noise, the background from which all foreground emerges, is an unformatted meaning-space constituted from other meanings, and which therefore implies a curating that must take place, a braiding of signals selected that brings forward a particular voice, a particular meaning. To come into the foreground, to make a clearing for this clear signal, there must be a mediation that discerns, that decides a protocol and revises all code so that sender and receiver share an address of knowing.[24]

So it was that the agonistic society of raucous political noise that surrounded Gropius and that led increasingly to the terrible sound of Schmitt's future Germany is filtered to bring forward the initial signal of the Bauhaus. Itten is the clarifier of the signal, the writer of an idealistic Weimar protocol, encoding the languages of making as individual, harmonious, and heteronomous—but given, in Goethe's famous words, to elective affinities. For Itten as for Schiller more than a hundred years before him in Weimar, the playfulness in individual creation, as Schiller argued in his *Aesthetic Education*, is as crucial to the life of art as it is to the art of living.[25]

What was at stake more generally in Germany was the restoration of German health, understood as a process of renewal that unified body, spirit, self, and country in the face of what was lost among the ruins. After the war, the movement of the *Wandervogel*—youth groups that embraced physical culture as a form of nationalist recuperation—spoke of *Aufbruch* (revolution) and *Gemeinschaft* (community) in a single healthful breath. They were thought of as disinherited youth, "a youth 'sensing in its incompleteness—*Halbheit*—the good and longing for a whole, harmonious humanity.'"[26] Of course, more frequently than not, that humanity was envisioned as whole only in its racially exclusive uniformity (Germanic noise from outside filtering in). Nor was the *Wandervogel* the only manifestation of yearning for wholeness that mixed bodily and spiritual exercise as a representation of incompleteness to be redressed. The *Wandervogel* attending the Bauhaus were joined by devotees under Itten's priestly example of Mazdaznan beliefs, a sect of Zoroastrianism that offered breathing exercises and vegetarianism as pathways to individual growth.

In keeping with the zeitgeist, the pedagogical scheme instantiated in Itten's *Vorkurs* marries the shapeliness of the progression of the courses to the flowering of creative individuality on the way, at least theoretically, to a unity of knowledge that resonates with Gropius's Bauhaus mandate. Each course is an individual disciplinary entity building the apprentice's unique expressiveness, beginning with the unfurling of the most basic exercises of the body: breathing, gesturing, marking. The expression is autographic, it comes through the body, through the hand's iterations, toward the most personal refinement. The pedagogy, the courses, and the apprentice are proposed as carriers of essence: the essence of drawing, the essence of each material, the essence of the apprentice's unfolding creativity into voice—mediation as purification. And yet essence wasn't seen as sufficient in itself, making the process of purification problematic from the first and amplifying the internecine noise that Gropius himself created in structuring the Bauhaus as he did.

While Itten's preliminary course preached essence and purity, a fundamental unity coming from within, Gropius had meanwhile produced a structural schism at the very center of the Bauhaus educational model: there were not one but two camps of instruction established. To the instructors of his apprentices, he offered the titles of Masters of Form (artists) and Masters of Craft (technical craftsman of traditional craft forms). At first, this seemed pragmatic and fit his totalist scheme of unification. In that very first document, his 1919 brochure, Gropius proclaims similarity and fusion (though perhaps he means learned affinity) in place of autonomy: "There is no essential difference between the artist and the craftsman. The artist is an exalted craftsman. [. . .] Proficiency in craft is essential to every artist. Therein lies the prime source of creative imagination. Let us then create a new guild of craftsmen."

Yet it would seem that a sentence is missing here. Shouldn't Gropius have written that, in turn, the craftsman is an exalted artist? His final proclamation is ambiguous. What is this new guild of craftsmen if by omission only one group of masters at the Bauhaus is exalted? Though it would seem that lack is implied all around. For the artist who seeks to get at the essence of things, essence is not enough. It is a never-enough—only the completion afforded by an excellence in craft leads to an exalted stature, while the craftsman seems simply to live on a lower plane. Before Itten has even arrived at his method, it would seem that Gropius is arguing that an initial principle of the Bauhaus model and the *Einheitskunstwerk* is that they can only reach their goal if the revelatory work of the artist is toward something not internal at all, but toward the practical production of useful things, which would be, in fact, the terra firma of the Masters of Craft.

But let us say that there's another elision, another leap of logic in Gropius's proclamation of a new guild, a leap that infers, in the spirit of the times, a pedagogical platform producing a new hybridity of producers whose interiority of spirit will have a productive form—a radically efficient assembly and unity of heterogeneous parts. Still, the introduction of the two separate groups of masters that Gropius established only bifurcates the reciprocity of craft and art as interdependent activities of a new art-in-life and life-in-art. The rejection of Itten's emphasis on interiority at first encouraged by Gropius now intensifies the trajectory toward the industrial, toward the idea also announced in his initial pamphlet—however tellingly paradoxical, considering his emphasis on the artist's improvement, not the craftsman's—that "the school is the servant of the [craft] workshop, and will one day be absorbed into it."[27]

In effect, the materiality of materials, the integration of forms, the interdisciplinarity of means toward a unified end always presented the autonomous artwork as a form that finally accommodates the noise within in order to move past it, just as the noise of the political must somehow be reduced to *sotto voce*. Gropius attempted to avoid political activities at the Bauhaus, to navigate shifting political waters, to continually beseech party officials in power for ever-diminishing funds among increasingly conservative hostility. What he envisioned and attempted was an apolitical way toward the Bauhaus's financial security through a revised pedagogy whose intention, however internally fractious, was to combine artistic and craft-based learning toward the standardized production of marketable goods. He theorized *through* practice, considering both maker and made as horizontalized components of art-in-life and life-in-art, anteceding in his own time what Gilles Deleuze would later describe for an informatic age as the "dividual" in place of the individual.[28]

The dividual is no longer perceived primarily as a political citizen under a regime of state power but as ever more an entity for commercial exploitation within a schema of "samples, data, markets." Gropius is intuitively on the way toward the dividualistic, a nodal structure both in the processual linkage of courses and in the idea of the new artist and his or her products that are all equally components in the serving of markets. The Bauhaus apprentice is turned away from a pedagogical economy of vertical development, celebratory in its interiority, toward a relational solution of standardized creative interdependency in the face of a fragmentary world, toward a nascent network aesthetics.

The intended purity of the Bauhausian signal is paradoxically its *im*purity, its purposeful integration of disciplines, methods, and approaches and its ultimate rejection of essence, isolated and inward. This expansive acclimation to noise, to the sustenance of background as foreground, recalibrates pedagogy as a more inclusively coded protocol. In 1922, in increasing conflict with Gropius's goals, Itten resigns (he can only hear one sound). Gropius defended his position, stating, "Recently, Master Itten demanded from us a decision either to produce individual pieces of work in complete contrast to the economically oriented outside world or to seek contrast with industry. [. . .] Let me at once clarify this: I seek unity in the *fusion*, not in the separation of these ways of life."[29] With Itten out, the curricular schematic now takes its place in history in its circular format as a network of material and skill-based courses. Its transfer of knowledge and data moves toward the central assembly of the *Bau* at the same time that it is centrifugal, dispersive—the production of products for the re-aestheticized retooling of a new world of *posts*: post-monarchic, post-war, post-agricultural, post-spiritual, post-individual—a reimagined social whole.

Seen as a network, the curriculum's categorical organization describes disciplinary entities of knowledge external to one another. Yet in the intention to articulate skills and knowledge as processual and teleological, with the building and products for its interior as acme and terminus, each of these rings and segments are sequential edges that create linked interoperable paths, things in communicative relation. In terms of these relations among things, as has been discussed, the curriculum is correlationist in its character. For Gropius, each discipline, in existing as a link to another, may have its own life but is only emergent in its *full* life through the other. In this fullness, it accomplishes its outward role as an element in its integrated production of artistic objects and practical goods for public consumption—a for-us that fulfills another "post" phase: post-Itten.

This relational condition of nodal entities within networks aligns itself with what Bruno Latour calls "formatting," which is an appropriate way to describe what training is, what master does to apprentice.[30] Formatting is the end result for another of Latour's notions captured by the word "plasma":

> No understanding of the social can be provided if you don't turn your attention to another range of unformatted phenomena. [. . .] I call this background *plasma*, namely that which is not yet formatted, not yet measured, not yet socialized, not yet engaged in metrological chains, and not yet covered, surveyed, mobilized, or 'subjectified.'"[31]

To the unformatted apprentice, materials and forms are plasma to be assigned purpose through an understanding of their internal properties toward the emergence of their related functions. The creativity of the apprentice, the plasmatic potentiality of the apprentice as maker, is like the materials to be encountered, formatted, and mastered:

inexhaustible but available to formal adaptation and practical use in the Bauhausian mold.[32] Gropius, by way of arguing his position, speaks of past academic models in a programmatic text he titles "The Theory and Organization of the Bauhaus," written just months after Itten's departure: "The fundamental pedagogic mistake of the academy arose from its preoccupation with the idea of the individual genius and its discounting the value of commendable achievement on a less exalted level."[33]

Along similar lines, Gropius wrote in his notes to faculty on February 3, 1922: "The Bauhaus has made a start in breaking with the usual academic training of artists to be 'little Raphaels' and pattern designers, and has sought to bring back to the people those creative talents who have fled the artistic working life, to their own and the people's detriment. It consciously strove to replace the principle of division of labor with that of unified collective work, which conceives the creative process of design as an indivisible whole."[34]

Now the exaltation of the artist is qualified, and so Gropius's nodal thinking, in rejecting the isolated figure of Romantic elevation in favor of a horizontalized pedagogical theory, formats a humbler apprentice, a dividual ultimately controlled by markets, producing relational things—networked producers for networks of marketable things.

The thingness implicit in this production process, the existential space of producers and products, of art-in-life and life-in-art once again, is an unfolding of heterogeneity that constitutes a nontotal total. On the most fundamental level, attention at the Bauhaus to interdependency among parts is intrinsic to practical training. Under Josef Albers, for example, students learn to "combine materials that exhibited haptic similarities to show how dissimilar materials could be used to reinforce visual effects."[35] The thingness of materials to which a workshop or course is devoted (as well as the objects produced) is scrutinized toward relational coordination, ultimately as a unified expression of *Bau.* Such nodal components affirm the conceptual Building while assembling its network of parts in practice, fulfilling the mandate of the *Einheitskunstwerk.*

On an institutional scale, human actors (apprentices, journeymen, junior masters, and masters in the full sequence of skill acquisition at the Bauhaus) and discipline-objects are entangled: a continually interchanged assembly that never totalizes but lies along the plane of potential completions of all buildings and each building in particular; a network of emerging surfaces in constructive play, support, and function that represent what consumption is. Consumption is a form of production, the production of taking away, of the endless absorption of resources, an ecology and economy. It is, once again, a never-enough, which is to say that as indexical and totalizing as the Bauhaus intends to be in its categorical, tiered curricular circuit, it is always dependent on the most fundamental level of relational development in the sense of lack that must be filled, refilled, endlessly filled with materials—the materials of knowledge and the materials of building—just as Tristan Garcia observes that "nothing else can be given to me except what I do not already have."[36]

This inadvertent koan for teaching is also a koan for networks in their perpetual state of transfer and ramification. The Bauhaus's pedagogical scheme and practice, with its linked nodal coursework and workshops as a form of network, affirms the unquenchable nature of consumption in knowledge and material production, and the way that the sequential linkage of disciplinary teaching and knowledge acquisition may be reiterative but is always operationally expansive. What this means in turn is that the educational action of the Bauhaus model depends on repetition and duration, making over and over to the point of mastery in the most explicit way of achieving the title of "Master"—at which blurred and liminal boundary the apprentice becomes an industrial producer. The lessons, having entered the body, are now output as component production that in aggregate become the house, the building, the city, and the economy and ecology of things.

In his 1923 text on the theory and organization of the Bauhaus, Gropius writes about the "standardization of units," of the ultimate accomplishment of buildings "conceived as an assembly of prefabricated and standardized parts."[37] He could as well be speaking of his teaching scheme as he is of material production, and Latour's metrological chains spring to mind once again. "Can we obtain some sort of universal agreement?" Latour asks rhetorically. "Of course we can! Provided you find a way to hook up your local instrument to one of the many metrological chains whose material network can be fully described."[38] Here is the moment of ulceration and eruption between Itten's insistently Romantic/subjective pedagogical drive and Gropius's assertion of an overt routinization, of the de-subjectivized, the formatted, the exteriorized.

The *Vorkurs*, with Itten's name attached as its inventor, is typically called the most radical and lasting component of the Bauhaus's educational legacy—the "Foundation" course taught in some version at practically every conventional art school to this day. Yet it isn't his version of the course that resounds, but the revisions that followed by Albers and László Moholy-Nagy. With their own systematic inquiries into color, material, form, and creative development, the expanded *Vorkurs* initiated the attempted holism of the overall curriculum. Albers begins his explanation of the preliminary course under the title "Concerning Fundamental Design":

> Economy of form depends on function and material. The study of the material must, naturally, precede the investigation of function. Therefore, our studies of form begin with studies of materials. [. . .] To experiment is at first more valuable than to produce; free play in the beginning develops courage. Therefore, we do not begin with a theoretical introduction; we start directly with the material. . . . [. . .] Learning in this way, with emphasis on technical and economical rather than esthetic considerations, makes clear the difference between the static and the dynamic properties of materials. It shows that the inherent characteristics of a material determine the way in which it is to be used. It trains the student in constructive thinking. [. . .] It counteracts the exaggeration of individualism without hampering individual development.[39]

Albers underscores the fundamental attitude intrinsic to the Bauhaus's revised pedagogy: the individual is encouraged to find the creative potential of his or her materials toward ends beyond the individual. As Jeffrey Saletnik notes, describing an article Albers published in 1924 about teaching at the Bauhaus in relation to traditional German pedagogy, "He questioned the emphasis placed upon the cultivation of the individual at the expense of the community" and "declared that schools should train students to meet the needs of contemporary life: 'a little history [and] a lot of work is what we're after.'"⁴⁰ In this overarching development of the apprentice, Albers's approach has much in sympathy with Moholy-Nagy, who had already expressed such concerns in a diary entry from May 1919, some four years before he comes to the Bauhaus from Berlin:

> During the war I became conscious of my responsibility to society and I now feel it even more strongly. My conscience asks unceasingly: is it right to become a painter at a time of social upheaval? Can I assume the privilege of becoming an artist for myself when everybody is needed to solve the problems of simply managing to survive? During the last hundred years art and life had nothing in common. The personal indulgence of creating art has contributed nothing to the happiness of the masses.⁴¹

Then, a year before joining the Bauhaus, in an essay titled "Constructivism and the Proletariat," he writes: "To be a user of machines is to be of the spirit of this century. It has replaced the transcendental spiritualism of past eras. [. . .] There is no tradition in technology, no class-consciousness."⁴² This thinking only underscores the Bauhaus's coexisting models of medieval guild society, socialism, the Wiener Werkstätte, and capitalism that point to the ideological instabilities, paradoxes, and unintended ironies inscribed in its history. In his alliance of the social and technological, in this flattening of economic and political distinctions of class and the ascent of technology, Moholy-Nagy affirms and echoes what Gropius had long been preaching and asserted anew with the school's exhibition of student and faculty work in 1923 that intended to show the world (under pressure from municipal authorities) what Bauhaus pedagogy had produced in its first four years. The title Gropius gave the show was "Art and Technology, A New Unity."⁴³ As Leah Dickerman notes, the exhibition succeeded in brushing away "the remaining cobwebs of mysticism" under Itten's influence, and what was put in place was a "thorough working over of the logic of the grid" that appears with regularity in Bauhaus designs.

The exhibition as an index of Bauhausian pedagogy presented unity precisely as a metrological chain of technology, industry, and standardization that includes artistic practice. It maps the methodological means by which the apprentice is formatted to produce works toward these ends. Yet Latour adds a caveat to his writing about universal agreement: "Provided there is also no interruption, no break, no gap, and no uncertainty along any point of transmission."[44] For Gropius and the Bauhaus, there are nothing but breaks and interruptions, continual noise he struggles to both accommodate and filter, adjusting his tolerance to a broader spectrum of signals.

Not only are there the ongoing perturbations of politics, not only drastic and constant funding problems, not only the contrarian subjectivity imposed by Itten in his educational approach but also, and endlessly to the last days of the Bauhaus's troubled life, the constant in-fighting among its teachers of art and teachers of craft—which was exacerbated by Gropius's decision, despite what he had said about the ascendance of craft, to pay the artists more and to refuse the craft masters voting rights in Bauhaus affairs. No matter what he writes and preaches, he is still being seduced by the conventional Romantic sense of artists as more individualistically prestigious. Hierarchy, à la Wagner, reaches from the *Bau* above all other expressive forms down to this bifurcation in pedagogical privileges in a system that struggles to accomplish actual commensuration.

When the Bauhaus is forced by political and economic pressures to leave Weimar, and then moves to Dessau in 1925, Gropius begins to call his nodes of practical training "laboratories" instead of workshops. The endorsement of standardized industrial means and dividualism for market production and consumption are evident, while Bauhaus pedagogy continues to be entrenched in artistic practices linked to flights of imagination and the oneiric. Bauhaus instructor Georg Muche underscores this when he writes in the school's magazine in 1926: "Art and technology are not a new unity; regarding their creative values, there is a significant difference between them. The limits of technology are set by reality, while art can only reach the level of true values if it aims at an ideal goal."[45] That goal is, therefore, contrasted with the practical; it is, in one form or another, proposed as superior to the practical, residing in some form of unearthly transcendence that rises from subjectivity and the pleasures of the senses. Yet it is the intensification in Dessau of the enchantment of art in tense relationship with the romance of machines and the logic of capital that concretizes the historical importance of the Bauhaus.[46]

In fact, it is only through these tensions of intersection in Dessau that Bauhaus pedagogy truly achieves its network condition: "Network is a place within which boundaries are drawn," Kai Eriksson states, "but at the same time the network itself is constantly brought about as a result of this boundary-drawing."[47] We can say of the Bauhaus, as we can of network aesthetics in principle, that openness is not itself the sole catalytic characteristic but instead the will of a particular protocol that enforces internodal relations. At the Dessau Bauhaus, Gropius's reassertion of the *Einheitskunstwerk* through technologically oriented teaching and production, in which object-based standardization is highlighted, holds the ongoing dilemma within of boundary-drawing that unsettles the network.

The words Gropius wrote in that first brochure in 1919 still linger, that art can't be taught, that it "rises above all methods," are in a sense a harbinger of the internal conflict to come. The Bauhaus's protocols among its teaching nodes form less and less of a circuit of contiguous concentric tiers of knowledge and more of a spiraling gyre, its internal pressures and conflicts accelerating its wobbling imbalance. It's precisely in this way that the conflicted pedagogical structure in Dessau embodies a network in which contingency thrives, constantly in motion, rewriting its own codes, struggling with overcoding, and in all of this producing something new and more sharply self-aware of its methods and goals: compellingly creative, often path-breaking, standardized, mass-produced objects nonetheless underwritten by the inner necessity of artistic materials and expressions. In the spirit of the school, these objects are woven together in the conversation of things with other things, discipline-objects with other discipline-objects, echoing that notion crucial to network aesthetics that Hegel stated: "what each is for the other as the other is for it."[48]

There can never be enough of this conversation, never enough production and consumption, and never enough even of the Gesamtkunstwerk per se because it, too, is foreseen as a lack, waiting to fulfill its true north of expanded relations, of a true othering. In an essay titled "Easel Painting, Architecture, and *Gesamtkunstwerk*," Moholy-Nagy states, "What we need is not the '*Gesamtkunstwerk*,' alongside and separated from which life flows by, but a synthesis of all vital impulses spontaneously forming itself into the all-embracing *Gesamtwerk* (life) . . ."[49]

In this, Moholy-Nagy also points to the consideration that the Bauhaus's tensions aren't the result of internecine struggles alone but were external as well—and should be. The *Gesamtwerk*'s formulation doesn't adhere to the ideologization of frictionless assembly that Gropius's initial schematic proposed for the Bauhaus in Weimar, with its three glorious stars advertising a supernal harmony within that still reflected the Romantic, inward genius of the artist. No, the Dessau Bauhaus and Moholy-Nagy's influence on it more fully reflect outside as much as inside, political and economic pressures that were always there, such that the aesthetic enclosure of the Gesamtkunstwerk was revealed as fragile, porous, the world and its contingencies seeping in, presenting instead this *Gesamtwerk*, which is, in fact, bracingly realistic and invigorating. So, Moholy-Nagy, pressing his agenda, remarks in his essay "Theater, Circus, Variety," which addresses the ambitions of Bauhaus theater, that "in today's theater, STAGE AND SPECTATOR are too much separated, too obviously divided into active and passive, to be able to produce creative relationships and reciprocal tensions."[50]

Moholy-Nagy wasn't alone in his idea that the Gesamtkunstwerk couldn't serve the times. Bertolt Brecht, whose theater shares an ideology of inclusiveness with Moholy-Nagy's notion of the *Gesamtwerk*, held the concept of the Gesamtkunstwerk in contempt. He stated: "So long as the expression 'Gesamtkunstwerk' means that the integration is a muddle, so long as the arts are supposed to be 'fused' together, the various elements will all be equally degraded, and each will act as a mere 'feed' to the rest. The process of fusion extends to the spectator, who gets thrown into the melting pot too and becomes a passive (suffering) part of the Gesamtkunstwerk. Witchcraft of this sort must of course be fought against."[51]

As Moholy-Nagy would have it, the *Gesamtwerk* is inclusive of a larger conception of what creative production is: a violence, a tumult, at once informed by ideological positions, aesthetic protocols, and artistic actions that are voluntary, revocable, and dynamic, as Darin Barney says of "network society."[52] To speak of the necessity of stage and spectator to be more interoperational is to speak of the agency of viewer-agents in a broader and deeper sense of viral infection, of a network far more open to external coding. The Bauhaus in Dessau can be seen as an exploit that hacked its previous pedagogical priorities. Pressures from without and within were mounting, and they were of a piece with Gropius's nature in the face of the tumultuous times to which, in his own way, he contributed. The proclamations of harmony rising from his radical vision always vibrated with a violence to the system that was felt both internally and externally, in the institutional structure he implemented that brought both creativity and strife to his faculty, and in the pugnacious dealings he initiated or was part of as the author of the Bauhaus, argument ornamented by the prospect of further argument.

A letter to a Lieutenant-General Hasse, November 24, 1923: "I have strongly rejected all attempts of political parties to use my institute."[53] A draft of a statement in April 1924: "The charges of a shift of emphasis from craftsmanship to constructivism is [sic] false."[54] A letter to Klee, dated October 13, 1926: "Your letter disturbed me, and I am unable to understand even today your refusal in a situation, difficult for all of us, which according to the events you are not judging correctly."[55] In a judgment by the district court in Dessau in favor of the plaintiff, Gropius, against Georg Büchlein, a local merchant and leader of the Citizens' Club, a public statement by a follower of Büchlein's is read to the court:

> If you, Herr Gropius, as the chief leader of this flock, were not so dishonorable, so thick-skinned, so cowardly, and so dishonest with yourself, you would have taken the consequences of the complete failure of your artistic abilities long ago. The thief, the intriguer, the coward lurks in every wrinkle of your sly, furtive face.[56]

Or on a less hyperbolic though hardly less inflammatory note, a report on the Bauhaus from 1922 by the artist and designer Vilmos Huszár, a colleague of Theo van Doesburg's in the De Stijl movement (Van Doesburg had hoped for a teaching job in the Weimar Bauhaus): "Everyone does what they feel like at the time, far removed from any strict discipline. [. . .] Where is there even an attempt to create a unified work of art, a unified configuration of space, form, color?"[57]

With its continuous breaks, gaps, and uncertainties, Gropius's networked schema of nodal disciplinary elements has the character of what Pierre Bourdieu calls "position-takings":

> When we speak of a *field* of position-takings, we are insisting that what can be constituted as a *system* for the sake of analysis is not the product of a coherence-seeking intention or an objective consensus (even if it presupposes unconscious agreement on common principles), but the product and prize of a permanent conflict; or to put it another way, that the generative, unifying principle of this "system" is the struggle, with all the contradictions it engenders.[58]

Field, system, and network accurately portray the dynamics of the Bauhaus and its configuration of coursework in which artist and craftsman, artist and technologist, workshop and laboratory, artist and industrial/commercial producer, art school and political scene, and iconomic and economic environments were in permanent conflict. Schmitt's vision of agonistic society, so close to Hugo Ball, shares something with Gropius's Bauhaus, too—more than might have been imagined. It's precisely this inconsistency, this network dynamic that allows the conflictual environment of standardization and homogeneity to exist alongside individual inspiration (the write/rewrite voluntarism of imagination toward its objects) and so to produce a network aesthetics of relational, modular, interoperable elements that, in fact, did not necessarily link. Everywhere within the historical record of the Bauhaus are these thin relationships of nomadic, shifting, co-dependent objects, be they courses or products, that are meant to be programmatically complementary.

Dickerman notes that the *Vorkurs* under Albers specifically eschews the nomination of knowledge in favor of experience, such that Albers writes, "we do not always create 'works of art,' but rather experiments; it is not our ambition to fill museums of art: we are gathering experience."[59] But she adds that experience is a freighted term, quoting Walter

Benjamin, who observed at the moment of the Bauhaus that any sense of normative experience was shattered, such was the Wilhelmine experience of Germany in light of the Great War and the calamitous upheavals, social and political, in its wake. For all its salubrious intentions, experience proves both an essential tool for the Bauhaus's radical teaching of unities and a matter of record of its internal discord mirroring the world outside its doors.

In all of this, we are hardly a breath away from Wagner's proclamation in "Art and Revolution," published, like "The Art-Work of the Future," seventy years before Gropius invents his new school: "To hold this art-work up to life itself as the prophetic mirror of its future appeared to me as a most weighty contribution toward damming the flood of revolution."[60] Gropius was far from alone in his desire to format a reaction to revolution that embodied socially useful expression through the integration of artistic disciplines to fuse art and life. Though he didn't profess to be a Marxist at the Bauhaus, the words hanging over the school's steel and glass entryway in Dessau could have been taken from the pages of *Das Kapital*: "Nothing can have value without being an object of utility. If the thing is useless, so is the labor contained in it."[61]

How closely those words align not only with Gropius's sentiments concerning the nexus of art, industry, and productivity in the fusion of artistic work and social benefit but also, unsurprisingly, with those of Anatoly Lunacharsky, the Russian playwright and cultural official who pronounced in October 1918, "A brotherhood of artists and architects will be born and will create not only temples and monuments to human ideals but also complete artistic towns. To link art with life—this is the task of the new art."[62]

Established in March 1920 by Lenin's decree, the Institute of Artistic Culture (INKhUK) runs parallel to the Bauhaus in myriad ways—at least briefly, as its existence was a mere four years, closing in 1924. Based on a program set out by Kandinsky, Varvara Stepanova, Aleksandr Rodchenko, and others in 1919, its ideas informed Vkhutemas, the "Higher Art and Technical Studios" that came into being at the same time, shared some personnel, sometimes conflicted in its approach to artistic production in support of the state's ambitions, and was itself shuttered in 1930 under pressure from Stalin. Nonetheless, the Russian formulations at the time rhyme closely with Bauhausian thinking, and there is some evidence that the year before Gropius founded the Bauhaus, he became aware of the new programmatic thinking coming out of Moscow similar to his own.[63]

The sources of resemblance run deeper. As early as 1905, Russian contemporary art practices, much in keeping with the Germans, fell under the influence of Ruskin's student mentioned earlier, William Morris, poet, visionary writer, and founder of the Arts and Crafts movement that was itself a model of practical interdisciplinarity. Its zenith was not coincidentally a building, the 1860 Red House, located in Bexleyheath, southeast London. Designed by Morris with Philip Webb, the paintings, furniture, textiles, stained glass, and a gamut of practical and decorative elements by Morris and his colleagues, within the container of the architecture itself, were conceived as a unified form. From art to politics, Morris's intricate sense of conjuncture underwrote his founding of the Socialist League in London, 1884.

In his novel *News from Nowhere*, published in 1893, the book's narrator falls asleep in Morris's time after going to a meeting of the Socialist League. He wakes up in a Socialist future, in which all property is common property and everybody does the work they want. At one point, the narrator's guide explains that "many of the things which used to be produced, slave-wares for the poor & mere wealth-wasting wares for the rich, ceased to be made. That remedy was, in short, the production of what used to be called art, but which has no name amongst us now, because it has become a necessary part of the labour of every man who produces."[64]

This is the logical conclusion of Gropius's own pan-disciplinary imaginary in which all laborers are creative co-agents of a production that embodies cultural and social unity. It is consonant with the aspirations of the Russians who would establish INKhUK, who sought a similar concord between the spiritual, ornamental, social, and practical. Art and industry were to be joined in a unified pedagogy. A speech delivered by P. S. Strakhov in St. Petersburg under the title "Technology and the Beauty of Life" precedes Gropius in arguing that artists should receive technical training and engineers reciprocally should receive training in aesthetics.[65] After the October Revolution, the emphasis on useful artistic practice only deepens. In 1918 the literary critic and cultural activist Osip Brik proposes a new school that would be an instrument of the new society: "An institute of material culture should be organized immediately where artists could be trained for work on the creation of new objects for proletarian use, and where they would work on creating the prototypes of these objects, these future works of art."[66]

INKhUK, akin to the Bauhaus, though whose political sphere demanded this specific proletarian trajectory, institutionalized a curriculum based on the systematic melding of disciplines toward productive ends—"the investigation of the analytical and the synthetic basic elements of the separate arts and of art as a whole."[67] The thinking at INKhUK and the work produced in Vkhutemas, the protean ground of Constructivist practices, instantiated the nodal interaction of disciplines. As Christina Lodder notes, "By studying painting in its color and surface form, architecture and sculpture in its spatial and volumetric form, music in its sound and time form, dance in its spatial and temporal form, and poetry in its rhythmic sound and time form, the INKhUK theoreticians intended to establish a scientific explanation for the intuitive element in creativity and so establish a scientific basis for art."[68]

Three types of problems were set out: "those related to the theory of different art forms; those related to the theory of the interaction of different art forms; and those related to what Kandinskii called monumental art or art as a whole."[69] The analysis of art was broken down into elements of material; color; space; time, or movement; form as a result of the interaction of all of these; and finally technique, or what we would call disciplines, including painting, mosaic, sculpture, and other artistic practices. At the root of the program was the ultimate emphasis on the utilitarian and the organization of life. As Rodchenko said: "All new approaches to art arise from technology and engineering and move towards organization and construction."[70]

Of course, technology, construction, and the whole of the modernist avant-garde's romance with machines was everywhere present in the artistic air. As I've said, the Futurists, Dadaists, and Duchamp's *Large Glass* assume the hybridizing of bodies and machines as the prerequisite (whether ecstatic, cautionary, or ruefully ironic) of the techno-topography to come. In Munich in the spring of 1920, the Soviet writer and diplomat Konstantin Umansky published the book *New Art in Russia 1914–1919*, in which he states that Tatlin developed Machine Art and writes: "Art is dead—Long live art, the art of the Machine with its construction and logic, its rhythm, its components, its metaphysical spirit—the art of the Counter-Reliefs."[71] The Dadaists read this in an adaptation of a section of the book for an article titled "Tatlinism or Machine Art," published in January 1920 in the journal *Der Ararat*. Five months later they produced a poster for an exhibition in Berlin that read: "Art is Dead. Long Live the Machine Art of Tatlin."[72] For Dada, the representation of machines is the perfect weapon to assault values of a failed humanism. For the Bauhaus and the Russian Constructivists, machines are turned clockwise: servants of a positive ethics, a way to embrace utilitarian means for the social whole.

As for the machinic revision of art and society that the Russians championed, so it was at the Bauhaus. In the biomechanical fantasias of Bauhaus theater, most formidably Oskar Schlemmer's *Triadisches Ballett*, first performed in 1922 in Stuttgart and then as the closing performance of the school's 1923 exhibition, the performers' bodies were rigged to the choreography of gridded Euclidean space; the figures abstracted in the spirit of a distanced, anti-Expressionist *Neue Sachlichkeit* (New Objectivity) that was entirely kindred with a technological sensibility; their bulbous, robotic bodies spinning in stiff revolutions like gears and tilting levers. So Juliet Koss summarizes, "This symbolic figure surpassed the limits of naturalism, providing an abstract, artificial model prepared for the challenges and delights of the posthumanist era."[73]

Schlemmer's theater work at the Bauhaus, which began officially when he took over the school's theater workshop in April 1923, seemed more than any other artistic expression there to reach wholly for the figuration of a contemporary Gesamtkunstwerk or even a more radical *Gesamtwerk*. *Triadisches Ballett*, more than any other single work of the Bauhaus in that period, captured the notion of the whole as more than human, truly horizontalized in its imagining of a new community, as

Koss suggests, of humans and nonhumans on an expanded plane: precise, explosive, metrological, encompassing.

Many of the works that issued from Schlemmer's workshop, including puppets and sets, music and lighting, reiterated the idea of the human as mechanical iterator, and the machine and machinic presenting something born of human systematicity and then exceeding the human. This posthuman, hybridized strain of transcendence was coincident with the embrace of a liberatory technological other that took seriously what Duchamp's mechanical bride presented as irony, though Schlemmer's theater was alive with its own seriocomic charm. As one observer wrote, "The 'new man' has become a 'marionette,' ruled by a higher, non-human and untamable power."[74] And yet Gropius was clear in his argument that the machine was always in service to the social turn in his shaping of the interdisciplinary artist: "The standardization of the practical machinery of life implies no robotization of the individual but, on the contrary, the unburdening of his existence from much unnecessary dead weight so as to leave him freer to develop on a higher plane."[75]

Meanwhile, the idea of the Soviet artist as *konstruktor* was imagined as a hybrid being, part artist, part engineer, creating a society in which it is no longer necessary to distinguish one from the other, nor the character of the works they produce. Boris Arvatov writes in a 1925 essay, "Everyday Life and the Culture of the Thing," that proletarian culture "will require the elimination of that rupture between things and people that characterized bourgeois society. [. . .] Proletarian society will not know this dualism of things."[76] The zeitgeist of the avant-garde reflected in the task of teaching, if locally inflected in Moscow and Dessau, nonetheless shared the sense of promise based on the ideologization of horizontalized being through the distributive powers of technology, craft, and artistic work, reaching toward the apex of a new productivism.

Educational space, certainly in the historical instances of the Bauhaus, INKhUK, and Vkhutemas, whether endorsed or suppressed, was political space, and it is all the more striking that the schools in Germany and Soviet Russia converge pedagogically from the antipodes of capitalism and communism. Their volte-face leads in both cases to prospects of dividualism: makers of discipline-objects-cum-practical-objects molded by networks of socioeconomic control that project the reformation of human use and so of human being. The pressure to produce the new hybridized creative entity—human and nonhuman, artist-konstruktor and artisan-architect, art-as-tool and tool-as-art—assertively converts the educational platform into a laboratory that seeks an inseparability between object production and social production. The artist who becomes a capitalist integer and the communist artist who is a laborer subsumed voluntarily or brutally into the social whole are both subject to contingencies of internecine historical struggles that bear down on their continuance.

"None of this," as Maria Gough writes about the fate of the Constructivists under Soviet industrialism—which can be said equally of the Bauhaus—"is to deny the latency of social engineering within Constructivism—a condition it shares with most other modernisms similarly convinced of the emancipatory potential of technological change."[77] The striving for a radical inclusiveness, for a new form of totalizing practice that could meet conceptual premises and external demands for profitable production simply tears apart these structures. For all of its extraordinary experimentation, its prodigiously creative faculty, its relentlessness under Gropius to foster an advanced interdisciplinary productivity, the Bauhaus was beaten down by political foes from within and without.

Its faculty and students can never agree on what the world should be. The signal-to-noise ratio, lifting and falling in quickening tempo, is a staccato modernist composition in itself. Gropius quits the Bauhaus in 1927, nine years after it began, exhausted. His replacement, Hannes Meyer, whose leftist politics are foregrounded in his leadership, lasts less than two years. National Socialism is ascendant. The Bauhaus, hounded out of Dessau, moves to Berlin under the new leadership of Mies van der Rohe, where it is no longer anything at all like a pedagogical revolution in interdisciplinary teaching and practice, but more narrowly an architecture program. In its final semester in the summer of 1933, when the Nazis shutter it, the winnowed Bauhaus has a total of nineteen students.[78]

As we've seen before, the unifying aesthetic impulse and that of social totalism verge on the chasm of implosive destruction. Boris Groys makes the argument in *The Total Art of Stalinism: Avant-Garde, Aesthetic Dictatorship, and Beyond*, however historically unreliable the argument is, that Stalin was the true Gesamtkunstwerk, a figure encompassing all practices in creative totalization, the total aesthetic being.[79] If this were so, it's best to use Moholy-Nagy's term and speak of Stalin as the *Gesamtwerk*, the utter fusion of life-in-art and art-in-life that he doesn't merely represent but *is*.

We remember the Rilkean *is* that instructs us in the equivalence of all things, of disgust and beauty, the real and the imagined, all made fluid, convivial—a talk among an immense and unending internodal symphony, an endless melody. If Stalin is imagined as the apodictic *is* for which the world is an infinitely elastic readymade, of course Hitler can assume the same creative zenith of aesthetic totalization in which all things as networks are little Hitlers. This is the total work of art as a totalitarianism logically extended from Hugo Ball's late theological conservatism, and it is conferred as a form of triumph by the Nazis, who champion Wagner's artistic project as a vessel of the Aryan spirit. The Bauhaus's circular schematic is recycled with pitch-black earnestness by the Nazis as a purely administrative diagram of control.

The Bauhaus is liquefied in 1933, like INKhUK, Vkhutemas, and the Constructivist movement in their own time. But liquefaction has its benefits. Its fluidity is a state of mixed bodies, traits dissolving, touching, reconfigured. Fluidity shares with networks the distributive condition, the nomadic state, the possibilities of intensities and flows. The fluid disciplines, of art, craft, technology, of meaning-making, of the conceptual and the practical, are momentarily combined in the stream of time. There is always a boundary, yet the entities within it do not unfold linearly but in a multiplicity of relational, interoperable connections, chattering with one another. The Bauhaus is a complex system of fluctuation and exchange, inclusive of interdisciplinary methods, a new pedagogy, but also a new creative type emerging (as networks are always platforms of emergence). The artist-engineer-proletariat-capitalist-producer, after all, is a type of invented reasoning machine produced in an imploding incubator that appears at the beginning of the twentieth century as an offshoot of the calamitous exigencies of war, revolution, technological acceleration, political experiment, and death and more death. In the case of Germany, and Russia as well, this formation of volatile sovereignty massively and violently denies otherness. In the face of this, if only for a moment, Walter Gropius as an othering machine attempts in Weimar and Dessau to reject the tyranny of sameness in the wake of bellicose disaster, his intensive new form of education an extraordinary experiment to undo stasis, which then, in an ultimate process of liquefaction, does what liquids do best: it spreads.

The Bauhaus becomes the primary pedagogical model for art schools across Europe, the United States, and Latin America for the rest of the twentieth century and into the twenty-first. The *Vorkurs*, as I've said, continues in various forms to be the standard "foundation" course for young artists. The hybridization of artistic "uselessness" (focused inwardly on the interrogation of its own means, and possibly antisocial) and productive usefulness (socially demonstrative and market-driven) touches every design program, architecture school, and interdisciplinary MFA program in some way. Deep in its genetic makeup, the group critique in art schools relies on permanent conflict, so present in the Bauhaus, of a community of simultaneously convivial and antagonistic producers enunciating territorial distinctions in making and thinking about making.

Gropius moves to Harvard, Josef and Anni Albers to Black Mountain College and to Yale, Moholy-Nagy to Chicago, where Mies also goes, both of them heading schools within what becomes the Illinois Institute of Technology. Mies ultimately spoke of the Bauhaus as a disembodied presence, simply as an idea: "The fact that it was an idea [. . .] is the cause of this enormous influence the Bauhaus had on every progressive school around the globe. You cannot do that with organization, you cannot do that with propaganda. Only an idea spreads so far."[80] Still, the Bauhaus in Dessau as a pedagogical apex and marquee actor in the formation of modernist aesthetics is more than an idea, of course, and in fact is prolonged through the images of an all-too-often unacknowledged figure of the Bauhaus, Lucia Moholy—Moholy-Nagy's wife from 1921 to 1934—whose sleek black-and-white photographs of the Bauhaus Dessau's exteriors and interiors, of its workshops and hall-ways and masters' houses, continue to circulate to this day as reliquary signs of what was and as Bauhaus advertisements in perpetuity.

For all of the ironies that implode the model of interdisciplinarity in the collapsing heart of the Bauhaus, what Gropius called "the common citizenship of all forms of creative work" has remained its abiding ped-agogical legacy and beyond it in complex, centrifugal, and varied regis-ters of being together.[81]

The Senses

PROPRIOCEPTION

••• To know where *is* is. Without looking, without smell. Where guidance begins, each limb calls its place, the inner ear directing its mechanical survey as if all the threaded navigations of the world were built into the blood so that knowing before knowing is a motor that whispers home-fulness to each body, and around me movement is a kind of singing each object makes, its mouth a form that lifts, a vibration I move through, re-butting permanence, feeling chance.

The objects in the gallery, aligned, opposed—a drawing of birds, some-thing glinting, a video low on a plinth, a heap of books, metal, wood—red with their magnetic poles. Their frictions turn me, a weight, a conversa-tion as I start and halt, feeling their colors, shine, an avoidance or assent, awake to the tightrope of each step that clarifies. And always forward, into, through, each limb implicitly a compass and ballast, eager to situate against the sibilant bendings of the Earth. For a moment the utopia of the moment, against the counterforce of unlove—movement as acceptance, the motive of the hunt.

Up above, the climb toward allegory, or first, as Dante taught, the de-scent on the tongue of fire before the reversal through grief into forgive-ness and release. My balance is that record, ours. The undergirding of all making gestures toward that state of the unseparate, the gelling proximity rotated, bent and lifted, of each thing placed, one with another, you to me as a coiled willingness of matter, break after break, set toward the seamlessly alive. I stood outside the door, listening, in a kind of vertigo, and the lintel of the blood called me to move across, there, into the inner ear of love's balance. The way when darkness on the horizon is the only light, movement is felt differently like an aperture opening or the suddenness of agreement. And turning then, accepting the invitation sight offered, I turned away, a scent unfolding of what forgiveness might be—*maleus, incus, stapes* amplifying waves of the unknown then becoming known, the otolith governing tilt.

Now, in the gallery, the level of my eyes parse difference and jointed meanings, as gravity and ambition impel me forward through the works assembled into an inquiry about concordance. I stop, as if each thing, even with my eyes closed, simply is, a mobile coalition of signals that enters me and slides, already half-erased by distraction, but remain under consciousness as residues, the mapped learning of routines an inventory of locomotion, inclination, recline.

To receive oneself in space is the long chain forward and back that scrawls its sense away from falling, my I in its hereness that gathering brings. And here I turn, animation and stillness, coming to the first place again in my mind. Being, a plank on a fulcrum, on one side all that I move through, on the other only afterness, the urge to find position, the signature of the flesh that writes its impercipience in space, and the networks of inhibition and excitation, of the ear's anterior and posterior canals, singing finally of what it was to be in *this* time, *for* this time, while I was here, and you—temporal, historical, the body as a gnomon between light and shadow, *quick now, here, now, always*. History, the sheer urge to find balance in the annals of movement, like the woven hope of the spider's web, or a snail's trace.

Seven

AFTERWORD AND FORWARD

• • • The formative nature of the interdisciplinary and networks is like geology, like symphonies, like spiders' webs, as I've said—something in us, in nature, that collects, weaves, bridges, snares, and holds, that aggregates. Which is, as this book has tried to present in many ways, the effects of the copula, of expressive causality, of every interior extruding the stickiness of shape. Bourriaud's derrick of European modernism drops its wrecking ball and foments the fragmentary, which finds its answer in the signals sent among things: attraction and assemblage. Networks are always an answer, intended or not, to the metaphysical question underlying the practical one of address and assignment, of how things should be with one another in life, networked life, the location of places strung together as concatenated meanings. This is the role of address. We have always looked to the stars.

If we consider where Wagner's first attempt at the artwork of the future has taken us, our twenty-first-century aspirations for community and connectivity take on a shapeliness of their own, in which all expressions move toward horizontality and lie across planes of interlinking protocols and nodes, often rough planes bristling with noise and intimately entwined with the turbulence and dangers of political life. So many changes over these more than 170 years have brought radically enlarged definitions of social organization, political organization, economic and technical systems of control, and with these what an artwork is and the ways in which constellated artistic disciplines reach toward compensatory commensurateness.

The roles of chance and contingency, of a fusing blur, of multiplicative effects, of networks with their infinitely rewritable codes, have shown that inside and outside oscillate perpetually, shifting the ground on the road to different intensities of totalizing ambitions. So Yuk Hui writes, "Becoming system means precisely the capacity to assimilate contingencies into its operation. That is to say, contingency is not something destructive that interrupts the causalities of the system, but rather that which allows the system to empower its internal dynamic."[1]

When the Bauhaus closed, in any case so bluntly deformed from its principles of radical disciplinary integration, many of its crucial figures performed their virological task of disseminating pedagogies that have led to the broadest forms of research-based art practices today that fall under the term "transdisciplinary" as well as "interdisciplinary." These practices are inclusive of every branch of esoteric and mainstream learning—whether quantum entanglement, post-post-structuralism, citations of the Frankfurt School, folklore or the reconstruction of various literary canons, gender studies, critical race theory, film theory, neurobiology, artificial intelligence—always expanding, based on each instance of artistic curiosity, need, and predilection. All instantiate the fundamental inclination toward the horizon of wholeness and the longing for (and questioning of) being together.

At the start of this book, I mentioned names of some of the contemporary artists who can easily be characterized by network aesthetic behaviors. It would be redundant to state them again, and so many more would need to be added as time passes. It's more useful to restate that from the first sentences of this history and theory of interdisciplinary practices, in which technology has carried its distributive capabilities continually farther and encouraged the erasure of divides, what has been described is that things in their thingness melt into other things, that there is always the instability and impermanence of fixed identity, the desire and demand for difference, the importance of identity as an assertion of collective rights, while there is also Adorno's argument for the necessity of non-identity, and in all, the reminder implicit in Lucretius's idea of the clinamen, of raining change at the base of matter that's timeless and fills the air.

The interdisciplinary is a speculum mirroring the world and a mirror for the world. In the interdisciplinary, there's a grasping for connection and structural evidence of a world that lives in an immense, still growing, and quickly growing meshwork of connectivity. What generative artificial intelligence now brings is still a more radical example of the active entanglement of all epistemic marks, of all knowledge and making infinitely open to combination, extraordinary and terrifying, creative and destructive, only echoing what we've seen as the double-sided nature of totalism's optimism and toxicity.

What emerges from this study of canonical European modernism's early interdisciplinary practices, in their range and adaptation to social urgencies, technological leaps, and political heterodoxies, is that each embodies traits of network aesthetics—an expression of wholenesses that are never total, but are communities of contingency and will, and that test the capacity to be self, other, and constituents within systems of communicative aggregation. Each practice is a fold-over space, streaming with strains of heterogeneous materials brought into constellated meaningfulness.

It can be said simply enough that interdisciplinary artists, now as before, find their ways toward understanding space, understanding their bodies, their notions of conscious self and of otherness, of isolated being and social action, of the legitimacy exchange of beings together. Each artist's attempt wants form, wants shape, and throws every energy into the making of what have been imagined as Gesamtkunstwerk, *Gesamtwerk*, *Einheitskunstwerk* . . . containers of the many-as-one, the monumental streaming of wholeness. Yet wholeness, it would seem, is only a horizon; and the interdisciplinary, finally, in its sense of melting and melding and flux, is a specimen of the frailty of things and the turbulence at the center of every life.

ACKNOWLEDGMENTS

Over the years that I've worked on this subject of the interdisciplinary urge in artistic practices and how it came to be, there have been many contributors to my thinking—people who have suggested different readings and other passageways. There have been colleagues and friends engaged in conversations, interview subjects, editors of my writing, supporters in different ways, starting with Glenn Lowry, director of New York's Museum of Modern Art, who first mentioned to me in passing one day at an art fair the prevalence of installation works on view (as a prime example of interdisciplinary art), which led me to begin to think about this and research an article about it for *The New York Times*. Subsequently, I based an entire series of course lectures on the subject at Yale University's School of Art, when I served there as a Senior Critic—for which I want to thank my former colleagues at Yale, Peter Halley, Jessica Stockholder, the late Chip Benson, and Robert Storr.

Many others have allowed me to think with them about the subject in general or about specific artists or, in fact, about themselves as practitioners. Cathy Leff, former director of the Wolfsonian at Florida International University, granted me time as a visiting scholar in the museum's library and archives while researching the Bauhaus. Jennifer

Tobias, then a librarian at the Museum of Modern Art, was endlessly helpful over many years as I did research there.

In various conversations with the artists Marina Abramović, Matthew Barney, Liam Gillick, Ann Hamilton, Thomas Hirschhorn, Kimsooja, Shirin Neshat, Raqs Media Collective, Shazia Sikander, Kiki Smith, Rirkrit Tiravanija, and Pablo Helguera, I learned more about the artists' concerns in the making of their objects, images, performances, and installations. And there are many fellow curators, theorists, and scholars to thank for their generosity of friendship and intellectual interrogation of the subject of interdisciplinary practice: Bruce Altshuler, Daniel Birnbaum, Francesco Bonami, Saskia Bos, Clémentine Deliss, Thierry de Duve, Emma Enderby, Albert Gelpi, Patrick Jagoda, David Joselit, Manuel DeLanda, Richard Flood, RoseLee Goldberg, Tim Griffin, Hou Hanru, Yuk Hui, Chrissie Iles, Daniel Kunitz, Patricia Olynyk, Stephanie Owens, Noam Segal, Terry Smith, Mick Wilson, Brian Kuan Wood, and Raphael Zagury-Orly.

For inviting me to bring the Yale lectures to the School of Visual Arts in New York, where I subsequently joined the faculty and founded the master's degree program in curatorial practice, I want to thank President David Rhodes, former Provost Jeffrey Nesin, and chair of the MFA in Art Practice, David A. Ross. I am grateful to Ursula K. Heise, then at Stanford University, for bringing me to the Modern Thought & Literature program to pursue my research. I want to thank Jeffrey T. Schnapp at Harvard University, Pamela M. Lee at Yale University, and Fred Turner at Stanford University, all of whom read versions of these chapters and offered their comments. Thanks must also go to Joseph Masheck, my first mentor as an undergraduate at Columbia University, who invited me to contribute to a Festschrift in his honor, the book *Mostly Modern: Essays in Art and Architecture*, published by Hudson Hills Press in 2015, in which an earlier version of my text on Cézanne—half of the chapter "Paul/Marcel. Two Bodies"—appeared.

My gratitude goes to Bronwyn Bevan for so many things, including her patience during the writing of this book and her thoughtful review of its pages.

And finally, I want to express my thanks to the various universities, academies, and organizations that invited me to lecture on the subjects that fill these pages: Bezalel Academy of Arts and Design, Tel Aviv; Central Academy of Fine Arts, Beijing; Curtin University, Perth; Dublin Institute of Technology; Independent Curators International, New York; Ohio State University, Columbus; Skidmore College, Saratoga Springs; Städleschule, Frankfurt am Main; Storefront for Art and Architecture, New York; Teachers College of Columbia University, New York; Universidad de los Andes, Bogotá; University of Chicago; University College London; University of Michigan, Ann Arbor; Valand Academy, Gothenburg; Washington University, St. Louis; and the Zurich University of the Arts.

NOTES

Chapter 1: A Cabinet of Concepts/Network Aesthetics

1. Albert Gelpi, *American Poetry After Modernism: The Power of the Word* (New York: Cambridge University Press, 2015), 3.

2. For an understanding of fragmentation in the modernist period, an essential book is Stephen Kern, *The Culture of Time and Space, 1880–1918* (Cambridge, MA: Harvard University Press, 1983).

3. Gertrude Stein, cited in Kern, *Culture of Time and Space,* 288. His chapter on the First World War is entitled "The Cubist War."

4. Umberto Boccioni et al., "The Exhibitors to the Public, 1912," in *Futurist Manifestos,* edited by Umbro Appolonio, translated by Robert Brain, R. W. Flint, J. C. Higgitt, and Caroline Tisdal (Boston: MFA Publications, 2001), 47.

5. Carol Oja, "George Antheil's *Ballet Mécanique* and Transatlantic Modernism," in *A Modern Mosaic: Art and Modernism in the United States,* edited by Townsend Ludington (Chapel Hill: University of North Carolina Press, 2000), 185.

6. See F. T. Marinetti and Filippo Tommaso, "The Futurist Manifesto," in *Futurism: An Anthology,* edited by Lawrence Rainey, Christine Poggi, and Laura Wittman (New Haven: Yale University Press, 2009), 49–53.

7. Le Corbusier, *Towards a New Architecture,* translated by Frederick Etchells (New York: Dover Publications, 1986), 95. Originally published as *Vers une architecture* (Paris: Les Éditions G. Crès et Cie, 1923).

8. Clement Greenberg, "Modernist Painting," in *Modern Art and Modernism: A Critical Anthology,* edited by Francis Frascina and Charles Harrison

(New York: Harper & Row, 1982), 5–10. Of course, Greenberg's formalism, doctrinal as he wished it to be, has been contested many times over. For example, see Robert Storr, "No Joy in Mudville: Greenberg's Modernism Then and Now," in *Modern Art and Popular Culture: Readings in High and Low*, edited by Kirk Varnedoe and Adam Gopnik (New York: The Museum of Modern Art, 1990), 160–91.

9. Hal Foster et al., *Art Since 1900: Modernism, Antimodernism, Postmodernism* (London: Thames & Hudson, 2004), 23.

10. Nicolas Bourriaud, *The Randicant* (New York: Lukas & Steinberg, 2009), 180–81. And see previous remarks concerning the modernist inclination toward images of fragmentation and its influence on subsequent art, 178.

11. Jacques Rancière, "Communists Without Communism?" in *The Idea of Communism*, edited by Costas Douzinas and Slavoj Žižek (London: Verso, 2010), 170.

12. Hal Foster, *Return of the Real: The Avant-Garde at the End of the Century* (Cambridge, MA: MIT Press, 2001), x.

13. In terms of contemporary cultural production, computation, and world-building, see Brian Kuan Wood, "Insurgency of Life," *e-flux journal*, no. 109 (May 2020).

14. In his essay "Curating, Exhibitions, and the *Gesamtkunstwerk*," the curator Hans Ulrich Obrist notes his own Gesamtkunstwerk genealogy, somewhat similar to my own, though reaching back to the French Revolutionary architecture of Étienne-Louis Boullée and the German romanticism of Philipp Otto Runge and Caspar David Friedrich. He relates this to Harald Szeemann's exhibition *Der Hang zum Gesamtkunstwerk*, held at the Kunsthaus Zürich, February–April 1983, that presents a different set of contemporary artists. Obrist remarks that Szeemann didn't see in the works he chose any kind of totalitarian urge, which implies, of course, that this urge is implicit in the Gesamtkunstwerk. See Obrist, *Ways of Curating* (New York: Faber and Faber, 2014), 30.

15. Though the term is used in an essay of the same title by Warren Sack in *Database Aesthetics: Art in the Age of Information Overflow*, edited by Victoria Vesna (Minneapolis: University of Minnesota Press, 2007), 183–210, his thinking is about interface design and bears no resemblance to my concerns. Patrick Jagoda's *Network Aesthetics* (Chicago: University of Chicago Press, 2016) is foundational, though my basis for this study in European modernism offers a different approach. Jagoda's book is not an art history text, does not cover the historical period or, for that matter, modernism in general, and focuses on American popular culture in novels, movies, TV shows, and video games as representative of interconnected contemporary life.

16. Jagoda, *Network Aesthetics*, 3.

17. Pamela M. Lee, *Forgetting the Art World* (Cambridge, MA: MIT Press, 2013), 21. Lee cites Lawrence Alloway's prescient essay "Network: The Art World Described as a System," *Artforum* 11, no. 1 (September 1972): 28–32.

18. The anthology *Networks*, edited by Lars Bang Larsen (Cambridge, MA: MIT Press, 2014), offers a range of essays on networks, network theory, and the cross-section of network thinking and artistic practice. It includes an excerpt from Roy Ascott's essay "Is There Love in the Telematic Embrace?" *Art Journal* 49, no. 3 (Fall 1990): 76–83.

19. Kris Cohen, *Never Alone, Except for Now: Art, Networks, Populations* (Durham: Duke University Press, 2017), 32.

20. Robert Frodeman, Julie Thompson Klein, Carl Mitcham, and J. Britt Holbrook, eds., *The Oxford Handbook of Interdisciplinarity* (Oxford: Oxford University Press, 2010). For an excellent study of the formation of academic literary studies and the incursion of interdisciplinarity, see Joe Moran, *Interdisciplinarity* (New York: Routledge, 2002).

21. Julie Thompson Klein, *Crossing Boundaries: Knowledge, Disciplinarities, and Interdisciplinarities* (Charlottesville: University Press of Virginia, 1996), 1.

22. Rosalind Krauss, "Sculpture in the Expanded Field," *October* 8 (Spring 1979): 30–44; Miwon Kwon, *One Place After Another: Site-Specific Art and Locational Identity* (Cambridge, MA: MIT Press, 2002).

23. Nicolas Bourriaud, *Relational Aesthetics*, translated by Simon Pleasance and Fronza Woods (Dijon: Les Presses du Réel, 2002). In relation to Bourriaud's text, see Claire Bishop, *Artificial Hells: Participatory Art and the Politics of Spectatorship* (London: Verso, 2012). See also Bishop, ed., *Participation* (London: Whitechapel, 2006); Rudolf Frieling, ed., *The Art of Participation: 1950 to Now* (New York: Thames & Hudson, 2008); and Bishop, *Disordered Attention: How We Look at Art and Performance Today* (London: Verso, 2024).

24. Claire Bishop, *Installation Art: A Critical History* (London: Tate Publishing, 2005), 133. Other studies devoted to installation art survey the field with an eye largely toward examples rarely reaching back past the last half century. None of them offers a full philosophical or theoretical grounding, as useful as they are. See Erika Suderburg, ed., *Space, Site, Situation: Situating Installation Art* (Minneapolis: University of Minnesota Press, 2000); Julie H. Reiss, *From Margin to Center: The Spaces of Installation Art* (Cambridge, MA: MIT Press, 2001); Mark Rosenthal, *Understanding Installation Art: From Duchamp to Holzer* (New York: Prestel, 2003); Nicholas de Oliveira, Nicola Oxley, and Michael Petry, *Installation Art in the New Millennium: The Empire of the Senses* (New York: Thames & Hudson, 2004).

25. Boris Groys, "Politics of Installation," *e-flux Journal*, no. 2 (January 2009).

26. Juliane Rebentisch, *Aesthetics of Installation Art*, translated by Daniel Hendrickson and Gerrit Jackson (Berlin: Sternberg Press, 2012), 108–9.

27. Rosalind Krauss, *"A Voyage on the North Sea": Art in the Age of the Post-Medium Condition* (London: Thames & Hudson, 1999). Krauss's text was originally delivered as the Walter Neurath Memorial Lectures at Birbeck College, University of London, in 1992. Related to this, Hal Foster remarks in an almost offhand

fashion, "now that the transgression of the mediums is tired," in an interview contributed to the publication *de-, dis-, ex-*. See Foster, "Trauma Studies and the Interdisciplinary: An Interview," *The Anxiety of Interdisciplinarity: de-, dis-, ex-,* vol. 2 (London: BACKless Books, 1998).

28. David Joselit, *After Art* (Princeton: Princeton University Press, 2013), 55.

29. See, for example, Dick Higgins's brief essay from 1966, "Intermedia," in *Multimedia: From Wagner to Virtual Reality*, edited by Randall Packer and Ken Jordan (New York: W. W. Norton & Company, 2001).

30. G.W.F. Hegel, *Phenomenology of Spirit*, translated by A. V. Miller (Oxford: Oxford University Press, 1977), 18.

31. Martin Heidegger, *Hegel's Phenomenology of Spirit*, translated by Purvis Emad and Kenneth Maly (Bloomington: Indiana University Press, 1988), 113.

32. Fred Moten, *The Universal Machine* (Durham, NC: Duke University Press, 2018), 251.

33. Gilles Deleuze and Félix Guattari, *A Thousand Plateaus: Capitalism and Schizophrenia*, translated by Brian Massumi (Minneapolis: University of Minnesota Press, 1987), 9.

34. Benjamin H. Bratton, *The Stack: On Software and Sovereignty* (Cambridge, MA: MIT Press, 2015), 197.

35. Luciana Parisi, *Contagious Architecture: Computation, Aesthetics, and Space* (Cambridge, MA: MIT Press, 2013), 66–67.

36. Alexander R. Galloway and Eugene Thacker, *The Exploit: A Theory of Networks* (Minneapolis: University of Minnesota Press, 2007), 30.

37. Ilya Kabakov, *On the "Total" Installation*, translated by Cindy Martin (Ostfildern: Cantz Verlag, 1995), 54.

38. Galloway and Thacker, *Exploit*, 32.

39. Bratton, *Stack*, 46.

40. See C. Gordon, ed., *Power/Knowledge: Selected Interviews and Other Writings, 1972–1977* (New York: Pantheon Books, 1980), 194–96.

41. Immanuel Kant, *Critique of Teleological Judgment* [1790], translated by James Creed Meredith (Oxford: Clarendon Press, 1928), 31, cited in Moran, *Interdisciplinarity*, 9.

42. For a related remark in describing this effect, see Pierre Bourdieu, *The Field of Cultural Production* (New York: Columbia University Press, 1993), 229.

43. Bratton, *Stack*, 46.

44. Gilles Deleuze and Claire Parnet, *Dialogues II* (New York: Columbia University Press, 2002), 69.

45. Fred Turner, *From Counterculture to Cyberculture: Stewart Brand, the Whole Earth Network, and the Rise of Digital Utopianism* (Chicago: University of Chicago Press, 2006), 25–26.

46. DeLanda, *Deleuze: History and Science* (New York: Atropos Press, 2010), 15.

47. Galloway and Thacker, *Exploit*, 67.

48. Clay Shirky, "Power Laws, Weblogs, and Inequality," cited in Galloway and Thacker, *Exploit*, 18.

49. Galloway and Thacker, *Exploit*, 34, 36.

50. Jagoda, *Network Aesthetics*, 29.

51. Bruno Latour, *Reassembling the Social: An Introduction to Actor-Network-Theory* (New York: Oxford University Press, 2005), 201–2.

52. Anna Munster, *An Aesthesia of Networks: Conjunctive Experience in Art and Technology* (Cambridge: MIT Press, 2013), 183.

53. Bratton, *Stack*, 37.

54. Legacy Russell, *Glitch Feminism* (New York: Verso, 2020), 19.

55. Maurice Merleau-Ponty, *Maurice Merleau-Ponty: Basic Writings*, edited by Thomas Baldwin (New York: Routledge, 2004), 129–30.

56. Latour, *Reassembling the Social*, 211–12.

57. Fredric Jameson, *The Hegel Variations: On the Phenomenology of Spirit* (London: Verso, 2010), 83.

58. This sequence of quotations from Hegel appears in: *Phenomenology of Spirit*, 113; 263–64; 145; 265; *Outlines of the Philosophy of Right*, translated by T. M. Knox (New York: Oxford University Press, 2008), 228. In *The Hegel Variations*, Jameson agitates for a reading of Hegel's complexity in the formation of his dialectical logic structure as a way to mediate the troubling teleology of the self subsumed by the state.

59. Michael Hardt and Antonio Negri, *Empire* (Cambridge, MA: Harvard University Press, 2000), 82.

60. Frantz Fanon, *Black Skin, White Masks*, translated by Richard Philcox (New York: Grove Press, 2008), 69.

61. Bratton, *Stack*, 49.

62. Latour, *Reassembling the Social*, 241–42.

63. Bratton, *Stack*, 69.

64. Bourriaud, *Randicant*, 188.

Chapter 2: Absolute Integration and Terminal Unity/Wagner's Way

1. Richard Wagner, *My Life*, authorized translation of *Mein Leben* (Munich: F. Bruckmann, 1911; London: Constable, 1911), 505–6, cited in Juliet Koss, *Modernism After Wagner* (Minneapolis: University of Minnesota Press, 2010), 9.

2. Wagner, *Speech to the Vaterlandsverein*, *Richard Wagner's Prose Works*, vol. 4, translated by William Ashton Ellis (London: Kegan Paul, Trench, Trübner, 1893–1899), 143. All translations from Ellis are modified for clarity to contemporary audiences. Cited earlier, I refer to Bourriaud's statement, "Indexed to progress and abundance, modernism is thus structured around the image of a derrick planted in the depths of the individual and society, a violent explosion of the visible." See Bourriaud, *The Randicant* (New York: Lukas & Steinberg, 2009), 180–81.

3. Wagner, "Art and Revolution," *Prose Works*, vol. 1, 24.

4. Ronald Taylor, *Richard Wagner: His Life, Art, and Thought* (London: Paul Elek, 1979), 94–96.

5. Friederich Nietzsche, *The Case of Wagner, Nietzsche Contra Wagner, and Selected Aphorisms*, translated by Anthony M. Ludovici (Edinburgh: T. N. Foulis, 1911), 72–73.

6. Wagner, "The Art-Work of the Future," *Prose Works*, vol. 1, 68. But it is worth noting that Wagner wasn't always so sanguine about the intrinsic value of society. In his 1864 essay "On State and Religion," he is less than complimentary about people generally. On page 10, we find this judgment: "We fall into astonishment at the quite incredible pettiness and weakness of the average human intellect, and finally into shamefaced wonder that it should ever have astonished us; for any proper knowledge of the world would have taught us from the outset that blindness is the world's true essence, and not Knowledge prompts its movements, but merely a headlong impulse, a blind impetus of unique weight and violence, which procures itself just so much light and knowledge as will suffice to still the pressing need experienced at the moment." See Wagner, "On State and Religion," *Prose Works*, vol. 4.

7. Wagner, "Art and Revolution," 31.

8. Wagner, "Art and Revolution," 33.

9. Wagner, "Art and Revolution," 35.

10. Wagner, "Art and Revolution," 43.

11. Wagner, "Art and Revolution," 43.

12. Wagner, "Art and Revolution," 64–65.

13. Quentin Meillassoux, *After Finitude: An Essay on the Necessity of Contingency*, translated by Ray Brassier (New York: Continuum, 2009), 104.

14. See in particular the discussion of identity, difference, and diversity in vol. 1, book 2, "The Doctrine of Essence" in G.W.F. Hegel, *The Science of Logic*, translated by George di Giovanni (Cambridge: Cambridge University Press, 2010), 356ff. This quotation is from an earlier discussion in vol. 1, book 1, "The Doctrine of Being," 51.

15. See the foreword by Martin Nicolaus to Marx's *Grundrisse* (New York: Penguin Books, 1993), 32.

16. Meillassoux, *After Finitude*, 70.

17. Alain Badiou, *Five Lessons on Wagner*, translated by Susan Spitzer (London: Verso, 2010), 82. Wagner himself noted in his letters and writings a relation to Hegel, sometimes respectfully and sometimes disparagingly. For a survey of the influence on Wagner of Hegel and Feuerbach, see George G. Windell, "Hegel, Feuerbach, and Wagner's *Ring*," *Central European History* 9, no. 1 (March 1976): 27–57.

18. Nietzsche, *The Case of Wagner, Nietzsche Contra Wagner, and Selected Aphorisms*, 31.

19. Koss, *Modernism After Wagner*, 13.

20. Koss, *Modernism After Wagner*, 11.

21. Wagner, "Art and Revolution," 24.

22. Wagner, "The Art-Work of the Future," 89.

23. Wagner, *Lohengrin: Opera in Three Acts*, bilingual edition, English version by Stewart Robb (New York: G. Schirmer, 1963), 1.3. Lohengrin: "Nie sollst du mich befragen, / noch Wissens Sorge tragen, / woher ich kam der Fahrt,/noch wie mein Nam und Art!" Elsa: "Nie, Herr, soll mir die Frage kommen!" Translation mine.

24. Wagner, "Art-Work of the Future," 95.

25. Wagner, "Art-Work of the Future," 98.

26. Wagner, "Opera and Drama," *Prose Works*, vol. 2, 236.

27. Wagner, "Opera and Drama," 376.

28. Nietzsche, *The Case of Wagner, Nietzsche Contra Wagner, and Selected Aphorisms*, 72–73.

29. Matthew Wilson Smith, *The Total Work of Art: From Bayreuth to Cyberspace* (New York: Routledge, 2007), 42.

30. Wagner, "Art and Revolution," 61. See Neil K. Friedman, "Gold Rules: The Politics of Wagner's *Ring*," in *Inside the Ring: Essays on Wagner's Opera Cycle*, edited by John Louis DiGaetani (Jefferson, NC: McFarland & Company, 2006), 69–94. See also Warren J. Darcy, "The Metaphysics of Annihilation: Wagner, Schopenhauer, and the Ending of the Ring" *Music Theory Spectrum* 16, no. 1 (Spring 1994): 1–40. The author speaks of the "rotational" structure of the final immolation scene of *Götterdämmerung*, calling it the "process of teleological genesis."

31. Bruno Latour, *Reassembling the Social: An Introduction to Actor-Network-Theory* (New York: Oxford University Press, 2005), 201–2.

32. Slavoj Žižek, *Tarrying with the Negative: Kant, Hegel, and the Critique of Ideology* (Durham, NC: Duke University Press, 1993), 141.

33. Edmund Husserl, *Logical Investigations*, vol. 2, translated by J. N. Findlay (London: Routledge and Kegan Paul, 1970), 558. This quote and those by Merleau-Ponty and Sartre are cited in Graham Harman, *Guerrilla Metaphysics: Phenomenology and the Carpentry of Things* (Peru, IL: Open Court, 2005), 22, 25, 50.

34. Maurice Merleau-Ponty, *The Visible and the Invisible*, translated by Alphonso Lingis (Evanston, IL: Northwestern University Press, 1968), 430.

35. Jean-Paul Sartre, *Being and Nothingness*, translated by Hazel E. Barnes (New York: Washington Square Press, 1984), 5.

36. Žižek, *Tarrying with the Negative*, 142.

37. Merleau-Ponty, *Visible and the Invisible*, 152.

38. Kai Eriksson, "Foucault, Deleuze, and the Ontology of Networks," *The European Legacy* 10, no. 6 (2005): 604.

39. Badiou, *Five Lessons on Wagner*, 69–70.

40. Wagner, "Opera and Drama," 174.

41. Stephen Hinton, *The Idea of Gebrauchsmusik: A Study of Musical Aesthetics in the Weimar Republic (1919–1933) with Particular Reference to the Works of Paul Hindemith* (New York: Garland, 1989).

42. Badiou, *Five Lessons on Wagner*, 41–42.

43. Richard Wagner, "Das Bühnenfestspielhaus zu Bayreuth," in *Richard Wagner: Gesammelte Schriften und Dichtungen*, vol. 9 (Leipzig: E. W. Fritzsch, 1873), 336, translation mine; Friedrich Kittler, "World-Breath: On Wagner's Media Technology" in *Opera Through Other Eyes*," ed. David J. Levin (Stanford: Stanford University Press, 1994), 232–33.

44. Wagner, "Das Bühnenfestspielhaus zu Bayreuth," 336.

45. Wagner, "Art-Work of the Future," 175.

46. Wagner, "Art-Work of the Future," 192–94.

47. Bratton, *The Stack*, 214.

48. Nietzsche, *The Case of Wagner, Nietzsche Contra Wagner, and Selected Aphorisms*, 22.

49. Nietzsche, *The Case of Wagner, Nietzsche Contra Wagner, and Selected Aphorisms*, 41.

50. Alexander R. Galloway and Eugene Thacker, *The Exploit: A Theory of Networks* (Minneapolis: University of Minnesota Press, 2007), 32. See page 22 of my text.

51. Theodor W. Adorno, *In Search of Wagner*, translated by Rodney Livingston (London: Verso, 2005), 143.

52. *Negative Dialectics*, translated by E. B. Ashton (London: Routledge & Kegan Paul, 1973), 341–42.

53. Adorno, *In Search of Wagner*, 44.

54. Koss, *Modernism After Wagner*, 21.

55. Wagner, "Speech to the Vaterlandsverein," *Richard Wagner's Prose Works*, translated by William Ashton Ellis, vol. 4 (London: Kegan Paul, Trench, Trübner, 1893–1899), 139.

56. Adorno, *Negative Dialectics*, 362.

57. Adorno, *Negative Dialectics*, 362.

58. Adorno, *Negative Dialectics*, 325.

59. Adorno, "Trying to Understand *Endgame*," *Notes to Literature*, vol. 2, translated by Shierry Weber Nicholsen (New York: Columbia University Press, 1992).

60. Adorno, *In Search of Wagner*, 52.

61. See, respectively, Adorno, "Trying to Understand *Endgame*," 362; *In Search of Wagner*, 101.

62. Adorno, *In Search of Wagner*, 47, 91, 90, 93.

63. Wagner, "What Is German?" *Prose Works*, vol. 4, 163.

64. Wagner, "Bayreuth (The Playhouse)," *Prose Works*, vol. 5, 330.

65. Smith, *Total Work of Art*, 25.

66. Badiou, *Five Lessons on Wagner*, 131.

67. Adorno, *In Search of Wagner*, 87.

68. Adorno, *In Search of Wagner*, 30.

69. Wagner, "On Franz Liszt's Symphonic Poems," *Prose Works*, vol. 3, 246. For the argument that Wagner saw the difficulty of imposing the absolute model of the Gesamtkunstwerk and changed his mind about the hierarchy of drama over music, see Bryan Magee, *Wagner and Philosophy* (New York: Allen Lane, 2000), 187.

70. Eriksson, "Foucault, Deleuze, and the Ontology of Networks," 601.

71. Darin Barney, *The Network Society* (Cambridge, UK: Polity Press, 2004), 156.

72. Wagner, "Opera and Drama," 168.

73. Deleuze and Guattari, *Thousand Plateaus*, 239.

74. For the Wagner anecdote concerning Hegel and for his assertion that Wagner most likely read the passage in Hegel and was influenced by it as a source for the organizational structure of the *Ring*, see Windell, "Hegel, Feuerbach, and Wagner's Ring," 41. For the Hegel quotation, see *Phenomenology of Spirit*, translated by A. V. Miller (New York: Oxford University Press, 1977), 2.

75. Eriksson, "On the Ontology of Networks," 321.

76. Merleau-Ponty, *Visible and the Invisible*, 127.

Chapter 3: Paul/Marcel: Two Bodies

1. Rainer Maria Rilke, *Letters on Cézanne*, translated by Joel Agee (New York: North Point Press, 2002), 67.

2. "Rappelez-vous l'objet que nous vîmes, mon âme, / Ce beau matin d'été si doux: / Au détour d'un sentier une charogne infâme / Sur un lit semé de Cailloux . . ." Charles Baudelaire, "Une Charogne," *Oeuvres Complètes*, vol. 1 (Paris: Éditions Gallimard, 1975), 31. Translation mine.

3. Slavoj Žižek, *Tarrying with the Negative: Kant, Hegel, and the Critique of Ideology* (Durham: Duke University Press, 1993), 131.

4. See for example, T. J. Clark, "The Environs of Paris," in *Critical Readings in Impressionism and Post-Impressionism: An Anthology*, edited by Mary Tompkins Lewis (Berkeley: University of California Press, 2007), 101–45.

5. Quoted in Joseph Masheck, *C's Aesthetics: Philosophy in the Painting* (Philadelphia: Slought Books, 2004), 54.

6. Masheck, *C's Aesthetics*, 57.

7. Masheck, *C's Aesthetics*, 70–71.

8. Louis Althusser and Étienne Balibar, *Reading Capital*, translated by Ben Brewster (London: Verso, 2009), 210.

9. Benjamin H. Bratton, *The Stack: Of Software and Sovereignty* (Cambridge, MA: MIT Press, 2015), 204.

10. Cited in Richard Schiff, *Cézanne and the End of Impressionism* (Chicago: University of Chicago Press, 1986), 151.

11. As Kai Eriksson notes, local decisions within networks can be "based on a kind of economy of power relations which does not posit a structure but rather posits a tension between nodes, setting up the whole topology of the network as antagonistic and asymmetric." See Eriksson, "On the Ontology of Networks," *Communication and Critical/Cultural Studies* 2, no. 4 (December 2005): 312.

12. Eriksson, "On the Ontology of Networks," 316.

13. Maurice Merlau-Ponty, "Cézanne's Doubt," in *Maurice Merleau-Ponty: Basic Writings*, edited by Thomas Baldwin (London and New York: Routledge, 2004), 281.

14. Merlau-Ponty, "Cézanne's Doubt," 279.

15. G.W.F. Hegel, *Phenomenology of Spirit*, translated by A. V. Miller (Oxford: Oxford University Press, 1977), 113.

16. Merleau-Ponty, "Cézanne's Doubt," 276–77.

17. Quentin Meillassoux, *After Finitude: An Essay on the Necessity of Contingency*, translated by Ray Brassier (New York: Continuum, 2009), 60.

18. For an analysis of Flaubert's novel and its influence on Cézanne's painting of the same subject, see Mary Tompkins Lewis, *Cézanne's Early Imagery* (Berkeley: University of California Press, 1989), 181–85.

19. Cited in Roger Caillois, "Mimicry and Legendary Psychasthenia," translated by John Shepley, *October* 31 (Winter 1984): 31.

20. Georg Büchner, *Complete Plays and Prose*, translated by Carl Richard Mueller (New York: Hill & Wang, 1963), 141.

21. Büchner, *Complete Plays and Prose* 31. The passage cited by Caillois can be found in Gustave Flaubert, *The Temptation of Saint Anthony*, translated by Lafcadio Hearn (New York: Modern Library, 2002), 190.

22. Jacques Rancière, "Deleuze, Bartleby, and the Literary Formula," in *The Flesh of Words: The Politics of Writing*, translated by Charlotte Mandell (Stanford: Stanford University Press, 2004), 149.

23. Joachim Gasquet, *Joachim Gasquet's Cezanne: A Memoir with Conversations*, translated by Christopher Pemberton (New York: Thames & Hudson, 1991), 168.

24. Gilles Deleuze and Félix Guattari, *A Thousand Plateaus: Capitalism and Schizophrenia*, translated by Brian Massumi (Minneapolis: University of Minnesota Press, 2005). On Artaud, see 150, 158–59; quoting Burroughs, 153.

25. Deleuze and Guattari, *Anti-Oedipus*, 12.

26. Deleuze and Guattari, *Thousand Plateaus*, 161.

27. Maurice Merleau-Ponty, *The Visible and the Invisible*, translated by Alphonso Lingis (Evanston, IL: Northwestern University Press, 1969), 83–84, 127. For a discussion of Merleau-Ponty's concept of flesh, see Graham Harman, *Guerrilla Metaphysics: Phenomenology and the Carpentry of Things* (Peru, IL: Open Court, 2005), 52–54.

28. Gasquet, *Joachim Gasquet's Cézanne*, 166–67.

29. Marc Augé, *Oblivion*, translated by Marjolijn de Jager (Minneapolis: University of Minnesota Press, 2004), 57.

30. Deleuze and Guattari, *Thousand Plateaus*, 150.

31. Merleau-Ponty, *Basic Writings*, 273.

32. For example, Thierry de Duve writes, "In 1910, three years behind the Cubists themselves, he [Duchamp] came up against Cézanne and paid him a tribute whose significance would show in the works only later, when Duchamp had finally traversed Cubism within a year, from 1911 to 1912." De Duve, *Pictorial Nominalism: On Marcel Duchamp's Passage from Painting to the Readymade*, translated by Dana Polan and Thierry de Duve (Minneapolis: University of Minnesota Press, 1991), 12.

33. De Duve, *Pictorial Nominalism*, 47–48.

34. De Duve, *Pictorial Nominalism*, 49.

35. David Joselit, *Infinite Regress: Marcel Duchamp, 1910–1941* (Cambridge, MA: MIT Press, 1998).

36. Kieran Lyons, "Military Avoidance: Marcel Duchamp and the 'Jura-Paris Road,'" *Tate Papers*, Spring 2006, accessed at www.work-web/research/tateresearch/tatepapers/06spring/lyons.htm.

37. For a superb account of the machine/man hybrid in modernist art and its technological, historical, psychological, literary, and Marxist underpinnings, see Hal Foster, *Prosthetic Gods* (Cambridge, MA: MIT Press, 2006). While what Foster has to say about the Futurists is of particular importance here, his insights regarding castration and perspective in *Etant donnés* are especially relevant to my thinking about the double figure of Duchamp/Rrose Sélavy. "Con celui qui voit" (The one who sees is a cunt), Jean-François Lyotard's remark cited by Foster on page 275 concerning looking through the peepholes at the work proposes a congruent notion with that of the viewer as rogue node who completes the circuit of the work.

38. Dawn Ades, Neil Cox, and David Hopkins, *Marcel Duchamp* (London: Thames & Hudson, 1999), 112–13.

39. Willis Domingo, "Meaning in the Art of Duchamp, Part II," *Artforum* 10, no. 5 (January 1972): 63–68.

40. Caroline Levine, *Forms: Whole, Rhythm, Hierarchy, Network* (Princeton: Princeton University Press, 2015), 113.

41. Deleuze and Guattari, *Thousand Plateaus*, 9.

42. Galloway and Thacker, *Exploit*, 46.

43. Marcel Duchamp, *The Writings of Marcel Duchamp*, edited by Michel Sanouillet and Elmer Peterson (New York: Da Capo Press, 1989), 26.

44. Joselit, *Infinite Regress*, 143.

45. Gilles Deleuze, "Postscript on the Societies of Control," *October* 59 (Winter 1992): 5.

46. Deleuze, "Postscript on the Societies of Control," 4.

47. Eriksson, "On the Ontology of Networks," 315.

48. Jones, *Postmodernsim and the En-Gendering of Marcel Duchamp* (Cambridge: Cambridge University Press, 1994), 144.

49. As noted above, this notion of accomplishment in a network is described with these words in Bratton, *The Stack*, 167.

50. Duchamp, *Writings of Marcel Duchamp*, 126.

51. Maurice Blanchot, *The Infinite Conversation*, translated by Susan Hanson (Minneapolis: University of Minnesota Press, 1993), 336.

52. Raymond Roussel, *How I Wrote Certain of My Books*, edited by Trevor Winkfield (Boston: Exact Exchange, 2005), 4–5.

53. Pierre Cabanne, *Dialogues with Marcel Duchamp*, translated by Ron Padgett (New York: Da Capo Press, 1987), 40.

54. Molly Nesbit and Naomi Sawelson-Gorse, "Concept of Nothing: New Notes by Marcel Duchamp and Walter Arensberg," in *The Duchamp Effect*, edited by Martha Buskirk and Mignon Nixon (Cambridge, MA: MIT Press, 1996), 159. See also Jean-Jacques Lecercle, *Philosophy Through the Looking Glass: Language, Nonsense, Desire* (Abingdon: Routledge, 2017).

55. Cited in George H. Bauer, "Duchamp's Ubiquitous Puns," in *Marcel Duchamp: Artist of the Century*, edited by Rudolf Kuenzli and Francis M. Naumann (Cambridge, MA: MIT Press, 1996), 132.

56. Marcel Duchamp and Francis Roberts, "I Propose to Strain the Laws of Physics," *ARTnews* 67, no. 8 (December 1968): 62.

57. Meillassoux, *After Finitude*, 99.

58. Galloway and Thacker, *Exploit*, 61.

59. Cabanne, *Dialogues with Marcel Duchamp*, 46–47.

60. Ades, Cox, and Hopkins, *Marcel Duchamp*, 79.

61. Deleuze, "Postscript," 4.

62. Cabanne, *Dialogues with Marcel Duchamp*, 39.

63. Cited in de Duve, *Pictorial Nominalism*, 173.

64. For an invaluable discussion of Duchamp's linguistic play and this example in particular, see Leah Dickerman, ed., *Dada: Zurich, Berlin, Hannover, Cologne, New York, Paris* (Washington, DC: National Gallery of Art, 2008), 379.

65. Sigmund Freud, "The Uncanny," *Writings on Art and Literature* (Stanford: Stanford University Press, 1997), 199–200.

66. Cited in de Duve, *Pictorial Nominalism*, 173.

67. Freud, "Uncanny," 216.

68. Ades, Cox, and Hopkins, *Marcel Duchamp*, 110.

69. For these two quotes, see Hector Obalk, "The Unfindable Readymade," *Tout-Fait* 1, no. 2 (May 2000), www.toutfait.com/issues/issue_2/Articles/obalk .html#N_3.

70. Michel Callon, "The Sociology of an Actor-Network: The Case of the Electric Vehicle" in *Mapping the Dynamics of Science and Technology: Sociology*

of Science in the Real World, edited by Michel Callon, John Law, and Arie Rip (Houndmills, UK: Macmillan, 1986), xvi.

71. Arturo Schwarz, *The Complete Works of Marcel Duchamp* (New York: Harry N. Abrams, 1970), 461, cited in Joselit, *Infinite Regress*, 67–68. In this regard, Joselit's discussion of "mensuration" as the gendered expression of measurement in *Network of Stoppages* and afterward in Duchamp's oeuvre is particularly compelling and relevant. Joselit, *Infinite Regress*, 60–62.

72. Deleuze and Guattari, *Thousand Plateaus*, 153.

73. Nesbit and Sawelson-Gorse, "Concept of Nothing," 175. There is a specifically Deleuzian implication stated in the same paragraph: "Language would reveal a sonority of organs without bodies, pure purposeless *bassesse*. Sound would be made to blink in rounds of Brissetism. More thickening. Endless rendez-vous. The pace was unrelentingly, unspecifically sexual." But, I would argue, not entirely unspecific. Rather, doubly specific.

74. G.W.F. Hegel, *Hegel's Science of Logic*, translated by A. V. Miller (Amherst, NY: Humanity Books, 1998), 107. Cited in Ralph Palm, "Hegel's Concept of Sublation: A Critical Interpretation," PhD diss., Katholieke Universeteit Leuven, Institute of Philosophy, 2009.

75. Duchamp quoted in Thierry de Duve, *Sewn in the Sweatshops of Marx*, translated by Rosalind E. Krauss (Chicago: University of Chicago Press, 2012), 65.

76. Jones, *Postmodernsim and the En-Gendering of Marcel Duchamp*, 194.

Chapter 4: Thing-Thingness and How Space Means

1. Doreen Massey, "Space-Time, 'Science' and the Relationship Between Physical Geography and Human Geography," *Transactions of the Institute of British Geographers* 24, no. 3 (September 1999): 274.

2. Steve Hinchliffe, "A Physical Sense of World," in *Spatial Politics: Essays for Doreen Massey*, edited by David Featherstone and Joe Painter (London: John Wiley & Sons, 2013), 188.

3. Graham Harman, *Guerrilla Metaphysics: Phenomenology and the Carpentry of Things* (Peru, IL: Open Court, 2005), 104.

4. Quentin Meillassoux, *After Finitude: An Essay on the Necessity of Contingency*, translated by Ray Brassier (New York: Continuum, 2009), 4.

5. Quentin Meillassoux, "Iteration, Reiteration, Repetition: A Speculative Analysis of the Sign Devoid of Meaning," in *Genealogy of Speculation: Materialism and Subjectivity Since Structuralism*, edited by Suhail Malik and Armen Avanessian (London: Bloomsbury, 2016), 126.

6. Tristan Garcia, *Forme et object: Un trait des choses* (Paris: Presses universitatires de France, 2011), 83. This translation is from a review of Garcia's book by Graham Harman, published in the online journal *Content*, 2, no. 1 (2012), www .continentcontinent.cc/index.php/continent/article/viewArticle/74. For the English translation, see Garcia, *Form and Object: A Treatise on Things*, translated

by Mark Allan Ohm and Jon Cogburn (Edinburgh: Edinburgh University Press, 2014).

7. Doreen Massey, *For Space* (London: Sage Publications, 2005), 139.

8. Maurice Merleau-Ponty, *The Visible and the Invisible*, translated by Alphonso Lingis (Evanston, IL: Northwestern University Press, 1969), 152, cited in Harman, *Guerrilla Metaphysics*, 57.

9. Jorie Graham, "The Way Things Work," in *Hybrids of Plants and of Ghosts* (Princeton: Princeton University Press, 1980), 3.

10. G.W.F. Hegel, *Phenomenology of Spirit*, translated by A. V. Miller (Oxford: Oxford University Press, 1977), 105. See B. Self-Consciousness, IV. The Truth of Self-Certainty.

11. Jacques Derrida, "Hostipitality," *Angelaki* 5, no. 3 (December 2000): 11.

12. Derrida, "Hostipitality," 4.

13. Massey, *For Space*, 68.

14. Massey, *For Space*, 10.

15. Henri Lefebvre, *The Production of Space*, translated by Donald Nicholson-Smith (Malden, MA: Blackwell Publishing, 1991), 184.

16. Maurice Merleau-Ponty, *Maurice Merleau-Ponty: Basic Writings*, edited by Thomas Baldwin (London and New York: Routledge, 2004), 106.

17. Judith Butler, "'How Can I Deny That These Hands and Body Are Mine?'" in *Senses of the Subject* (New York: Fordham University Press, 2015), 17–35.

18. Massey, *For Space*, 54.

19. Gaston Bachelard, *The Poetics of Space*, translated by Maria Jolas (Boston: Beacon Press, 1994), 229–30. Rilke's quotation, in a different translation than the one used in Bachelard, is from *The Notebooks of Malte Laurids Brigge*, translated by Burton Pike (London: Penguin, 2009), 54–55.

20. Michel de Certeau, *The Practice of Everyday Life*, translated by Steven Rendall (Berkeley: University of California Press, 1988), 119–20.

21. Merleau-Ponty, *Basic Writings*, 113.

22. Theodor W. Adorno, *Negative Dialectics*, translated by E. B. Ashton (London: Routledge & Kegan Paul, 1973), 191.

23. Ernesto Laclau, *New Reflections on the Revolution in Our Time*, translated by Jon Barnes (London: Verso, 1990), 84, cited in Massey, *For Space*, 44–45.

24. Ilya Prigogine, *The End of Certainty: Time, Chaos, and the Laws of Nature* (London: Free Press, 1997), 55.

25. Victor Burgin, *In/Different Spaces: Place and Memory in Visual Culture* (Berkeley: University of California Press, 1996), 43.

26. In this regard, I refer to Yve-Alain Bois, "Painting: The Task of Mourning," in *Painting as Model* (Cambridge, MA: MIT Press, 1990).

27. Tung-Hui Hu, *A Prehistory of the Cloud* (Cambridge, MA: MIT Press, 2015), 1–2.

28. For this and the previous quote, see Burgin, *In/Different Spaces*, 43–44.

29. Marc Augé, *Non-Places: Introduction to an Anthropology of Supermodernity*, translated by John Howe (London: Verso, 1995), 32.

30. Michel Serres, *Hermes: Literature, Science, Philosophy* (Baltimore: Johns Hopkins University Press, 1983), 44–45.

31. Massey, *For Space*, 141.

32. Martin Heidegger, *Poetry, Language, Thought*, translated by Albert Hofstadter (New York: HarperCollins, 1971), 154.

33. Fred Moten, *The Universal Machine* (Durham, NC: Duke University Press, 2018), 141–42. See also Édouard Glissant, *The Poetics of Relation*, translated by Betsy Wang (Ann Arbor: University of Michigan Press, 1997).

34. Gilles Deleuze, *The Fold: Leibniz and the Baroque*, translated by Tom Conley (Minneapolis: University of Minnesota Press, 1992), 7.

35. Bruno Latour, *Reassembling the Social: An Introduction to Actor-Network-Theory* (New York: Oxford University Press, 2005), 242.

36. Kai Eriksson, "On the Ontology of Networks," *Communication and Critical/Cultural Studies* 2, no. 4 (December 2005): 322.

37. Yuk Hui, *Recursivity and Contingency* (London: Roman and Littlefield International, 2019), 242.

Chapter 5: A Waltz Before Hitler/Hugo Ball and the Dictatorship of Unreason

1. Hugo Ball, *Flight Out of Time: A Dada Diary*, translated by Ann Raimes (Berkeley: University of California Press, 1996), 9.

2. Ball, *Flight Out of Time,* 233.

3. Ball, *Flight Out of Time,* 102, entry for March 30, 1917.

4. Ball, *Flight Out of Time,* 37.

5. Walter Benjamin, "The Storyteller," in *Illuminations: Essays and Reflections*, translated by Harry Zohn (New York: Schocken Books, 1969), 84, cited in T. J. Demos, "Zurich Dada: The Aesthetics of Exile," in *The Dada Seminars*, edited by Leah Dickerman with Matthew S. Witkovsky (Washington, DC: Center for Advanced Study in the Visual Arts, National Gallery of Art, in association with D.A.P., 2005), 8.

6. See Kern, "The Cubist War," in *Culture of Time and Space,* 287–312.

7. Ball, *Flight Out of Time,* 231.

8. Ball, *Flight Out of Time,* 67.

9. Ball, *Flight Out of Time,* 87, 90, 98.

10. Ball, *Flight Out of Time,* 11.

11. Ball, *Flight Out of Time,* 50.

12. Francis Heylighen, "Why Is Open Access So Successful? Stigmergic Organization and the Economics of Information," in *Open Source Jahrbuch 2007*, edited by B. Lutterbeck, M. Bärwolff, and R. A. Gehring (Berlin: Lehmanns Media, 2007), http://pespmc1.vub.ac.be/Papers/OpenSourceStigmergy.pdf.

13. Benjamin H. Bratton, *The Stack: Sovereignty and Software* (Cambridge, MA: MIT Press, 2015), 44.

14. Georges Hugnet, "The Dada Spirit in Painting," in *The Dada Painters and Poets: An Anthology,* 2nd ed., edited by Robert Motherwell (Cambridge, MA: Harvard University Press, 1988), 131–32.

15. Tristan Tzara, "Lecture on Dada" (1922), quoted in William Rubin, *Dada, Surrealism, and Their Heritage* (New York: Harry N. Abrams, 1968), 11–12. See also Motherwell, ed., *Dada Painters and Poets,* 250.

16. Ball, *Flight Out of Time,* 61.

17. Hal Foster, ed., *The Anti-Aesthetic: Essays on Postmodern Culture* (Port Townsend, WA: Bay Press, 1983). The very notion of the anti-aesthetic is at the core of modernism, as Foster states in his preface to this seminal anthology, and that core takes fundamental form at Cabaret Voltaire and its subsequent formulation and distribution as Dada.

18. Hans Richter, "Zurich Dada 1915–1920," in *Dada: Art and Anti-Art,* translated by David Britt (London: Thames & Hudson, 1997), 19.

19. Richter, *Dada,* 27.

20. Bratton, *Stack,* 288–89.

21. Richter, *Dada,* 17–21.

22. Kris Cohen, *Never Alone, Except for Now: Art, Networks, Populations* (Durham, NC: Duke University Press, 2017), 103.

23. Ball, *Flight Out of Time,* 57.

24. Ball, *Flight Out of Time,* 57.

25. Kern, *Culture of Time and Space,* 294.

26. Ball, *Flight Out of Time,* 134.

27. Henri Bergson, *Time and Free Will: An Essay on the Immediate Data of Consciousness,* translated by F. L. Pogson (New York: Dover, 2001), 127–28.

28. Bergson, *Time and Free Will,* 128.

29. For details of the performance, see Marius Hentea, *TaTa Dada: The Real Life and Celestial Adventures of Tristan Tzara* (Cambridge, MA: MIT Press, 2014), 70.

30. Bratton, *Stack,* 40.

31. Matthew S. Witkovsky, "Pen Pals," in *The Dada Seminars,* edited by Leah Dickerman with Matthew S. Witkovsky (Washington, DC: Center for Advanced Study in the Visual Arts, National Gallery of Art, in association with D.A.P., 2005), 279.

32. Ball, *Flight Out of Time,* 63.

33. Richard Huelsenbeck, *En Avant Dada: A History of Dadaism,* 1920, excerpted in Motherwell, ed., *Dada Painters and Poets,* 23.

34. For John Elderfield's remarkable scholarly detective work that ultimately supports Ball and Heulesenbeck's paternity of the word in his afterword, see Ball, "'Dada': The Mystery of the Word," *Flight Out of Time,* 238–55.

35. Ball, *Flight Out of Time,* 60, 63.

36. Ball, *Flight Out of Time*, 219–21.

37. Michel Foucault, *The Order of Things: An Archaeology of the Human Sciences* (New York: Vintage Books, 1973), 36.

38. Walter Benjamin, "On Language as Such and on the Language of Man," in *Reflections: Essays, Aphorisms, Autobiographical Writings*, translated by Edmund Jephcott (New York: Harcourt Brace Jovanovich, 1978), 314–32. See also Anson Rabinbach, *In the Shadow of Catastrophe: German Intellectuals Between Apocalypse and Enlightenment* (Berkeley: University of California Press, 2001), 73.

39. Ball, *Flight Out of Time*, 68.

40. Ball, *Flight Out of Time*, 221.

41. Ball, *Flight Out of Time*, 30, 28.

42. Ball speaks about Kandinsky's poems in a lecture simply titled "Kandinsky," which he gave at the short-lived Galerie Dada on April 7, 1917. See *Flight Out of Time*, 222–34.

43. Ball, *Flight Out of Time*, 70–71.

44. T. J. Demos, "Zurich Dada: The Aesthetics of Exile," in *The Dada Seminars*, edited by Dickerman with Witkovsky, 18–20.

45. Ball, *Flight Out of Time*, 66.

46. Cited in Kai Eriksson, "Foucault, Deleuze, and the Ontology of Networks," *The European Legacy* 10, no. 6 (2005): 603.

47. Hugo Ball, "Carl Schmitt's Political Theology," translated by Matthew Vollgraff, *October* 146 (Fall 2013): 77.

48. Carl Schmitt, *Political Theology: Four Chapters on the Concept of Sovereignty*, translated by George Schwab (Chicago: University of Chicago Press, 2005), 5, 7. This thinking about Schmitt in relation to Ball is greatly indebted to Trevor Stark's brilliant essay "*Complexio Oppositorium*: Hugo Ball and Carl Schmitt," *October* 146 (Fall 2013): 31–64.

49. Cited by George Schwab in his introduction to *Political Theology*, xlv.

50. Schmitt, *Political Theology*, 13.

51. Schmitt, *Political Theology*, 63.

52. Schmitt, *Political Theology*, 3.

53. Giorgio Agamben, *State of Exception*, translated by Kevin Attell (Chicago: University of Chicago Press, 2005), 39, 54.

54. Bratton, *Stack*, 357.

55. See Daniel Hedrick, *The Invisible Weapon: Telecommunications and International Politics, 1851–1945* (New York: Oxford University Press, 1991), 138–42, cited in Witkovsky, "Pen Pals," 292.

56. Leah Dickerman, "Dada Gambits," *October* 105 (Summer 2003): 3–12.

57. Quoted in Matthew S. Witkovsky, "Chronology," in *Dada: Zurich, Berlin, Hannover, Cologne, New York, Paris*, edited by Leah Dickerman (Washington, DC: National Gallery of Art in association with D.A.P./Distributed Art Publishers, New York, 2005), 426–27.

58. Walter Benjamin, "The Work of Art in the Age of Mechanical Reproduction," in *Illuminations: Essays and Reflections*, edited by Hannah Arendt, translated by Harry Zohn (New York: Schocken, 1969), 238.

59. Ball, *Flight Out of Time*, 90.

60. Ball, *Flight Out of Time*, 19.

61. T. J. Demos, "Circulations: In and Around Zurich Dada," *October* 105 (Summer 2003): 155.

62. Stark, "*Complexio Oppositoruim*," 57.

63. Ball, *Flight Out of Time*, 208.

64. Stark, "*Complexio Oppositorium*," 62–63.

65. Ball, *Flight Out of Time*, 82.

66. Stark, "*Complexio Oppositorium*," 55.

67. Ball, *Flight Out of Time*, 65. See also Hal Foster, "A Bashed Ego: Max Ernst in Cologne" in *The Dada Seminars*, edited by Dickerman with Witkovsky; and Foster, "Dada Mime," *October* 105 (Summer 2003).

68. See, for example, Ball, "The German-Jewish Conspiracy to Destroy Morality," in *Critique of the German Intelligentsia*, translated by Brian L. Harris (New York: Columbia University Press, 1993), 149–99.

69. Ball, *Flight Out of Time*, 210. John Elderfield, in his introduction to Ball's diary, thinks that Ball may have been fantasizing in hindsight, given his turn to theology. Yet he acknowledges Huelsenbeck's remembrance.

70. Richard Huelsenbeck, "*En Avant Dada*: A History of Dadaism," in *Dada Painters and Poets*, edited by Motherwell, 31.

71. Agamben, cited in Matthew Vollgraff, "Afterword: Hugo Ball's Theology," *October* 146 (Fall 2013): 94–95.

72. Ball, *Flight Out of Time*, 90.

73. Ball, *Flight Out of Time*, 165.

74. Ball, "Carl Schmitt's Political Theology," 79.

75. Ball, "Carl Schmitt's Political Theology," 90.

76. Ball, "Carl Schmitt's Political Theology," 91.

77. Ball, "Carl Schmitt's Political Theology," 73–74.

78. Stark, "*Complexio Oppositorium*," 62.

79. Ball, "Carl Schmitt's Political Theology," 91.

80. Ball, *Critique*, 161.

81. Ball, "Carl Schmitt's Political Theology," 80.

Chapter 6: Liquefying the Bauhaus

1. Gropius married Gustav Mahler's widow, Alma, in 1915. He and the serially unfaithful Alma divorced five years later. In 1923 he married Ise Frank.

2. Walter Gropius, "Program of the Staatliche Bauhaus in Weimar," in *The Bauhaus: Weimar, Dessau, Berlin, Chicago*, edited by Hans M. Wingler (Cambridge, MA: MIT Press, 1986), 31–33. Four-page brochure with woodcut illustration, *Cathedral*, by Lyonel Feininger.

3. Those compatriots included Mikhail Larionov, Natalia Goncharova, and Kazimir Malevich. See Éva Forgács, *The Bauhaus Idea and Bauhaus Politics*, translated by John Bátki (New York: Central European University Press, 1995), 11–12.

4. While most art schools around the world today still replicate the material-based heuristic pedagogy of the Bauhaus's *Grunkurs*, Jeffrey Saletnik notes that its principles bespeaking universalist ideology have also been reconsidered negatively in recent years. Saletnik, *Josef Albers, Late Modernism, and Pedagogic Form* (Chicago: University of Chicago Press, 2022). Thierry de Duve writes about the replacement of the Bauhaus model by a conceptual approach in the time of postmodernism. See de Duve, "When Form Has Become Attitude—and Beyond," in *Theory in Contemporary Art Since 1985*, edited by Zoya Kocur and Simon Leung (London: Blackwell Publishing, 2005).

5. Walter Gropius, "Recommendations for the Founding of an Educational Institution as an Artistic Counseling Service for Industry, the Trades, and the Crafts" in *Bauhaus*, edited by Wingler, 23.

6. Nicholas Fox Weber, *The Bauhaus Group: Six Masters of Modernism* (New Haven: Yale University Press, 2011), 37–38.

7. Forgács, *Bauhaus Idea*, 11.

8. Rainer K. Wick, *Teaching at the Bauhaus*, translated by Stephen Mason and Simon Lèbe (Ostfildern-Ruit: Hatje Cantz, 2000), 57.

9. Wick, *Teaching at the Bauhaus*, 59.

10. John Ruskin, "The Nature of Gothic," *The Stones of Venice, Volume II: The Sea-Stories,* chapter 6 (New York: John B. Alden, 1885), 165.

11. See Frank Whitford, *Bauhaus* (London: Thames & Hudson, 1984).

12. Forgács, *Bauhaus Idea*, 11–12.

13. Jeffrey T. Schnapp, "Border Crossings," *Critical Inquiry* 21, no. 1 (Autumn 1994): 84. Schnapp's focus is on the aesthetico-political renovation of theater between the two world wars, specifically the convergence of notions of totality as politically felicitous in Germany and Italy, as made evident in Gropius's Bauhaus and the Italy of Giuseppe Terragni's Casa del Fascio.

14. Schnapp, "Border Crossings," 86.

15. Peter Gay, *Weimar Culture: The Outsider as Insider* (New York: W. W. Norton, 2001), 9. Fitch also became a Gropius biographer.

16. Walter Gropius, *Scope of Total Architecture* (New York: Collier Books, 1962), 19.

17. Carl Schmitt, *The Concept of the Political: Expanded Edition*, translated by George Schwab (Chicago: University of Chicago Press, 2007, based on the 1932 publication), 64. The 1932 edition was an outgrowth of a 1927 article with the same title.

18. Gropius in Wingler, ed., *Bauhaus*, 32.

19. Gropius, "Address to the Students of the Staatliche Bauhaus, Held on the Occasion of the Yearly Exhibition of Student Work in July 1919," in *Bauhaus*, edited by Wingler, 36.

20. "In the Arbeitsrat the architect Otto Bartning elaborated a plan for train-ing in the arts and crafts. He proposed the abolition of professorships, and the restoration of the old *master/apprentice* relationship, with the renewed usage of these terms. This would clearly demarcate the new style of education. [. . .] To turn towards the Middle Ages was now an innovative, avant-garde gesture." Forgács, *Bauhaus Idea*, 11. The abbreviated reference to the Arbeitsrat is to the Arbeitsrat für Kunst (AfK), or Work Council for Art, established in November 1918, with Bruno Taut as its leader, and subsequently led by Gropius, who took over from Taut in February 1919. Bartning was also a member of the AfK. See, for example, Taut's program for the AfK, reproduced in *German Expressionism, Documents of the Wilhelmine Empire to the Rise of National Socialism*, edited by Rose-Carol Washton Long (Berkeley: University of California Press, 1993), 193–94.

21. For an excellent, highly detailed analysis of the Bauhaus courses and their productions, see *Bauhaus: A Conceptual Model*, edited by Bauhaus-Archiv Berlin, Museum für Gestaltung, Stiftung Bauhaus Dessau, and Klassik Stiftung Weimar (Ostifilden: Hatje Cantz, 2009).

22. Quoted in Johannes Itten, *Design and Form: The Basic Course at the Bau-haus and Later, Revised Edition* (New York: Van Nostrand Reinhold, 1975), 12.

23. Michel Serres, *Genesis*, translated by Geneviève James and James Nielson (Ann Arbor: University of Michigan Press, 1997), 7.

24. As Alexander R. Galloway and Eugene Thacker write: "Information, for [Norbert] Wiener, is a statistical choice from among the 'noise' of the surrounding world, and as such it implies an apparatus with the ability to instantiate the very act of choice or selection." Galloway and Thacker, *The Exploit: A Theory of Net-works* (Minneapolis: University of Minnesota Press, 2007), 55.

25. Friederich Schiller, *Letters on the Aesthetic Education of Man*, translated by Elizabeth M. Wilkinson and L. A. Willoughby (Oxford: Clarendon Press, 1967).

26. Gay, *Weimar Culture*, 77–78.

27. Gropius in Wingler, ed., *Bauhaus*, 32.

28. Deleuze, "Postscript on the Societies of Control," *October* 59 (Winter 1992): 5.

29. Wick, *Teaching at the Bauhaus*, 37.

30. Bruno Latour, *Reassembling the Social: An Introduction to Actor-Network-Theory* (New York: Oxford University Press, 2005), 244–46. For a useful discussion of Latour's notions of relations among things in terms of plasma and formatting, see Graham Harman, *Prince of Networks: Bruno Latour and Meta-physics* (Melbourne: re.press, 2009), 128–34.

31. Latour, *Reassembling the Social*, 243–44.

32. Thierry de Duve makes a case for distinctions between the academic Beaux Arts pedagogical model and that of the Bauhaus, comparing the Beaux Arts belief in talent versus the Bauhaus embrace of creativity, the old model's métier versus the modernist investment in the medium. As he states: "The *métier* gets practiced,

the medium gets questioned; the *métier* gets transmitted, the medium communicates or gets communicated; the *métier* gets learned, the medium gets discovered; the *métier* is a tradition, the medium is a language; the *métier* rests on experience, the medium relies on experimentation." See de Duve, "When Form Has Become Attitude—and Beyond," 23.

33. Walter Gropius, "The Theory and Organization of the Bauhaus," in *Bauhaus: 1919–1928*, edited by Herbert Bayer, Walter Gropius, and Ise Gropius (New York: Museum of Modern Art, 1938), 21.

34. Gropius in Wingler, ed., *Bauhaus*, 51.

35. Saletnik, *Josef Albers, Late Modernism, and Pedagogic Form*, 58.

36. Tristan Garcia, *Form and Object: A Treatise on Things*, translated by Mark Allan Ohm and Jon Cogburn (Edinburgh: Edinburgh University Press, 2014), 80.

37. Gropius, *Bauhaus: 1919–1928*, 28.

38. Latour, *Reassembling the Social*, 228–29.

39. Josef Albers, "Concerning Fundamental Design," in *Bauhaus: 1919–1928*, 114–16.

40. Saletnik, *Josef Albers, Late Modernism, and Pedagogic Form*, 38.

41. László Moholy-Nagy quoted in Whitford, *Bauhaus*, 127.

42. Whitford, *Bauhaus*, 128.

43. Leah Dickerman, "Bauhaus Fundaments," in *Bauhaus 1919–1933: Workshops for Modernity*, edited by Barry Bergdoll and Leah Dickerman (New York: Museum of Modern Art, 2009), 19. Catalogue published in conjunction with the exhibition of the same name, organized at the Museum of Modern Art by Barry Bergdoll and Leah Dickerman, November 8, 2009–January 25, 2010.

44. Latour, *Reassembling the Social*, 229.

45. Georg Muche, quoted in Forgács, *Bauhaus Idea*, 112.

46. On the subject of the Bauhaus's commercial interests, see, for example, Frederick J. Schwartz, "Utopia for Sale," in *Bauhaus Culture: From Weimar to the Cold War*, edited by Kathleen James-Chakraborty (Minneapolis: University of Minnesota Press, 2006), 115–38. See also Regina Bittner, "The Bauhaus on the Market: On the Difficult Relationship Between the Bauhaus and Consumer Culture" in *Bauhaus: A Conceptual Model*, 331–36.

47. Kai Eriksson, "On the Ontology of Networks," *Communication and Critical/Cultural Studies* 2, no. 4 (December 2005): 311.

48. G.W.F. Hegel, *Phenomenology of Spirit*, translated by A. V. Miller (Oxford: Oxford University Press, 1977), 263–64.

49. Laszlo Moholy-Nagy, "Easel Painting, Architecture, and Gesamtkunstwerk," in *Painting, Photography, Film*, translated by Janet Seligman (Cambridge, MA: MIT Press, 1987), 17, quoted in Schnapp, "Border Crossings," 85.

50. Laszlo Moholy-Nagy, "Theater, Circus, Variety," translated by Arthur S. Wensinger, in *The Theater of the Bauhaus*, edited by Walter Gropius and Arthur S. Wensinger (Baltimore: Johns Hopkins University Press, 1996), 49–72.

51. *Brecht on Theater*, edited and translated by John Willett (New York: Hill and Wang, 1996), 37–38.

52. Darin Barney, *The Network Society* (Cambridge, UK: Polity Press, 2004), 156.

53. Walter Gropius, "Letter of Complaint Dated November 24, 1923 to Lieutenant-General Hasse, Military Commandant in Thuringia," in *Bauhaus*, edited by Wingler, 76.

54. Walter Gropius, "The Intellectual Basis of the Staatliche Bauhaus in Weimar," in *Bauhaus*, edited by Wingler, 77.

55. Walter Gropius, "Correspondence of September-October 1926 on the Question of a Salary Cut," in *Bauhaus*, edited by Wingler, 120.

56. "Verdict in the Case Against Georg Büchlein, Merchant, July 29, 1927," in *Bauhaus*, edited by Wingler, 128.

57. Vilmos Huszár, "Das Staatliche Bauhaus in Weimar," *De Stijl*, 5, no. 9 (1922): 136, quoted in Magdalena Droste, *Bauhaus 1919–1933* (Cologne: Taschen, 2002), 54.

58. Pierre Bourdieu, *The Field of Cultural Production*, translated by Richard Nice (New York: Columbia University Press, 1993), 34.

59. Bergdoll and Dickerman, eds., *Bauhaus 1919–1933*, 17.

60. Richard Wagner, "Art and Revolution," in *Richard Wagner's Prose Works*, vol. 1, translated by William Ashton Ellis (London: Kegan Paul, Trench, Trübner, 1893–1899), 24. Translation modified for clarity.

61. Karl Marx, *Capital: A Critique of Political Economy, Volume 1*, translated by Ben Fowkes (New York: Vintage Books, 1977), 131.

62. Christina Lodder, *Russian Constructivism* (New Haven: Yale University Press, 1983), 59.

63. Wick, *Teaching at the Bauhaus*, 62.

64. William Morris, *News from Nowhere*, chapter 18, "The Beginning of the New Life" (Hammersmith, UK: Kelmscott Press, 1893), 192. The novel was originally published in 1890 in serial form in the journal *Commonweal*.

65. Wick, *Teaching at the Bauhaus*, 74.

66. Lodder cites various sources for the establishment of the program at INKhUK, including this quote from Brik, in *Russian Constructivism*, 279, note 36. See also Maria Gough, *The Artist as Producer: Russian Constructivism in Revolution* (Berkeley: University of California Press, 2005). Gough writes about various aspects of INKhUK throughout her book.

67. Lodder, *Russian Constructivism*, 79.

68. Lodder, *Russian Constructivism*, 79.

69. Lodder, *Russian Constructivism*, 79.

70. Lodder, *Russian Constructivism*, 88.

71. Lodder, *Russian Constructivism*, 234.

72. Lodder, *Russian Constructivism*, 234–35.

73. Juliet Koss, *Modernism After Wagner* (Minneapolis: University of Minnesota Press, 2010), 221.

74. Hans Heinz Stuckenschmidt, quoted in Droste, *Bauhaus 1919–1933*, 103.

75. Gropius, *Scope of Total Architecture*, 20.

76. Christina Kiaer, *Imagine No Possessions: The Socialist Objects of Russian Constructivism* (Cambridge, MA: MIT Press, 2005), 30.

77. Gough, *Artist as Producer*, 192.

78. See Adrian Sudhalter, "14 Years Bauhaus: A Chronicle," in *Bauhaus 1919–1933*, edited by Bergdoll and Dickerman, 337.

79. Boris Groys, *The Total Art of Stalinism: Avant-Garde, Aesthetic Dictatorship, and Beyond*, translated by Charles Rougle (London: Verso, 2011). Christina Kiaer argues that Groys is historically inaccurate in his account. See Kiaer, *Imagine No Possessions*, 27.

80. Mies van der Rohe, quoted in Saletnik, *Josef Albers, Late Modernism, and Pedagogic Form*, 7.

81. Gropius, *Scope of Total Architecture*, 20.

Chapter 7: Afterword and Forward

1. Yuk Hui, *Recursivity and Contingency* (London: Rowman & Littlefield International, 2019), 251.

BIBLIOGRAPHY

Ades, Dawn, Neil Cox, and David Hopkins. *Marcel Duchamp*. London: Thames & Hudson, 1999.

Adorno, Theodor W. *In Search of Wagner*. Translated by Rodney Livingston. London: Verso, 2005.

———. *Negative Dialectics*. Translated by E. B. Ashton. London: Routledge & Kegan Paul, 1973.

———. "Trying to Understand *Endgame*." Translated by Shierry Weber Nicholsen. In *Notes to Literature*, vol. 2, 241–75. New York: Columbia University Press, 1992.

Agamben, Giorgio. *State of Exception*. Translated by Keven Attell. Chicago: University of Chicago Press, 2005.

Alloway, Lawrence. "Network: The Art World Described as a System." *Artforum* 11, no. 1 (September 1972): 28–32.

Althusser, Louis, and Étienne Balibar. *Reading Capital*. Translated by Ben Brewster. London: Verso, 2009.

Augé, Marc. *Non-Places: Introduction to an Anthropology of Supermodernity*. Translated by John Howe. London: Verso, 1995.

———. *Oblivion*. Translated by Marjolijn de Jager. Minneapolis: University of Minnesota Press, 2004.

Bachelard, Gaston. *The Poetics of Space*. Translated by Maria Jolas. Boston: Beacon Press, 1994.

Badiou, Alain. *Five Lessons on Wagner*. Translated by Susan Spitzer. London: Verso, 2010.

Ball, Hugo. *Critique of the German Intelligentsia*. Translated by Brian L. Harris. New York: Columbia University Press, 1993.

———. *Flight Out of Time: A Dada Diary*. Translated by Ann Raimes. Introduction by John Elderfield. Berkeley: University of California Press, 1996.

Barney, Darin. *The Network Society*. Cambridge, UK: Polity Press, 2004.

Baudelaire, Charles. "Une Charogne." In *Oeuvres Complètes,* vol. 1. Paris: Éditions Gallimard, 1975.

Bauer, George H. "Duchamp's Ubiquitous Puns." In *Marcel Duchamp: Artist of the Century*, edited by Rudolf Kuenzli and Francis M. Naumann. Cambridge, MA: MIT Press, 1996.

Bauhaus-Archiv Berlin, Museum für Gestaltung, Stiftung Bauhaus Dessau, and Klassik Stiftung Weimar, eds. *Bauhaus: A Conceptual Model*. Ostfildern: Hatje Cantz, 2009.

Bayer, Herbert, Walter Gropius, and Ise Gropius, eds. Bauhaus: 1919–1928. New York: Museum of Modern Art, 1938.

Benjamin, Walter. *Illuminations: Essays and Reflections*. Translated by Harry Zohn. New York: Schocken Books, 1969.

———. *Reflections: Essays, Aphorisms, Autobiographical Writings*. Translated by Edmund Jephcott. New York: Harcourt Brace Jovanovich, 1978.

Bergdoll, Barry, and Leah Dickerman, eds. *Bauhaus 1919–1933: Workshops for Modernity*. New York: Museum of Modern Art, 2009.

Bergson, Henri. *Time and Free Will: An Essay on the Immediate Data of Consciousness*. Translated by F. L. Pogson. New York: Dover, 2001.

Bishop, Claire. *Artificial Hells: Participatory Art and the Politics of Spectatorship*. London: Verso, 2012.

———. *Disordered Attention: How We Look at Art and Performance Today*. London: Verso, 2024.

———. *Installation Art: A Critical History*. London: Tate Publishing, 2005.

———, ed. *Participation*. London: Whitechapel, 2006.

Bois, Yve-Alain. *Painting as Model*. Cambridge, MA: MIT Press, 1990.

Bois, Yve-Alain, and Rosalind E. Krauss. *Formless: A User's Guide*. New York: Zone Books, 1997.

Bourdieu, Pierre. *The Field of Cultural Production*. Translated by Richard Nice. New York: Columbia University Press, 1993.

Bourdon, David. "The Razed Sites of Carl Andre." *Artforum* 5, no. 2 (October 1966): 14–17.

Bourriaud, Nicolas. *The Randicant*. New York: Lukas & Steinberg, 2009.

———. *Relational Aesthetics*. Translated by Simon Pleasance and Fronza Woods. Dijon: Les Presses du Réel, 2002.

Bratton, Benjamin H. *The Stack: On Software and Sovereignty*. Cambridge, MA: MIT Press, 2015.

Brecht, Bertolt. *Brecht on Theater.* Edited and translated by John Willett. New York: Hill and Wang, 1996.

Bredekamp, Horst. "From Walter Benjamin to Carl Schmitt, via Thomas Hobbes." *Critical Inquiry* 25, no. 2 (Winter 1999): 247–66.

Bridle, James. *New Dark Age: Technology and the End of the Future.* London: Verso, 2019.

Büchner, Georg. *Complete Plays and Prose.* Translated by Carl Richard Mueller. New York: Hill & Wang, 1963.

Burgin, Victor. *In/Different Spaces: Place and Memory in Visual Culture.* Berkeley: University of California Press, 1996.

Butler, Judith. *Senses of the Subject.* New York: Fordham University Press, 2015.

———. *Subjects of Desire: Hegelian Reflections in Twentieth-Century France.* New York: Columbia University Press, 1987.

Cabanne, Pierre. *Dialogues with Marcel Duchamp.* Translated by Ron Padgett. New York: Da Capo Press, 1987.

Cage, John. "An Autobiographical Statement." *Southwest Review* 76, no. 1 (Winter 1991): 65–66.

Caillois, Roger. "Mimicry and Legendary Psychasthenia." Translated by John Shepley. *October* 31 (Winter 1984): 16–32.

Callon, Michel. "The Sociology of an Actor-Network: The Case of the Electric Vehicle." In *Mapping the Dynamics of Science and Technology: Sociology of Science in the Real World,* edited by Michel Callon, John Law, and Arie Rip, 19–34. Houndmills, UK: Macmillan, 1986.

Clark, T. J. "The Environs of Paris." In *Critical Readings in Impressionism and Post-Impressionism: An Anthology,* edited by Mary Tompkins Lewis, 101–45. Berkeley: University of California Press, 2007.

Cohen, Kris. *Never Alone, Except for Now: Art, Networks, Populations.* Durham, NC: Duke University Press, 2017.

Darcy, Warren J. "The Metaphysics of Annihilation: Wagner, Schopenhauer, and the Ending of the Ring." *Music Theory Spectrum* 16, no. 1 (Spring 1994): 1–40.

de Certeau, Michel. *The Practice of Everyday Life.* Translated by Steven Rendall. Berkeley: University of California Press, 1988.

de Duve, Thierry. *Pictorial Nominalism: On Marcel Duchamp's Passage from Painting to the Readymade.* Translated by Dana Polan and Thierry de Duve. Minneapolis: University of Minnesota Press, 1991.

———. *Sewn in the Sweatshops of Marx.* Translated by Rosalind E. Krauss. Chicago: University of Chicago Press, 2012.

———. "When Form Has Become Attitude—and Beyond." In *Theory in Contemporary Art Since 1985,* edited by Zoya Kocur and Simon Leung, 21–33. London: Blackwell Publishing, 2005.

DeLanda, Manuel. *Deleuze: History and Science*. New York: Atropos Press, 2010.

———. *A Thousand Years of Nonlinear History*. New York: Zone Books. 1997.

Deleuze, Gilles. *Difference and Repetition*. Translated by Paul Patton. New York: Columbia University Press, 1995.

———. *The Fold: Leibniz and the Baroque*. Translated by Tom Conley. Minneapolis: University of Minnesota Press, 1992.

———. "Postscript on the Societies of Control." *October* 59 (Winter 1992): 3–7.

Deleuze, Gilles, and Félix Guattari. *Anti-Oedipus: Capitalism and Schizophrenia*. Translated by Robert Hurley, Mark Seem, and Helen R. Lane. New York: Penguin Books, 2009.

———. *A Thousand Plateaus: Capitalism and Schizophrenia*. Translated by Brian Massumi. Minneapolis: University of Minnesota Press, 2005.

———. *What Is Philosophy?* Translated by Hugh Tomlinson and Graham Burchell. New York: Columbia University Press, 1994.

Deleuze, Gilles, and Claire Parnet. *Dialogues II*. New York: Columbia University Press, 2002.

Demos, T. J. "Circulations: In and Around Zurich Dada." *October* 105 (Summer 2003): 147–58.

———. "Zurich Dada: The Aesthetics of Exile." In *The Dada Seminars*, edited by Leah Dickerman with Matthew S. Witkovsky, 7–29. Washington, DC: Center for Advanced Study in the Visual Arts, National Gallery of Art, in association with D.A.P., 2005.

de Oliveira, Nicholas, Nicola Oxley, and Michael Petry. *Installation Art in the New Millennium: The Empire of the Senses*. New York: Thames & Hudson, 2004.

Derrida, Jacques. "Hostipitality." *Angelaki: Journal of the Theoretical Humanities* 5, no. 3 (December 2000): 3–18.

Dickerman, Leah, ed. *Dada: Zurich, Berlin, Hannover, Cologne, New York, Paris*. Washington, DC: National Gallery of Art in association with D.A.P., 2005.

Dickerman, Leah, with Witkovsky, Matthew S., eds. *The Dada Seminars*. Washington, DC: Center for Advanced Study in the Visual Arts, National Gallery of Art, in association with D.A.P., 2005)

Domingo, Willis. "Meaning in the Art of Duchamp, Part II." *Artforum* 10, no. 5 (January 1972): 63–68.

Droste, Magdalena. *Bauhaus 1919–1933*. Cologne: Taschen, 2002.

Duchamp, Marcel. *The Writings of Marcel Duchamp*. Edited by Michel Sanouillet and Elmer Peterson. New York: Da Capo Press, 1989.

Eriksson, Kai. "Foucault, Deleuze, and the Ontology of Networks." *The European Legacy* 10, no. 6 (2005): 595–610.

———. "On the Ontology of Networks." *Communication and Critical/Cultural Studies* 2, no. 4 (December 2005): 305–23.

Fanon, Frantz. *Black Skin, White Masks*. Translated by Richard Philcox. New York: Grove Press, 2008.

Finn, Ed. *What Algorithms Want: Imagination in the Age of Computing*. Cambridge, MA: MIT Press, 2017.

Flaubert, Gustave. *The Temptation of Saint Anthony*. Translated by Lafcadio Hearn. New York: Modern Library, 2002.

Forgács, Éva. *The Bauhaus Idea and Bauhaus Politics*. Translated by John Bátki. New York: Central European University Press, 1995.

Foster, Hal, ed. *The Anti-Aesthetic: Essays on Postmodern Culture*. Port Townsend, WA: Bay Press, 1983.

———. "A Bashed Ego: Max Ernst in Cologne." In *The Dada Seminars*, edited by Leah Dickerman with Matthew S. Witkovsky, 127–49. Washington, DC: Center for Advanced Study in the Visual Arts, National Gallery of Art, in association with D.A.P., 2005.

———. "Dada Mime." *October* 105 (Summer 2003): 166–76.

———. *Prosthetic Gods*. Cambridge, MA: MIT Press, 2006.

———. "Trauma Studies and the Interdisciplinary: An Interview." *The Anxiety of Interdisciplinarity: de-, dis-, ex-*. Vol. 2. London: BACKless Books, 1998.

Freud, Sigmund. "The Uncanny." *Writings on Art and Literature*. Stanford: Stanford University Press, 1997.

Friedman, Neil K. "Gold Rules: The Politics of Wagner's *Ring*." In *Inside the Ring: Essays on Wagner's Opera Cycle*, edited by John Louis DiGaetani, 69–94. Jefferson, NC: McFarland & Company, 2006.

Frieling, Rudolf, ed. *The Art of Participation: 1950 to Now*. New York: Thames & Hudson, 2008.

Foucault, Michel. The Order of Things: An Archaeology of the Human Sciences. New York: Vintage Books, 1973.

Frodeman, Robert, Julie Thompson Klein, Carl Mitcham, and J. Britt Holbrook, eds. *The Oxford Handbook of Interdisciplinarity*. Oxford: Oxford University Press, 2010.

Galloway, Alexander R. *Protocol: How Control Exists After Decentralization*. Cambridge, MA: MIT Press, 2004.

Galloway, Alexander R., and Eugene Thacker. *The Exploit: A Theory of Networks*. Minneapolis: University of Minnesota Press, 2007.

Garcia, Tristan. *Form and Object: A Treatise on Things*. Translated by Mark Allan Ohm and Jon Cogburn. Edinburgh: Edinburgh University Press, 2014.

Gasquet, Joachim. *Joachim Gasquet's Cezanne: A Memoir with Conversations*. Translated by Christopher Pemberton. New York: Thames & Hudson, 1991.

Gay, Peter. *Weimar Culture: The Outsider as Insider*. New York: W. W. Norton, 2001.

Glissant, Édouard. *The Poetics of Relation*. Translated by Betsy Wing. Ann Arbor: University of Michigan Press, 1997.

Gombrich, E. H. *Aby Warburg: An Intellectual Biography*. Chicago: University of Chicago Press, 1986.

Gough, Maria. *The Artist as Producer: Russian Constructivism in Revolution.* Berkeley: University of California Press, 2005.

Graham, Jorie. *Hybrids of Plants and of Ghosts.* Princeton: Princeton University Press, 1980.

Gropius, Walter. *Scope of Total Architecture.* New York: Collier Books, 1962.

Groys, Boris. *Going Public.* Translated by Steven Lindberg and Matthew Partridge. Berlin: Sternberg Press, 2010.

———. *The Total Art of Stalinism: Avant-Garde, Aesthetic Dictatorship, and Beyond.* Translated by Charles Rougle. London: Verso, 2011.

Hardt, Michael, and Antonio Negri. *Empire.* Cambridge, MA: Harvard University Press, 2000.

Harman, Graham. *Guerrilla Metaphysics: Phenomenology and the Carpentry of Things.* Peru, IL: Open Court, 2005.

———. "Object-Oriented France: The Philosophy of Tristan Garcia." *Continent* 2, no. 1 (2012). http://www.continentcontinent.cc/index.php/continent/article/viewArticle/74.

———. *Prince of Networks: Bruno Latour and Metaphysics.* Melbourne: re.press, 2009.

Hedrick, Daniel. *The Invisible Weapon: Telecommunications and International Politics, 1851–1945,* 138–42. New York: Oxford University Press, 1991.

Hegel, Georg Wilhelm Friedrich. "The Doctrine of Essence." Volume 1, Book 2 of *The Science of Logic.* Translated by George di Giovanni. Cambridge: Cambridge University Press, 2010.

———. *Hegel's Science of Logic.* Translated by A. V. Miller. Amherst, NY: Humanity Books, 1998.

———. *Outlines of the Philosophy of Right.* Translated by T. M. Knox. New York: Oxford University Press, 2008.

———. *Phenomenology of Spirit.* Translated by A. V. Miller. Oxford: Oxford University Press, 1977.

Heidegger, Martin. *Hegel's Phenomenology of Spirit.* Translated by Purvis Emad and Kenneth Maly. Bloomington: Indiana University Press, 1988.

———. *Poetry, Language, Thought.* Translated by Albert Hofstadter. New York: HarperCollins, 1971.

Hentea, Marius. *TaTa Dada: The Real Life and Celestial Adventures of Tristan Tzara.* Cambridge, MA: MIT Press, 2014.

Heylighen, Francis. "Why Is Open Access So Successful? Stigmergic Organization and the Economics of Information." In *Open Source Jahrbuch 2007,* edited by B. Lutterbeck, M. Bärwolff, and R. A. Gehring. Berlin: Lehmanns Media, 2007. http://pespmc1.vub.ac.be/Papers/OpenSourceStigmergy.pdf.

Higgins, Dick. "Intermedia." In *Multimedia: From Wagner to Virtual Reality,* edited by Randall Packer and Ken Jordan. New York: W. W. Norton & Company, 2001.

Hinchliffe, Steve. "A Physical Sense of World." In *Spatial Politics: Essays for Doreen Massey*, edited by David Featherstone and Joe Painter, 178–88. London: John Wiley & Sons, 2013.

Hinton, Stephen. "Gebrauchsmusik." Grove Music Online. http://www .oxfordmusiconline.com.

Hugnet, Georges. "The Dada Spirit in Painting." In *The Dada Painters and Poets: An Anthology*, 2nd ed., edited by Robert Motherwell. Cambridge, MA: Harvard University Press, 1988.

Hui, Yuk. *Recursivity and Contingency*. London: Roman and Littlefield International, 2019.

Husserl, Edmund. *Logical Investigations*. Translated by J. N. Findlay. London: Routledge and Kegan Paul, 1970.

Itten, Johannes. *Design and Form: The Basic Course at the Bauhaus and Later, Revised Edition*. New York: Van Nostrand Reinhold, 1975.

Jameson, Fredric. *The Hegel Variations: On the Phenomenology of Spirit*. London: Verso, 2010.

Jones, Amelia. *Postmodernism and the En-Gendering of Marcel Duchamp*. Cambridge: Cambridge University Press, 1994.

Joselit, David. ———. *After Art*. Princeton: Princeton University Press, 2013.

———. *Infinite Regress: Marcel Duchamp, 1910–1941*. Cambridge, MA: MIT Press, 1998.

Kabakov, Ilya. *On the "Total" Installation*. Translated by Cindy Martin. Ostfildern: Cantz Verlag, 1995.

Kant, Immanuel. Critique of Teleological Judgment [1790]. Translated by James Creed Meredith. Oxford: Clarendon Press, 1928.

Katz, Vincent. *Black Mountain College: Experiment in Art*. Cambridge, MA: MIT Press, 2013.

Kern, Stephen. *The Culture of Time and Space, 1880–1918*. Cambridge, MA: Harvard University Press, 1983.

Kiaer, Christina. *Imagine No Possessions: The Socialist Objects of Russian Constructivism*. Cambridge, MA: MIT Press, 2005.

Kittler, Friederich. "World-Breath: On Wagner's Media Technology." In *Opera Through Other Eyes*," edited by David J. Levin. Stanford: Stanford University Press, 1994.

Klein, Julie Thompson. *Crossing Boundaries: Knowledge, Disciplinarities, and Interdisciplinarities*. Charlottesville: University Press of Virginia, 1996.

Koss, Juliet. *Modernism After Wagner*. Minneapolis: University of Minnesota Press, 2010.

Krauss, Rosalind. "Sculpture in the Expanded Field." *October* 8 (Spring 1979): 30–44.

———. *"A Voyage on the North Sea": Art in the Age of the Post-Medium Condition*. London: Thames & Hudson, 1999.

Kwon, Miwon. *One Place After Another: Site-Specific Art and Locational Identity.* Cambridge, MA: MIT Press, 2002.

Laclau, Ernesto. *New Reflections on the Revolution in Our Time.* Translated by Jon Barnes. London: Verso, 1990.

Laclau, Ernesto, and Chantal Mouffe. *Hegemony and Socialist Strategy: Towards a Radical Democratic Politics.* London: Verso, 2001.

Larsen, Lars Bang, ed. *Networks.* Whitechapel Documents of Contemporary Art. Cambridge, MA: MIT Press, 2014.

Latour, Bruno. *Reassembling the Social: An Introduction to Actor-Network-Theory.* New York: Oxford University Press, 2005.

———. *We Have Never Been Modern.* Translated by Catherine Porter. Cambridge, MA: Harvard University Press, 1993.

Lee, Pamela M. *Forgetting the Art World.* Cambridge, MA: MIT Press, 2013.

Lefebvre, Henri. *The Production of Space.* Translated by Donald Nicholson-Smith. Malden, MA: Blackwell Publishing, 1991.

Lewis, Mary Tompkins. *Cézanne's Early Imagery.* Berkeley: University of California Press, 1989.

Lodder, Christina. *Russian Constructivism.* New Haven: Yale University Press, 1983.

Long, Rose-Carol Washton, ed. *German Expressionism: Documents of the Wilhelmine Empire to the Rise of National Socialism.* Berkeley: University of California Press, 1993.

Lyons, Kieran. "Military Avoidance: Marcel Duchamp and the 'Jura-Paris Road.'" *Tate Papers.* Spring 2006. http://www.work-web/research/tateresearch/tatepapers/06spring/lyons.htm.

Magee, Bryan. *Wagner and Philosophy.* New York: Allen Lane, 2000.

Mallarmé, Stéphane. "The Book, Spiritual Instrument." Translated by Michael Gibbs. In *The Book, Spiritual Instrument,* edited by Jerome Rothenberg and David Guss, 14–20. New York: Granary Books, 1996.

Marinetti, Filippo Tommaso. "The Futurist Manifesto." In *Futurism: An Anthology.* Edited by Lawrence Rainey, Christine Poggi, and Laura Wittman. New Haven: Yale University Press, 2009. Originally published in *Le Figaro* 20 (1909): 39–44.

Marx, Karl. *Capital: A Critique of Political Economy.* Vol. 1. Translated by Ben Fowkes. New York: Vintage Books, 1977.

Masheck, Joseph. *C's Aesthetics: Philosophy in the Painting.* Philadelphia: Slought Books, 2004.

Massey, Doreen. *For Space.* London: Sage Publications, 2005.

———. "Space-Time, 'Science' and the Relationship Between Physical Geography and Human Geography." *Transactions of the Institute of British Geographers* 24, no. 3 (September 1999): 261–76.

Meillassoux, Quentin. *After Finitude: An Essay on the Necessity of Contingency.* Translated by Ray Brassier. New York: Continuum, 2009.

Menand, Louis. *The Marketplace of Ideas: Reform and Resistance in the American University*. New York: W. W. Norton & Company, 2010.

Merleau-Ponty, Maurice. *Maurice Merleau-Ponty: Basic Writings*. Edited by Thomas Baldwin. London and New York: Routledge, 2004.

———. *Sense and Non-Sense*. Translated by Hubert and Patricia Dreyfus. Evanston, IL: Northwestern University Press, 1964.

———. *The Visible and the Invisible*. Translated by Alphonso Lingis. Evanston, IL: Northwestern University Press, 1969.

Michelson, Annette, ed. *Andy Warhol*. October Files. Cambridge, MA: MIT Press, 2001.

Moholy-Nagy, Laszlo. "Theater, Circus, Variety." Translated by Arthur S. Wensinger. In *The Theater of the Bauhaus*, edited by Walter Gropius and Arthur S. Wensinger, 49–72. Baltimore: Johns Hopkins University Press, 1996.

Moran, Joe. *Interdisciplinarity*. New York: Routledge, 2002.

Morris, William. *News from Nowhere*. Hammersmith, UK: Kelmscott Press, 1893.

Moten, Fred. *The Universal Machine*. Durham: Duke University Press, 2018.

Munster, Anna. *An Aesthesia of Networks: Conjunctive Experience in Art and Technology*. Cambridge, MA: MIT Press, 2013.

Nesbit, Molly, and Naomi Sawelson-Gorse. "Concept of Nothing: New Notes by Marcel Duchamp and Walter Arensberg.". In *The Duchamp Effect*, edited by Martha Buskirk and Mignon Nixon, 130–75. Cambridge, MA: MIT Press, 1996.

Nicolaus, Martin. "Foreword." In *Grundrisse* by Karl Marx. New York: Penguin Books, 1993.

Nietzsche, Friedrich. *The Case of Wagner, Nietzsche Contra Wagner, and Selected Aphorisms*. Translated by Anthony M. Ludovici. Edinburgh: T. N. Foulis, 1911.

Obalk, Hector. "The Unfindable Readymade." *Tout-Fait* 1, no. 2 (May 2000). http://ww.toutfait.com/issues/issue_2/Articles/obalk.html#N_3.

Obrist, Hans Ulrich. "Curating, Exhibitions, and the *Gesamtkunswerk*." In *Ways of Curating*. New York: Faber and Faber, 2014.

Palm, Ralph. *Hegel's Concept of Sublation: A Critical Interpretation*. PhD diss., Katholieke Universeteit Leuven, Institute of Philosophy, 2009.

Parisi, Luciana. *Contagious Architecture: Computation, Aesthetics, and Space*. Cambridge, MA: MIT Press, 2013.

Prigogine, Ilya. *The End of Certainty: Time, Chaos, and the Laws of Nature*. London: Free Press, 1997.

Rabinbach, Anson. *In the Shadow of Catastrophe: German Intellectuals Between Apocalypse and Enlightenment*. Berkeley: University of California Press, 2001.

Rancière, Jacques. "Communists Without Communism?" *The Idea of Communism*, edited by Costas Douzinas and Slavoj Žižek, 167–77. London: Verso, 2010.

Rebentisch, Juliane. *Aesthetics of Installation Art*. Translated by Daniel Hendrickson and Gerrit Jackson. Berlin: Sternberg Press, 2012.

Reiss, Julie H. *From Margin to Center: The Spaces of Installation Art.* Cambridge, MA: MIT Press, 2001.

Richter, Hans. *Dada: Art and Anti-Art.* Translated by David Britt. London: Thames & Hudson, 1997.

Rilke, Rainer Maria. *Letters on Cézanne.* Translated by Joel Agee. New York: North Point Press, 2002.

———. *The Notebooks of Malte Laurids Brigge.* Translated by Burton Pike. London: Penguin, 2009.

Roberts, Francis. "I Propose to Strain the Laws of Physics." *Art News* 67, no. 8 (December 1968): 62.

Rosenthal, Mark. *Understanding Installation Art: From Duchamp to Holzer.* New York: Prestel, 2003.

Roussel, Raymond. *How I Wrote Certain of My Books.* Edited by Trevor Winkfield. Boston: Exact Exchange, 2005.

Rubin, William S. *Dada, Surrealism, and their Heritage.* New York: Museum of Modern Art, 1968.

Ruskin, John. *The Stones of Venice, Volume II: The Sea-Stories.* New York: John B. Alden, 1885.

Russell, Legacy. *Glitch Feminism.* New York: Verso, 2020.

Sack, Warren. "Network Aesthetics." In *Database Aesthetics: Art in the Age of Information Overflow*, edited by Victoria Vesna, 183–210. Minneapolis: University of Minnesota Press, 2007.

Saletnik, Jeffrey. *Josef Albers, Late Modernism, and Pedagogic Form.* Chicago: University of Chicago Press, 2022.

Sartre, Jean-Paul. *Being and Nothingness.* Translated by Hazel E. Barnes. New York: Washington Square Press, 1984.

Schiff, Richard. *Cézanne and the End of Impressionism.* Chicago: University of Chicago Press, 1986.

Schiller, Friederich. *Letters on the Aesthetic Education of Man.* Translated by Elizabeth M. Wilkinson and L. A. Willoughby. Oxford: Clarendon Press, 1967.

Schmitt, Carl. *The Concept of the Political: Expanded Edition.* Translated by George Schwab. Chicago: University of Chicago Press, 2007.

———. *Political Theology: Four Chapters on the Concept of Sovereignty.* Translated by George Schwab. Chicago: University of Chicago Press, 2005.

Schnapp, Jeffrey T. "Border Crossings." *Critical Inquiry* 21, no. 1 (Autumn 1994): 80–123.

Schwartz, Frederick J. "Utopia for Sale." In *Bauhaus Culture: From Weimar to the Cold War*, edited by Kathleen James-Chakraborty, 115–38. Minneapolis: University of Minnesota Press, 2006.

Schwarz, Arturo. *The Complete Works of Marcel Duchamp.* New York: Harry N. Abrams, 1970.

Serres, Michel. *Genesis*. Translated by Geneviève James and James Nielson. Ann Arbor: University of Michigan Press, 1997.

——. *Hermes: Literature, Science, Philosophy*. Edited by Josué V. Harari and David F. Bell. Baltimore: Johns Hopkins University Press, 1983.

Shirky, Clay. "Power Laws, Weblogs, and Inequality." *Clay Shirky's Writings About the Internet*. Last modified February 10, 2003. http://www.shirky.com /writings/powerlaw_weblog.html.

Smith, Matthew Wilson. *The Total Work of Art: From Bayreuth to Cyberspace*. New York: Routledge, 2007.

Smith, Terry, Okwui Enwezor, and Nancy Condee, eds. *Antinomies of Art and Culture: Modernity, Postmodernity, Contemporaneity*. Durham: Duke University Press, 2008.

Stark, Trevor. "*Complexio Oppositorium*: Hugo Ball and Carl Schmitt." *October* 146 (Fall 2013): 31–64.

Stevens, Wallace. "Of Mere Being." In *The Palm at the End of the Mind*, edited by Holly Stevens. New York: Vintage Books, 1990.

Suderburg, Erika, ed. *Space, Site, Intervention: Situating Installation Art*. Minneapolis: University of Minnesota Press, 2000.

Taylor, Ronald. *Richard Wagner: His Life, Art, and Thought*. London: Paul Elek, 1979.

Tisdall, Caroline. *Art into Society, Society into Art*. London: ICA, 1974.

Turner, Fred. *From Counterculture to Cyberculture: Stewart Brand, the Whole Earth Network, and the Rise of Digital Utopianism*. Chicago: University of Chicago Press, 2006.

Wagner, Richard. *Gesammelte Schriften und Dichtungen*. Vol. 9 Leipzig: E. W. Fritzsch, 1873.

——. *Lohengrin: Opera in Three Acts*. Bilingual edition. English version by Stewart Robb. New York: G. Schirmer, 1963.

——. *My Life*. Authorized translation of *Mein Leben*. Munich: F. Bruckmann, 1911; London: Constable, 1911.

——. *Richard Wagner's Prose Works*. Translated by William Ashton Ellis. London: Kegan Paul, Trench, Trübner, 1893–1899.

Weber, Nicholas Fox. *The Bauhaus Group: Six Masters of Modernism*. New Haven: Yale University Press, 2011.

Whitford, Frank. *Bauhaus*. London: Thames & Hudson, 1984.

Wick, Rainer K. *Teaching at the Bauhaus*. Translated by Stephen Mason and Simon Lèbe. Ostfildern-Ruit: Hatje Cantz, 2000.

Windell, George G. "Hegel, Feuerbach, and Wagner's *Ring*." *Central European History* 9, no. 1 (March 1976): 27–57.

Wingler, Hans M., ed. *The Bauhaus: Weimar, Dessau, Berlin, Chicago*. Cambridge, MA: MIT Press, 1986

Witkovsky, Matthew S. "Pen Pals." In *The Dada Seminars*, edited by Leah Dickerman with Matthew S. Witkovsky, 269–93. Washington, DC: Center for Advanced Study in the Visual Arts, National Gallery of Art, in association with D.A.P., 2005.

Žižek, Slavoj. *Tarrying with the Negative: Kant, Hegel, and the Critique of Ideology.* Durham: Duke University Press, 1993.

INDEX

Note: Entries containing "n" indicate endnotes.

· · ·   **Sensing Media**
Aesthetics, Philosophy,
and Cultures of Media
EDITED BY WENDY HUI KYONG CHUN
AND SHANE DENSON

What does it mean to think, feel, and sense with and through media? In this cross-disciplinary series we present books and authors exploring this and related questions: How do media technologies, broadly defined, transform artistic practices and aesthetic sensibilities? How are practices, encounters, and affects entangled with the deep infrastructures and visible surfaces of the media environment? How do we "make sense"—cognitively, perceptually, and culturally—of media?

We are especially interested in contributions that open our understanding of media aesthetics beyond the narrow confines of Western art and aesthetic values. We seek works that reestablish the environmental connections between art and technology as well as between the aesthetic, the sensible, and the philosophical. We invite alternative epistemologies and phenomenologies of media rooted in the practices and subjectivities of Black, Indigenous, queer, trans, and other communities that have been unjustly marginalized in these discussions. Ultimately, we aim to sense the many possible worlds that media disclose.

—

Adrian J. Ivakhiv, *The New Lives of Images: Digital Ecologies and Anthropocene Imaginaries in More-than-Human Worlds*

Maja Bak Herrie, *Thinking Through Data: How Outliers, Aggregates, and Patterns Shape Perception*

The DISCO Network, *Technoskepticism: Between Possibility and Refusal*

Timon Beyes, *Organizing Color: Toward a Chromatics of the Social*

Edmund Mendelssohn, *White Musical Mythologies: Sonic Presence in Modernism*

Ioana B. Jucan, *Malicious Deceivers: Thinking Machines and Performative Objects*

Vilém Flusser, *Communicology: Mutations in Human Relations?*, edited by Rodrigo Maltez Novaes, foreword by N. Katherine Hayles

Mark Amerika, *My Life as an Artificial Creative Intelligence*

The authorized representative in the EU for product safety and compliance is:
Mare Nostrum Group
B.V Doelen 72
4831 GR Breda
The Netherlands

www.ingramcontent.com/pod-product-compliance
Lightning Source LLC
Chambersburg PA
CBHW020855180526
45163CB00007B/2513